YOUR AMERICA

YOUR AMERICA

DEMOCRACY'S LOCAL HEROES

JOHN SICELOFF

JASON MALONEY

INTRODUCTION BY
DAVID BRANCACCIO

palgrave
macmillan

Grateful acknowledgment is made to Chelsea Green for permission to reprint an
excerpt from: Diane Wilson, *An Unreasonable Woman: A True Story of Shrimpers,
Politicos, Polluters and the Fight for Seadrift, TX* (White River Junction, VT:
Chelsea Green Publishing, 2005). Copyright © 2005 by Chelsea Green
Publishing. Reprinted by permission of Chelsea Green Publishing.

Photograph of crowd at beginning of chapter 1 © Step It Up 2007; photograph of
shrimp boats at beginning of chapter 12 © Diane Wilson; all other photographs
© JumpStart Productions.

First published in 2008 by
PALGRAVE MACMILLAN™
175 Fifth Avenue, New York, N.Y. 10010 and
Houndmills, Basingstoke, Hampshire, England RG21 6XS.
Companies and representatives throughout the world.

PALGRAVE MACMILLAN is the global academic imprint of the Palgrave
Macmillan division of St. Martin's Press, LLC and of Palgrave Macmillan Ltd.
Macmillan® is a registered trademark in the United States, United Kingdom and
other countries. Palgrave is a registered trademark in the European Union and
other countries.

ISBN-13: 978-0-230-60533-6
ISBN-10: 0-230-60533-8

Library of Congress Cataloging-in-Publication Data
Siceloff, John.
    Your America : democracy's local heroes / John Siceloff, Jason Maloney.
        p.   cm.
    Includes bibliographical references and index.
    ISBN 0–230–60533–8
    1. Social reformers—United States—Biography.   2. Social action—United
States—History.   I. Maloney, Jason.   II. Title.
HN65.S556   2008
303.48'4092273—dc22
[B]
                                                                    2007052849

A catalogue record of the book is available from the British Library.

Design by Letra Libre

First edition: July 2008
10 9 8 7 6 5 4 3 2 1
Printed in the United States of America.

*This book is dedicated to all those
who enlarge the geography of hope.*

CONTENTS

YOUR AMERICA

INTRODUCTION

by David Brancaccio

ONCE MET THE WOMAN WITH THE GRIMMEST JOB ON EARTH. HER NAME WAS Clea. A graduate of the University of Arizona, she dug up mass graves for evidence of war crimes for a living. Happily, my job is not that grisly. As anchorman and roving reporter for one of the most serious programs of investigative journalism on television, I am thrust on a regular basis into crucially significant but often grave stories. On any given week I might find myself traveling with one of our investigative teams to examine (take your pick): torture and other human rights abuses, degradation of our environment or powerful people who abuse their power to swindle or oppress. Raking through this muck on a regular basis would not be a recipe for living a life of zestful hope were it not for one other important feature of my work: regular contact with the sorts of heroes you'll meet in this book.

I have the honor of spending time with these heroes at the rate of about once a week. The effect on me and, judging from audience response, the effect on our viewers is exhilarating, provocative and inspiring. As I write this, I have just come from an encounter with Bill McKibben, an environmental writer who has come up with a cure for public and political inaction on global warming. Realizing that e-mails and letters to the editor go only so far, McKibben teamed with some smart people in their early twenties to figure out how to get politicians in cities and towns across America face to face and eye to eye with real people demanding policy action now on climate change.

The week before, I spent a pleasant autumn morning in a farmhouse in a stretch of the Appalachians in Virginia getting some straight talk from

Anthony Flaccavento who has come up with an innovative system to persuade local farmers to grow nice, healthy vegetables instead of killer tobacco.

Like the folks in this book, Flaccavento and McKibben do not claim to be saints possessed with some otherworldly altruistic drive. Neither is rich; they are not converting vast stock options into traditional charities. Neither has given up the satisfactions of family living for lives of monastic forbearance. These are folks who have figured out that we imperfect mortals have a personal capacity to fix things that are broken in our world if we realize that we each have the capacity to help. We just have to have our eyes open, on the lookout for the need.

A few years ago, I spent some time watching people imbued with the entrepreneurial spirit learn some basic skills about starting their own small businesses. In the windowless conference room of a hotel strangely situated next to the Universal Studios theme park in Hollywood, I took notes as people without apparent connections to power and privilege went through the small business equivalent of the Hollywood pitch meeting: They each had a few moments to dazzle an expert with their business innovation.

Some of the pitches seemed promising; others were plain goofy. However, I did detect one universal element of each proposal that I do see universally echoed in the stories of the heroes in this book. Each of the budding entrepreneurs had identified a gap or void in the market. Even in the great kaleidoscope of commerce, they saw needs not met that they were prepared to fill with their new business idea. Opportunities, they called them.

At the small business conference, the ultimate goal of the participants was clear: personal profit. Spotting that hole of need in the market was a way to put some money in their pockets. The heroes in this book are driven by something beyond profit. They are also able to identify holes of need and also see them as opportunities, but these voids are not in the fabric of wholesale or retail. Our heroes managed to spot the many, pressing places where social systems have left critical voids in urgent need of filling with social innovation. Like traditional entrepreneurs, the heroes here do not just talk about the breakdown, void, or need. They take action to fill it.

What is especially interesting to me is that these heroes are not just figuring out ways to work on small problems. The stories show that individuals can take on the biggest of social challenges. A few winters ago, I was walking down a main street in Michigan ravaged by the offshoring of jobs as a consequence of globalization. Peering into the window of a pawn shop in Greenville, my eyes were attracted to a heap of gleaming bits of metal. The pile, about the size of a minor snow drift, was made up of stainless steel sockets that fit into the handles of wrenches. As manufacturing jobs moved to foreign lands, the good folks of Greenville, Michigan, had been forced to pawn their livelihoods, their very hand tools, in order to raise cash.

Many people see what globalization does to American manufacturing jobs as a vast problem, nearly intergalactic in scope, a law of physics that cannot be faced down by mere mortals. That was not the view of the owner of Huckleberry's restaurant across the street from the pawn shop. Mike Huckleberry got actively engaged when word came that the local Electrolux refrigerator factory was going to move its jobs away. In the spirit of the legendary pamphleteer Tom Paine, Huckleberry used the paper placemats on the tables in his restaurant to stir up concrete action. Some of his placemats read: "Dear politicians. In spite of continued raises and perks for yourselves, you have allowed NAFTA and unfair world trade policies to take its toll on hard-working Americans, their families and the communities they live in, as well as our great community. In spite of it, we have news for you. Greenville is bigger than Electrolux."

Placemats led to discussions among patrons about the town's economic challenges. The restaurant became a forum, Greenville's Hyde Park Corner. Did Congress rescind NAFTA? Not at last check. What Huckleberry's actions did do, however, is create what is known as social capital, the key ingredient to civic life and community development, when people come together to engage social issues. This social capital will be a crucial part of any bid by Greenville, Michigan, to fashion a new future for itself.

That is what the heroes whom we get to meet regularly on our weekly broadcasts and whose stories are detailed in this book are driving toward—a new, better future. Faced with a need, they did not settle for phoning their favorite AM radio demagogue or demigod, depending on your point of view, so that they could wait on hold for forty minutes in exchange for a forty-second chance to vent their spleens into the ether. They took action and that is what our democracy needs if it is to flourish.

In the mountains of Aspen, Colorado, not long ago, I had a heart-to-heart with one of our country's deepest thinkers on the subject of political communication, and the importance of citizen action came up. Orville Schell, dean of the journalism school at the University of California-Berkeley, sees a dangerous disruption in what might be called the food chain of democracy. In this chain, information about a problem should lead to discussion, then to action, then to correction. Schell argues that too often this chain is broken at the top because too many citizens do not want to accept the results of rigorous journalistic or scientific inquiry. But the chain can also break closer to the bottom, that is, if concerned members of the community, faced with the facts, remain inert. If there is no action there is no correction. The stories in this book show that all around us, people are taking personal action. If the stories inspire others, then our democracy will be all the stronger.

DAVID BRANCACCIO is the host and senior editor of the public television show *NOW on PBS*. A broadcaster for twenty-eight years, he spent a decade as host of the public radio program *Marketplace*, winning a DuPont-Columbia University Award and a George Foster Peabody Award. He is the author of the book *Squandering Aimlessly*.

1

THE POLITICS OF
EMPOWERMENT

OW DO YOU GET STARTED IF YOU WANT TO MAKE A DIFFERENCE IN AMERICA? That's the question we asked each of the people profiled in *Your America*.

What's fascinating is what we didn't hear. These folks didn't get their start working for political parties. Their credentials weren't burnished in think tanks—progressive, conservative or libertarian. They weren't on the payroll of advocacy groups.

They didn't become grassroots activists because somebody paid them or trained them to do it. These people began working for change in their communities because they cared passionately about an issue close to their lives. Something wasn't working, and they wanted to fix it. They became involved.

All of them share a special quality that's almost disappeared from public debate. They are authentic. They became involved because they were part of a community that was directly impacted by a problem. These folks didn't pull into town one day and start telling people what they had to do to improve their lives. They wanted to fix things because they wanted a better world for themselves and their families and others like them.

Their causes vary enormously. Wynona Ward helps abused women. Rueben Martinez gets books to young Latinos. Diane Wilson pushes chemical companies to stop polluting. They discovered within themselves the capacity to make change. Each became empowered.

With their actions, they help point the nation toward solutions for urgent policy issues. And that is what democracy is all about—people solving problems. Grassroots activists stand alongside the folks who get elected and make laws. Both are important. Right now, the civic activists are especially important because many of those elected officials have let us down in the democracy department. They're on the phone with the guys who sent them fat campaign contributions. When regular citizens dial up, their calls go to voice mail.

If you have ever spoken up at a PTA meeting, or volunteered at the local library, you've engaged in grassroots activism. It takes all kinds. Case in point: Diane Wilson. She took her shrimp boat out to the bay waters where a big company was discharging toxic waste. Her plan was to sink the boat and maybe die in the process. That didn't happen, thank goodness. But we're not all wired to be Diane Wilson. Many of us don't hear that clarion call for total sacrifice. The good news is that there are lots and lots of ways to make a difference that fit right into the life you are leading today.

For those who want to make change happen, what are the lessons of the civic activists profiled in *Your America?* The first thing that leaps out is what they didn't do. They didn't start with banners and barricades. Protest wasn't their thing. Each found a route to change that was built around action. Some worked within a troubled institution. John Walsh transformed the treatment of foster care kids by working within the government system that was causing the problems. Bunny Greenhouse, as a top official at the U.S.

Army Corps of Engineers, demanded transparency and accountability in contracting.

Others worked from the outside to make reform happen. Peggy Buryj, mother of a U.S. Army soldier killed in Iraq, pushed the army to improve its handling of casualties. Robert Moses created a program to improve the teaching of algebra to poor and minority kids, and in the process, created a national model for transforming education and investing in young people.

How did they achieve success? They built movements. They knew that the power of one was only the starting point. They looked around for others who cared, and got them involved. And the involvement wasn't simply a matter of signing a petition, or forwarding an e-mail or writing a check for twenty bucks. They called on people to give time and energy—to be active.

That's how empowerment spreads and grows. The activists showed with the power of example that each person can make change happen. Each successful grassroots movement tilts the country toward a healthy future and away from partisan bickering and cynicism.

Who exactly did these grassroots activists recruit for their movements? They started with people in exactly the same situation. Lucas Benitez, immigrant tomato picker, got other tomato pickers to join the effort to get a better wage. But Benitez didn't stop there. He wanted people who could put pressure on the fast-food companies that bought the tomatoes. He found some unlikely allies: students and religious groups. The students created the "Boot the Bell" boycott movement against Taco Bell. The religious leaders condemned Taco Bell for exploiting workers and chipped away at its brand image. Moral leadership, consumer power and worker solidarity—together, they made a very effective movement.

Other grassroots activists found common ground across divisions of politics and ideology. Lynn and Devonna Owens wanted to save family cattle ranches in the high valleys of Montana. But they knew that ranchers were no match for the real estate developers. They needed allies. So Lynn and Devonna, ranchers who were the children of ranchers, made common ground with their ancient enemies, the environmentalists, in order to preserve their way of life. Ranchers, environmentalists and wealthy vacation homeowners joined together. They all valued the open range, even though their motivations varied. Some wanted a great view, some wanted a place to graze cattle and some wanted a habitat for predators.

For grassroots activists, how do you measure success? The goal for the Owenses was to save the ranching way of life in Madison Valley. Success was all about keeping the developers at bay.

Others found success in one community but didn't stop there. They wanted to scale up their activism and reach more people. After Lucas Benitez and the Coalition of Immokalee Workers triumphed over Taco Bell, they turned their attention to other fast-food companies. They've won against McDonald's and now they're setting up for new battles.

Bill Graham is using the power of example to spread the word. He turned around the town of Scottsburg, Indiana, by focusing on infrastructure for the digital age. Now he's on the road all over the country showing other communities how to do the same thing. John Walsh built the Foster Children's Project to speed troubled children through foster care. Now his project is serving as a "best practices" example for other communities.

Not everyone will hear the call to change the entire system, as John Walsh did. There are people who pitch in to help as after-school tutors or coaches for sports teams. Others volunteer as mentors for troubled kids. Service and volunteerism, powered by altruism, often achieve good things. But here lies an important distinction about how change happens. At its core, grassroots activism is not about altruism and helping others. It's about gaining power to help yourself and others like you to make a better world for all. The folks you'll read about in *Your America* told us they didn't become activists just to plug holes in an ever-more-leaky safety net. They went to work to help build a better way of doing things, to create an America where ideas, priorities and solutions percolate up from the grassroots.

The people profiled in *Your America* are among the hundreds of local heroes whose stories have appeared on the public television show *NOW on PBS*. For the dozen people who appear in the book, we (the coauthors) went across the country to do new interviews and investigate exactly how they had achieved success. We also asked *NOW*'s producers and reporters to write first-person accounts about their encounters with these remarkable people. You'll find their verbal snapshots at the end of each chapter.

As we did our research, two themes emerged. These people embraced activism because of a deeply felt need, a personal mission. And they were determined to scale up because they wanted to help lots of people.

Wynona Ward didn't want anybody to endure the abuse that she had suffered. She found a way to help abused women with legal advice and transportation to and from court. She could have kept her activism small scale and personal, driving around in her SUV and working by herself. But she wanted to help more and more women. She built Have Justice Will Travel into a major force in Vermont and a national example. She spends half her time fundraising and now has a budget that supports five full-time lawyers. Her group has been able to assist thousands of women.

Katie Redford, as a novice lawyer, came up with a new legal approach to go after an American corporation doing business in Burma, a country with one of the worst human rights records in the world. When she won tens of millions of dollars for Burmese villagers, lots of folks would have stopped right there. After all, it took Redford years and years of work and endless legal maneuvering to prevail. But for Katie Redford, that was only the beginning. She and her husband, Ka Hsaw Wa, continued to expand the work of their group EarthRights International, and now have an annual budget of over $1 million. They are using the power of the law to stop unsavory conduct by U.S. corporations all over the world.

Jackie Thrasher's successful run for the Arizona House of Representatives is an example of activism on a national scale. Her victory wouldn't have happened without years of groundwork to get the money out of politics with a system of publicly financed, clean elections. There are organizations that promote clean elections all over the country, and they have been prime movers in the successful referendum campaigns in Arizona, Maine and elsewhere. Thrasher and other citizen legislators who have been the beneficiaries of clean elections are the muscle that keeps the movement alive and growing. Thrasher divides her time between teaching middle school and debating laws in the state capitol. You couldn't invent a better example of a grassroots activist. She and the dozens of others who won by running clean show all the good things that happen when the torrent of private money is eliminated from elections.

How did Robert Moses scale up his work helping poor and minority students learn algebra? As a young man, Moses worked all over the South as an organizer in the civil rights movement. But decades later, when he created the math program, he started out slowly. He spent years in a couple of schools, fine tuning the approach. He networked with teachers and administrators and parent organizations and educational foundations. With these groups, he created a broad, diverse base for the movement. From the beginning, Moses's aim was to make the Algebra Project into a national movement. He laid the groundwork by training facilitators and teachers and securing funding sources. When he had all the parts in place, he rolled out the program across the country. The growth has been explosive. The Algebra Project went from helping a handful of schoolkids to working with over 10,000 children a year. And Moses says that's only the beginning.

You have to hand it to Moses—the man knows how to take a good idea and make it grow. But there's another lesson at the very core of Moses' approach. He has always believed in the transformative power of the individual. He doesn't look at students as "units" that passively accept new information. He believes change only happens through empowerment. In his view, students first have to embrace their own ability to make a difference. He is creating a "culture of change" where students themselves push for more learning, more resources and more opportunities.

For half a century, Robert Moses has helped people discover that empowerment is the key to citizenship in our democracy. He is pushing the country toward a better place, and at the same time he is creating a new generation of activists and cocreators of democracy. It's an approach that can work for all of us, in communities across the nation. The local heroes of *Your America* point the way forward.

2

HAVE JUSTICE, WILL TRAVEL

WYNONA WARD

WHAT SHE'S DONE:
Ward has helped thousands of women in Vermont to confront domestic violence and abuse.

LOCAL HERO HIGHLIGHT:
She went from driving trucks to getting a law degree to inventing a new way to help rural women in trouble.

HOW DO YOU GET STARTED IN CIVIC ACTIVISM? YOU BECOME EMPOWERED. You believe that what you do will make a difference in the world. That's a difficult leap for many Americans. How do you even begin pushing for change when the forces of the status quo are so enormous and so powerful?

Wynona Ward has an answer for that. In fact, the challenge for her was even greater. How do you become empowered if you grow up in poverty, if you have an inadequate education, if you have a job that barely supports you? Wynona Ward was able to overcome all of that and achieve amazing things. She built on what would have destroyed most people: She was abused as a young girl. Now she has become a forceful and effective advocate for others who have experienced violence and abuse at home.

Wynona Ward grew up in the 1950s in a rural, remote part of Vermont. Her family lived in what she describes as a four-room, tarpaper shack in a tiny hillside town called West Fairlee. When you drive through West Fairlee today, you'll find a single gas station–general store that sits near the junction of Route 113 and Beanville Road. Imagine, then, what it was like half a century ago. The nearest big shopping district is still across the Connecticut River in Lebanon, New Hampshire, a drive of about thirty miles. You lose your cell phone signal as soon as you exit the nearest interstate, fifteen miles away. The only signs that modernity might have reached these parts are the forests of satellite dishes that cling to the sides of houses to bring in a television signal. Until Ward was in high school, her home had no television, not even a telephone.

Ward's childhood was not a happy one. Her father, who worked on and off as a miner, ruled the household through intimidation, violence and abuse. Ward vividly remembers an incident in her youth, in 1957, when she and her siblings watched in horror as her father, enraged that their mother did not have dinner ready and had not stocked the fridge with beer, nearly choked her to death right before their eyes. The children were able to pull him off and save their mother's life. They earned a beating of their own for their trouble, but were all damaged far more and far longer by the trauma of what they'd witnessed.

And there was also sexual abuse. Ward, trapped in an impoverished family in rural Vermont, says she made it through one day at a time. She felt no one was there to protect her or help her. Looking back, she says nothing was as difficult as the helplessness and hopelessness she felt watching her mother be beaten almost to the point of death. "When my father sexually abused me, it was very traumatic. But what was much more traumatic for me and much more difficult for me to deal with was when I watched him beat my mother, choke my mother, throw things at her," remembered Ward in 2002 when *NOW on PBS* first met up with her.

When Wynona was seventeen, Harold Ward, her sweetheart since eighth grade, asked her to marry him. Wynona didn't think twice. They couldn't afford a place of their own, so she moved up the hill to the converted single-room schoolhouse Harold shared with his family in neighboring Vershire Heights. Harold's mother was ill, and the family welcomed Wynona's assistance and embraced her as a new member of the family. For years, Wynona never told Harold of her ordeals, obeying a code of silence that she says was an unspoken rule of rural Vermont life at the time. They cobbled together money for an eighteen-wheeler and began life on the road. Wynona and Harold hauled cargo that ranged from refrigerated food to parts of the sets of Broadway musicals such as *Les Miserables*. Together they logged over a million miles and visited every one of the lower forty-eight states.

It was on one of these treks across the country that Wynona's past caught up to her. She received a call from back home saying that her brother, Richard, had sexually abused his and Wynona's nine-year-old niece. The news hit Wynona with a jolt: She couldn't believe that her brother, who had often tried to protect her from abuse when they were young, was doing the same thing their father had done. The victim's mother—Wynona's sister—was calling for advice as to what to do. Wynona insisted her sister go to the police, even though she knew that would bring down the wrath of their father. She immediately made plans to return home to see how she could help.

Ward had made a life for herself that took her away from West Fairlee and what she had endured as a child. This fresh tragedy would have sent many people—maybe most people—fleeing even farther away. But that is not how Wynona Ward reacted. She was drawn back to help out the young girl who had been abused by her brother. "It was very painful for me to learn that he had done this. But more than that it was painful for me to realize what this child had to be feeling. It took me back to my own childhood where I was abused in a similar way. And I said, 'It has to stop. It has to stop here. It can't keep going on.'"

Wynona and Richard Ward had both been abused by their father. She knew in clinical detail how much her brother had suffered as a child. And she also knew that domestic abuse often repeats itself through generations, so that victims go on to become perpetrators later in life. She had sympathy for Richard, but she was absolutely determined to halt the cycle of violence that had begun in the small shack in West Fairlee.

A few years before, Wynona had decided to tell Harold about her own difficult history. He was as understanding and supportive with the news about Richard as he had been then. They headed back to Vermont. They had just finished a run to New Jersey and could make it home in several hours. At first, Wynona had to face the painful realities of the case involving her brother. In order to make sure he was rendered unable to abuse children—by putting him behind bars—Ward would have to battle her own parents and reopen the wounds of the abusive relationship she'd had with her father. The family split in two. The parents lined up behind her brother, urging him to deny any allegations of wrongdoing. Wynona and her sister vowed to keep the brother locked up until he sought help for his problems.

Wynona began to work directly with her niece. She took her in, spent time with her, comforted her and even physically protected her all the way through the successful prosecution that sent Ward's brother to jail. It was a time of highly charged emotion for Wynona. Her weeks of work with the young victim fueled anger and even rage at her brother. She remembers sitting on the front porch of their house with a .357 Magnum on the day she knew her brother would be passing by on his way home after getting out, briefly, on bail. She shudders to think what she would have done if the car had slowed. Today, she uses that memory to remind her to maintain a necessary distance when taking on a new case.

The saga with Ward's brother didn't end with the guilty verdict. When, two years later, Richard—still in total denial of any wrongdoing—lodged a plea for medical parole, Wynona spearheaded an all-out fight to keep him behind bars and away from the community. And she did all she could to convince him to admit what he'd done and begin the process of healing himself through treatment. Her advice fell on deaf ears. Only after long battles in court and the denial of medical parole did Richard finally accept counseling. Eventually Wynona was able to resume a relationship with him.

Wynona Ward had changed. The orbit of pain, violence and abuse in her family empowered her. She saw that she could make a difference with her brother Richard, and she did. Now Ward moved another step along the path to civic activism. She decided to take action to help the wider community.

Through the years of involvement in her brother's case, Wynona became convinced that what she had worked so hard for in her own life could be expanded to the greater community. Many others were afflicted by the same cycle of abuse that had so ravaged her family, and she found herself driven to help victims of domestic violence end that cycle. It was a profound turning point. Ward made a decision to restart her life to help others who were facing what she herself had endured.

She realized that her first step would be to finish her education, even if it meant having classmates young enough to be her children. Back in the 1970s she'd done two years at Boston University but had to stop when she ran out of money. Now, almost twenty years later, she tracked down a program at Vermont College of Norwich University that would allow her to complete her degree while still working alongside her husband, Harold, driving the rig. And so Ward did her homework in the back of the truck's cabin, crisscrossing the country. She kept in contact with her instructors by letter and FedEx. Finally, in 1995, she earned her college degree.

At first, Wynona thought she could be most helpful to victims of abuse as a social worker or child psychologist. But by the time she'd finished college, she'd decided on a more proactive way to help victims of domestic abuse. Rather than counsel people and help them cope after a crime had been committed, she would become a prosecutor and make sure perpetrators would be taken out of communities as efficiently as possible. The aim was to stop them before they were able to inflict more damage. This meant more education, and more time. So she enrolled in Vermont Law School, a reputable nonprofit school located in South Royalton, at the foot of the valley just over the mountain from where she and Harold were living. Completing her undergraduate studies by the light of a truck cabin was one thing, law school was another matter entirely. The time had come for Wynona to come off the road for good. Harold stayed behind the wheel another year, long enough for Wynona to really pour herself into the law books and get started, but eventually he too came home to stay.

Ward had already decided what she needed to do with her life. But just how to achieve it became a journey in itself. Each step along the way she refined her approach and honed in on a path that would maximize her ability to help. After diving into her studies at Vermont Law School and working on a summer internship with the Vermont attorney general's child protective unit, she came to the realization that as a prosecutor she would not have very much interaction with victims. The way the system worked, she would be able to get abusers locked up but would have, at best, only a handful of opportunities a year to help people. At the same time she realized that the rural isolation she had grown up in—and the code of silence she'd observed—stood almost as much in the way of justice and relief as the abusers themselves.

Often, she found, women and children were trapped in abusive situations largely because they had no means at all of seeking help and had nowhere to go. Not only did many of them lack telephones, driver's licenses and cars, many lacked any ability to support themselves and their families financially once they left the abusive situation. Rural Vermont, she discovered, required a different approach to getting victims legal help. "The difference between rural domestic violence and domestic violence in urban areas is the difficulty in reaching out for these services, the difficulty in getting them," she says. "You can't hop on a bus and go downtown and fill out the welfare papers here. You've got to have transportation, it's a very big problem." Transportation, of course, was something Ward already had a lot of experience with.

Wynona Ward says she got the idea for her organization, Have Justice Will Travel, as she was finishing up law school. It would become a hybrid of sorts: part law firm, part counseling service and part taxi fleet. If women and children in rural Vermont were having such a hard time getting out of abusive situations and finding their way to social and legal services, she would bring the services to them, driving her hulking old Dodge Ramcharger right to their homes, no matter how isolated they were. She learned about abuse cases from police reports, victims abuse hotlines, personal referrals and word of mouth. Her approach was designed to reassure the victims. Ward talked to them at their own kitchen tables rather than whisking them off to a law office far away. Her every-woman appearance helped. She looked like one of them, aside from the sophisticated glasses with thin metal rims. And her follow-up also emphasized the personal—often simply offering a ride so clients could make it to court to follow legal proceedings all the way to the end.

Ward made some astute choices. She saw the justice system wasn't working well, but she didn't attack the courts. She set out to make the system work much, much better. The state did have the infrastructure to deal with parts of the puzzle, but it took Ward's ingenuity to bring all the pieces together. During the seven years that elapsed from her brother's trial through college and law school, Ward came up with an ingenious solution to the problem she was tackling.

Transportation is a particular concern in Vermont because the state has only two real highways, both of which run roughly north to south. Traveling up and down the state is usually no problem, but going east to west is a really big deal. Here you are at the whim of state roads, usually two-lane affairs as likely to be dirt or gravel as paved. Distances of thirty miles to do the shopping may sound trivial to someone from Texas, but when you take into account the mountainous terrain and narrow roads, which in winter are often impassable, the distance seems a world away. And public transportation? You can forget about it. In Vermont, rural means remote. And low population means that most communities are small and that for many citizens the distances between home and the nearest social service can be great.

But before Ward could officially start driving around the state representing battered woman and children, she still had one more obstacle to overcome. Ward had to pass the state bar exam before she could officially practice as a lawyer. Though she'd had an excellent academic track record, she failed her first attempt. This was not especially unusual; a significant percentage of first-timers fail. So she got ready for a second try and studied nonstop. Again she failed. The Vermont bar exam is made up of three sections: a written part, an ethics survey and multiple-choice questions. Ward had passed the essay and ethics sections right away and did not need to repeat those parts. It was the multiple-choice section where she was hung up. On her second try she missed by only two wrong answers. She remembers her husband, Harold, joking at the time, "Well at least you didn't miss by only one!" That dubious distinction was reserved for her third attempt.

It had now been six years since news of her brother's crime had brought her back from life on the road and set her on an unswerving course dedicated to helping victims. She was tantalizingly close. She had worked out all the steps she needed to realize her dream, and the only thing holding her back was one multiple-choice test. No matter how hard she'd studied, she had been blocked. It was so bad that a professor urged Ward to seek medical advice to see if she had a learning disability. The wife of another one of her professors, a neuropsychologist, examined her. Ward's brain, it turned out, had difficulty processing certain kinds of information—including the type needed to answer multiple-choice questions. But that brought up another mystery: The disability was normally only associated with severe physical brain trauma at an early age. Ward had no memory or record of anything like that happening to her.

She began to research her early history and discovered that she'd been taken to a nearby hospital when she was just over a year old. The official explanation given by Ward's mother was that she'd fallen out of a highchair and hit her head. Ward requested the medical files and was shocked to read the doctor's assessment that her injury was consistent with having been swung around with "great centrifugal force for an extended period." One doctor speculated that she'd been unconscious for hours before she'd been brought to the hospital. Because questions were not asked in those days about suspicions of domestic abuse, Wynona had been treated and released. But it was all there in the records for her to read. It was her most chilling moment. The abuse Ward had suffered in that shack in West Fairlee nearly forty years earlier still had the capacity to haunt her hopes and dreams for the future.

The realization that her father's abuse was still affecting her was sickening to Ward. By then her father had died. "The world's a better place for it," muttered Ward of his passing. Her father had gone to his grave in total denial of his crimes. Now it was as if he was reaching back from the beyond, committing one final atrocity. It took an enormous effort of will for Wynona to go forward. But she was not going to let her father's sickness win.

Fortunately, the Vermont Bar Association was understanding when Wynona explained to them that she had been diagnosed with a learning disability. Ward asked for and was granted extra time for the multiple-choice section. This time she passed easily. The year was 2000: Have Justice Will Travel was officially born.

For a long while, Have Justice, as it is known across the state, was just Wynona, a one-woman operation. She received funding from a group called Equal Justice Work, enough to get her started. Later, she would receive grants from the Vermont Women's Fund, Ashoka and the Department of Justice in Washington, D.C., to keep going. Her operating costs were not high but she did need to make enough to live on and to pay her not insignificant student loans. "I have to pay $605 a month until I am seventy-eight!" says Ward. From the start, she insisted that all the services she provided be given free to families in need. In a state where the average attorney bills at a hundred dollars an hour, Ward receives a salary of only $45,000. Given her average work week of eighty hours, this works out to less than eleven dollars an hour, higher than minimum wage, perhaps, but as low as you will find for a practicing lawyer.

Her office in the early days was her 1986 Dodge Ramcharger, not the most fuel-efficient choice—but just try driving across Route 110 in January in a Corolla. Today she has upgraded to a used Ford Explorer for which she was able to secure vanity tags with "HJWT" on them. The vehicle is kitted out for work on the road—she has a laptop, a printer and a set of portable legal files—and for the special rigors of Vermont isolation. Much of the state and many of the places Ward goes (and even her home) have no conventional cellular phone service at all. Harold insisted she get an extra-high-frequency car antenna which is mounted on top of the cab so at least some of the time she can pull in enough bars to make a call. Ward has memorized many of the locations on hilltops around the state where she can reliably place and receive calls while traveling.

It wasn't long before Have Justice began receiving a lot of attention—and a lot of work. From the start, says Ward, there was never any shortage of clients. In fact, then, as now, Ward says the hardest part of her job was having to turn people away. She even receives the occasional call from out of state, someone who has learned of the program from some of the national press coverage Ward has earned. Have Justice only works in Vermont, and even then is struggling to provide full statewide coverage. But Wynona keeps a nationwide legal services handbook nearby so that callers from far away in search of help can at least be given some advice.

Case referrals come to Have Justice from a variety of sources, but the greatest are legal advocacy and victim support groups and law enforcement. Not surprisingly for a place with such rural traditions, word of mouth also brings in a significant number of calls. It is Ward's job alone to determine if she can take a new case (although she jokes that her staff tries to keep her away from the phone because she can't say no). Her top priority is taking cases that demonstrate the greatest need—when the women who have been abused don't have the financial resources to get a lawyer.

In a traditional case, an instance of domestic abuse against a woman or mother with children, Ward will start by helping to secure a Relief from Abuse Order from the state to put an immediate stop to the violence. Because Ward travels with everything she needs in the car, she can draft documents and get signatures right on the spot and then file them on her way to her next appointment. And if a case cannot be solved that quickly, Have Justice will remain involved all the way through divorce and child custody proceedings, whatever it takes to ensure the violence is fully ended. (Wynona's longest case lasted four years from start to finish, amassing over 1,000 billable hours of attorney time.) And throughout the process, the program brings in a whole host of social services: child care, financial advice, job placement assistance, visitation supervision, housing referrals. Sometimes she even delivers furniture to help get victims up and running. The idea is to approach the case with an entire battery of services and support so that victims have every degree of ability to seek relief and justice without worrying for their safety and welfare. Ward uses the phrase "wraparound support" to define the approach.

And then there is transportation. Even as the organization has matured, the "Will Travel" aspect of the mission remains a cornerstone. In those early years when Ward was a one-woman operation, she logged more than 30,000 annual miles visiting clients and seeing their cases through the court system, roughly equivalent to having traversed the entire state, top to bottom, 150 times.

Wynona Ward went from empowerment to action. She has now moved to the next point along the path to civic activism: scaling up. She sought out public and private funds to expand her operation, and she succeeded. Have Justice's current operating budget, about half a million dollars a year, typically comes half from government grants and half from public and private foundations. Last year a donor gave the organization a seventy-five-acre property worth $612,000, their biggest single contribution to date. Today,

Have Justice Will Travel has four dedicated offices around the state. Still, much of the work Ward and her associates do is in the original manner: home visits and lots of miles on the road.

According to Have Justice's 2006 Annual Report, 1,960 women and children (and even one man) "have received the entire spectrum of HJWT services." This breaks down to 491 individual cases; but when you look at the numbers of people who have received some counseling but not full legal representation the number skyrockets to over 1,000 cases and more than 10,000 individuals. The statistic that Ward is most proud of is that fewer than 10 percent of the women she has assisted over the years have put themselves back into the abusive situations from which they fled.

NOW first learned of Have Justice Will Travel in 2002. The television program, then called *NOW with Bill Moyers,* ran a feature segment on Ward's operation. *NOW* interviewed a woman named Connie Button, a seventh generation Vermonter, who told of the great sense of shame she'd felt at being a victim of domestic abuse. That was until she met up with Wynona Ward in 1999 and sought help. Button's sentiments are typical of those who have received the services of Have Justice.

Ward has maintained close relationships with many of her former clients but is always on guard to make sure she doesn't get too close. She knows the visceral anger from the abuse she suffered still lurks within her and is careful not to allow it to cloud her lawyer's judgment, which needs to be clear and dispassionate. "You can't let yourself sit on the porch with the .357 all the time," she observes.

One of Ward's greatest victories is having one of her former clients, Brandy Todd, now work for the organization as a paralegal. Todd helps run an offshoot of Have Justice called Women in Transition, which helps victims get on with their lives, teaching them survival skills (like how to open a checking account), offering job search training, and providing them with mentoring and encouragement. Often women who have benefited from the program return to become mentors.

Over the years, Have Justice Will Travel has grown significantly. Ward outgrew using the backseat of her SUV as her headquarters and slowly her work began invading the house she and Harold shared. She jokes that they'd worked and lived in the same small place together while driving the eighteen-wheeler, so why would this be any different? But eventually stacks of legal documents had taken over every room. The house that Harold's grandparents had lived in—a small three-bedroom ranch house just down the hill—came up for sale, and in 2004 Wynona moved the official head- quarters there, right across the street from a huge red cattle barn. Her com- mute from home to office is only about fifty yards. It's an easy stroll, although with winter ice and snow the return uphill can be challenging.

Wynona now has five other full-time attorneys working on staff in ad- dition to a handful of legal assistants and administrative personnel. Interns from nearby Dartmouth College and Ward's alma mater, Vermont Law School, also help with cases. Physically, the operation has grown to include affiliate offices in Bennington and Brattleboro, in the southwest and south- east corners of the state respectively, taking the burden of the entire south- ern tier away from Ward's home office in Vershire, roughly in the middle of the state. In the four counties on the western side of Vermont, which run from Rutland up to the Canadian border, she has started a legal assistance program called LEAP, which she hopes is a precursor to full Have Justice representation some time in the near future.

But these days what Ward is most excited about is her newest addition: Have Justice is expanding to the most remote part of the state, called the Northeast Kingdom. In the summer of 2006, she added a new office on the massive tract of land the group was given (anonymously) in a town called Brownington. At first, the donation of house and land was more burden than benefit: The taxes were sky-high and she regularly had to send Harold on the ninety-minute drive up there to mow the lawn and make small re- pairs on the buildings. She's already had to sell a sliver of the land in order to make her first-year tax payment. But now she's converted the garage on the property into a full office and is looking to hire a part-time attorney to staff it. Until then, it falls to Ward herself to run the operation. She hopes to one day turn the main house, which she now rents to vacationers, into a temporary safe house for victims and their families.

This expansion is very significant: The property is in the middle of remote Orleans County—only fifteen miles from Quebec—and will allow Have Justice to offer full services throughout the entire Northeast Kingdom, the state's poorest and most violence-afflicted region. This is the forgotten corner of the state, the least touched by the advance of vacationing investment bankers and urban dropouts. In this part of Vermont there are no Ben & Jerry's outlets. Every problem created by isolation and lack of resources elsewhere in Vermont is multiplied once you enter this pocket.

These days Ward is only able to spend about 50 percent of her time working on cases. It seems to frustrate her deeply, but she is resigned to it. She knows the only way that she can continue to grow the organization is to do fundraising and apply for grants in order to be able to hire more lawyers and represent the last corners of the state that she has yet to reach. "While I'd rather be able to work with twenty women directly, I know that if I get enough funding we can help 200 people a year," says Ward. For Ward, fundraising is not that unlike life on the road behind the wheel of a rig: If you don't drive, you don't make money.

Publicity has played a big role in her ability to raise money and expand the organization, and there certainly has been no shortage of recognition for her hard work. When she started to get feedback from an article she'd written about her work in a bar association publication early on, she was told by a board member, a publicist, that she was getting her fifteen minutes of fame. Now, years later, she keeps asking him when her fifteen minutes will be over. Accolades have come from all over, from discreet nods in the local market to declarations from Capitol Hill. Patrick Leahy, Vermont's senior senator proclaimed, "[Have Justice] is a shining example for grassroots domestic violence assistance on a national level. I have met this extraordinary woman many times, and I never fail to be inspired and humbled by her dramatic personal story and her venture into a nontraditional career." Wynona's copy of the Congressional Record of his statement is signed "To Wynona Ward with pride." Ward has received a long list of awards, has appeared in print, radio and television many times, and speaks frequently on campuses and before community groups across the country.

Although Ward has no real plans to expand her own program across state lines, she does dream of one day establishing a Have Justice Will Travel Institute that would encourage others to replicate what she has done in Vermont in places all around the country—anywhere people may suffer from both domestic abuse and the ill effects of rural isolation. The thought she left *NOW on PBS* with back in 2002 holds just as true today: "Different donors have asked me, 'Well, how are you going to expand Have Justice? There's only one Wynona.' But I say to them, 'No you're wrong. There are many Wynonas out there.'"

PRODUCER'S SNAPSHOT: WYNONA WARD

Even standing a couple of thousand feet up in the Vermont mountains, an eighteen-wheel Diamond Reo truck looms large enough to be intimidating—but not half as nerve-wracking as the gaze of Harold Ward. "Harold": Could there be a more incongruous name for a 200-pound truck driver with a ZZ Top beard down to his chest? Harold looked like the kind of guy who can see a knife fight coming and still drain his beer.

He was wary of doing interviews but had agreed to speak to me, and I convinced him to stand outside by the truck, which he did patiently as I fumbled with my camera in the cold. I got my equipment set up, blathering on about Thanksgiving plans. Harold watched without saying a word. I took the camera around to the other side of the Diamond Reo cab and composed a shot of him through the open passenger and driver doors.

Harold had put over a million miles on this truck. Inside the cab was a clarifying detail. Above the 12,000-pound front axle was a gas pedal with a tiny metal foot attached to it—something that looked like an antique holiday cookie cutter or a measuring device from the ladies' shoe section at Macy's.

He had jerry-rigged it because his wife, Wynona, had had trouble reaching the gas pedal. I asked him about it, and Harold got all pussycat on me. Chatty, even. He had a lot of affection for that Diamond Reo—it was the one thing in life that he loved even half as much as Wynona. Harold was eager to tell me how he had helped to construct and repair almost every accessory in the cabin. But talking about the gas pedal booty, all he really wanted to discuss was Wynona and her commitment to drive alongside him. She needed it, so why wouldn't he do it?

If someone you care for needs something, why, you go out there and make it happen. That's exactly the outlook on life that Wynona Ward shared with me again and again during that trip. About her brother and his victim. About her clients. About her growing staff that she funded at her own expense, eating lunch they'd all heat up in her kitchen . . . with Harold.

I had been warned before I arrived that there would be no cell phone coverage—something a New Yorker can't easily imagine. There wasn't. It's a real problem in these hills, as each year a handful of travelers die because they can't get a signal to phone for help. Most are elderly. One horrific story after another leads the local news: a man who died in the snow in front of his wife because she couldn't reach 911, or another trapped in his car for more than a day after he ran off the road.

As I followed Wynona in her oversized SUV, the level of her audacity grew on me. She is completely alone out there. She is driving from one (and let's call it what it is) crime scene to another. She wouldn't be there if things hadn't already turned violent. And yet there she is, unafraid, quietly, determinedly, shockingly and brazenly big as life, helping those who would be virtually helpless without her.

Wynona Ward is courageous. She's not a firebrand. Her determination burns within. It's a quality seen in novels and movies, and it's rarely believable even then. To see this kind of courage in real life, up close, doesn't happen very often. But when it does, it's often a slow burn. Wynona's bravery comes through in what she does. Harold and the others around her see it at work day in, day out, year after year.

Wynona is literally a moving target to those who would wish her harm. But she also embodies the very best of her community: a soft-spoken, herbal-tea-drinking, velvet hammer of a wake-up call. It wasn't anything she set out to do or become. To Wynona, there was a need, so why wouldn't she do it?

To know Wynona's past is to understand even more clearly how exceptional she is. The literature about boys who are abused shows a clear pattern, that many grow up to become abusers. Surprisingly, there's not a lot of research showing definitive effects abuse has on girls when they become adults. Somehow Wynona found the strength to get from that childhood to where she is today. And to see her relationship with Harold is to know that in this way, too, she must be exceptional. To give and receive that kind of love takes leaps and bounds of faith from the least scarred amongst us. But to have experienced what Wynona did as a child, and then to love and live as she does today requires the most extraordinary courage.

And more than assistance or even justice, it's courage that Wynona has delivered again and again on those winding roads.

THE PRODUCER: ROBE IMBRIANO has worked for *NOW on PBS*, but he's also produced for Peter Jennings, Bill Moyers, Ted Koppel and Oprah Winfrey, winning numerous awards along the way. His company, Crystal Stair Productions, is dedicated to bringing stories of the marginalized to a national audience.

3

TOMATOES OF WRATH

LUCAS BENITEZ

WHAT HE'S DONE:

Benitez has transformed the lives of the worst-paid people in America, getting them better pay and better work conditions.

LOCAL HERO HIGHLIGHT:

He created an alliance of workers and consumers, took on two of the biggest fast-food companies in the world, and won.

HOW DO YOU STICK UP FOR THE LITTLE GUY IF YOU *ARE* THE LITTLE GUY? That was the question that faced Mexican immigrant Lucas Benitez, a laborer in the tomato fields of south Florida. He and the hundreds of others working under the hot sun were barely earning enough to live on. They were subjected to brutal treatment from their employer—not just verbal abuse but beatings. For years, the workers put up with the abuse and the low pay, until Lucas Benitez spoke up and sparked a revolution.

Benitez is a stocky, barrel-chested farm worker who left his home in Guerrero, Mexico, fourteen years ago, bound for Immokalee, Florida, to join members of his mother's family. He got day work immediately, harvesting winter tomatoes and cucumbers. He soon learned the ropes of working the fields as a migrant, heading to north Florida to pick oranges, and traveling to Georgia, Alabama and the Carolinas during the spring and summer to harvest everything from pecans to peaches.

But Lucas Benitez always came back to Immokalee. "It became my home base," he explained in an interview. "With all the winter crops here, you can get work for seven, even eight months." In fact, Immokalee had a lot in common with the towns Benitez had left behind in rural Mexico. It's a small city in the southwest of Florida, off the main roads, miles inland from the coast. The town center is an intersection of three roads, surrounded by a maze of small streets. People are outside everywhere in the town, walking, riding bikes, standing on corners in discussions, sitting on verandas. It's a startling contrast to nearby Naples, with its sealed environments of air conditioning and SUVs. The city's buildings are mostly single story, often brightly painted in purples, lime greens, and oranges. The diverse cultures of America meet here. One wooden shack, painted vibrant red with purple trim, stands at a prominent corner in town. Tejano music pours out of the open doorway and a tangle of men stand outside watching the foot traffic go by. There's no sign that says "Bar"—in fact no sign of any kind—but the waste bin is piled high with empty bottles of Olde English and King Kobra.

The planted median on Main Street proudly displays flags printed with the words "Immokalee, my home." But there is no mistaking that Immokalee is a very poor city. Chickens dart back and forth from the shade offered by verandas and parked vans. Main Street is surrounded by one run-down trailer park after another.

The locals call the trailer parks *campos*. These are home to the people who pick America's tomatoes. Some structures are actual trailers, with a rusting hitch on the front, but they haven't been on the road in decades. Residents have added rickety wooden verandas and attached propane tanks for cooking. Benitez crowded in with his mother's family in a trailer when he first arrived, but eventually he and his brother rented their own tiny run-down trailer. It was barely big enough to fit two small mattresses. There was no heater or air conditioning. "We just went there to sleep," he says. "It was not a nice place." In these cramped conditions, Benitez's life took shape. He applied for and got a green card and legal residency. He courted a woman who also worked in the fields; they are now married and have a one-year-old boy.

The choices for housing for the town's workers are simply terrible. Few workers have the money to own a house, and most can't come up with the funds for a deposit on a rental apartment. The landlords at the *campos* know it. The rent for a trailer can be as high as $1,500 a month. At these prices, workers cannot afford to house their families with them in Immokalee (Lucas is an exception). The mostly male workforce crowds into the cheapest option, cinder-block barracks with long rows of doors. Each door leads to a single small room with a single window. Each room is packed—home to as many as eight farm workers.

How bad is it? There's no kitchen. The workers share a one-ring burner for cooking. Some of the landlords won't allow air conditioners—they don't want to pay the extra costs for electricity. The rooms are hot, humid and cramped. It's a transient community. Many workers stay for a while and move on. But there are always new arrivals, hungry for work, who come to fill the beds.

Immokalee is a flashback to a distant world of colonies and underdevelopment. The dilapidated town is populated by poor, mostly migrant workers, living in deplorable housing rented to them by rich white landowners. And the forces of law and order? The police officers of Collier County are mostly white. Their cruisers roll through Immokalee, driven by burly young men with crew cuts.

During harvest time there are 20,000 workers thronging Immokalee. The working population is diverse. There's a sharp line between Caribbean blacks (mainly Haitian) and Latino workers. The Latinos have come from all over Central and South America, mostly from Guatemala and Mexico. Some of Immokalee's Latino laborers don't even speak Spanish. They communicate with each other in Q'anjob'al and Mam and other Mayan languages.

The workday begins at four thirty in the morning. Workers gather at a series of parking lots around town. At the largest lot, thousands turn up, walking from their assorted *campos*. Around dawn, old school buses arrive—stripped down, no longer yellow. Workers pile onto the buses and are taken out to the fields that surround the town for miles around.

Once in the fields, workers move quickly up and down the rows of tomato plants. The tool of their trade is a wide plastic bucket. Full of tomatoes, the bucket weighs around thirty-two pounds. Doesn't sound like much? Try filling it, lifting it, carrying it all day. The amount workers earn in a day is wholly dependent on how quickly they can deliver their buckets from sunup to sunset. Each full bucket adds forty-five cents to their pay. It is grueling work, carried out in heat that can exceed ninety degrees and almost completely without shade.

This is the part of the food chain that most Americans never see: an entire class of people working in backbreaking conditions for less than fifty dollars a day. If a worker were able to work six days every week and stay through both of Immokalee's two harvesting seasons, the annual salary would top out at $15,000. And that's assuming what never happens—agreeable weather each day and employers whose needs are spread out evenly over the season.

Immokalee may seem distant, but it's not. Every time you and I shop at the supermarket, we benefit from the rock-bottom pay that farm workers receive. A century ago, American families spent fully one-fourth of their income on food. Today the figure is less than 10 percent. Partly, that's due to the mechanization and industrialization of agriculture. But those low salaries in the fields are a big factor too.

Farm worker salaries are so low that many workers don't even earn the minimum wage mandated by law. Why? The workers are transients, moving from harvest to harvest. And it's estimated that around 30 percent of the farm workers in America are illegal aliens. Farm workers may be the most disempowered group of people in America today.

In these stark conditions, Lucas Benitez found something that gave him hope and a chance to organize. The workers are pretty much left alone after the sun goes down. "In the North, you live in central housing, owned by the boss. You can't even look for your own place because how are you going to get to work? So the boss controls everything. You can't organize. Here people live on their own. No one needs a car, you can walk everywhere you need to go. Also there are two growing seasons so people can stay here longer and this makes it less transient than other places."

It wasn't long after he arrived in Immokalee that Benitez began talking with other workers, during the half-hour lunch break in the fields. There was no place to go for lunch, and no trees for shade, so the workers would gather next to the bus parked on the side of the fields, leaning against the hot metal to get a few minutes' respite from the sun.

Benitez did a lot of listening. Long-time residents told him that wages had been the same for decades. The workers told him stories of threats and beatings. In the voices of his fellow workers, Benitez also heard fear—fear of losing work, of being abused by the growers. They worried that if they spoke up, the growers would target them as troublemakers and refuse to let them work in the fields.

Benitez knew that any effort to get better conditions would need to be unanimous in order to avoid retaliation. But he wasn't discouraged. Benitez and a half-dozen other workers began getting together regularly to talk. The small group's first action was to conduct an informal survey. What were workers worried about? What did they want? The results were clear: Workers wanted better pay, and they wanted respect from their employers.

In the run-down *campos,* Benitez saw the seeds of community. He organized meetings for discussion. He began to nurture what he calls the "expectation of possibilities." For these workers, expecting something different and better was a revolutionary idea. Their lives were organized around endless repetition, doing the same job day after day, year after year. Benitez offered hope. He told them the system could be changed so that workers would get a better deal.

The "expectation of possibilities"—empowerment begins with this phrase. If you think things will never get better, you will never work for change. It's only when you believe change is possible that you become open to the opportunity to make that change happen. When you expect a better life and throw yourself into the struggle to achieve it, you are empowered.

And that was the start of the Coalition of Immokalee Workers, or CIW. The nascent workers' group knew their first challenge was to deal with their bosses, the growers. And these weren't the kind of people who were in the mood for negotiations. There were barriers of race, class, language and culture. The workers of Immokalee say the growers come from an anachronistic, backward way of thinking. The workers called them *rancheros,* a culture out of synch with modern values. "They use the n-word all the time," declared one member of the CIW during a group interview at their headquarters. Lucas Benitez, cofounder of the group added, under his breath and in Spanish, "And not only for black people."

In the days before the CIW was formed in Immokalee, workers say the crew leaders, or *contratistas,* would commonly patrol the fields with guns holstered at their hips. The purpose, they say, was intimidation—to make them feel like workers on a prison chain gang. It was a common occurrence for a foreman to deny a worker payment, claiming they "forgot" or that the worker had not performed the work. Many went unpaid, the guns of the *contratistas* a convincing reason not to raise a dispute.

Then came the first steps toward change. Benitez and a few others set up the Coalition for Immokalee Workers in 1994. At first they used the local Catholic church for meetings. Later they rented out a small, storefront space just steps from Main Street. To this day, the group's structure and decision-making process is egalitarian in the extreme. All members, including all staff, must be actively engaged in field work. And all decisions are made by consent of the entire group. Plans and decisions are made at standing-room-only gatherings each Wednesday after work.

Anybody can be a member of CIW as long as they work in the fields. To get an official membership card for a year-and-a-half term, you pay ten dollars, but this is voluntary. Benitez was interested in inclusion and action. He wanted everybody to participate, everyone to decide and everyone to act. He believed the power of the entire workforce was the only way to win against the *rancheros*.

In one of CIW's earliest victories, Benitez says that they were able to recover over $100,000 in back wages in their first year of operation. But the tasks ahead were still daunting. The workers wanted more pay. The *rancheros* refused to budge. Benitez and the others recall the time a local reporter asked a *ranchero* for comment on a hunger strike being staged by the coalition over wages. He was quoted as saying, "A tractor doesn't tell the farmer how to run his farm." That said it all: *Rancheros* viewed their workers as nothing more than shovels and spades.

Benitez and his colleagues worked hard to organize the workers to fight for their rights. They spoke with other workers as equals, not as bosses. Among CIW staff members there are no official distinctions or titles. For coalition work, the staff gets paid the same rate as the workers in the fields—six dollars an hour. Gerardo Reyes, a gangly thirty-year-old farm worker, explains: "The community sees that this helps the community. There is no corruption. No one has their own private interest." There is a central committee tasked with devising strategies, but even this body is run strictly as a group. When an issue requires investigation, a *formacion* (special group) is assembled from the general membership to take responsibility for the matter.

Before each gathering, pamphlets are circulated throughout the *campos,* attached to the sides or trailers or stapled to palm trees. For members of the community who can't read or don't understand Spanish, the main operating language of the group, staff members create drawings to depict the issues at hand. There is a need to constantly advertise, says staff member Cruz Salucio, a twenty-three-year-old who recently arrived from Guatemala, because there is constant turnover in the community. At the meetings, workers sit on the floor, on a beat-up old couch, at makeshift desks made with folding banquet tables and metal chairs. A poster of Martin Luther King Jr. hangs on the wall. A framed photograph of Zapatista revolutionary Subcomandante Marcos, wearing his signature balaclava and smoking his pipe, hangs opposite the entrance. And a massive mural adorns the central wall, depicting a series of workers, each labeled with a nation of origin—Haiti, Guatemala, Mexico, U.S.A.—standing together with clenched fists raised and the words "One United Force" above them in Spanish and Creole.

The meetings are a free-for-all in which all members are encouraged to speak about their issues. This has lead to a lot of venting of concerns, which Benitez acknowledges is a form of therapy for the community. "Therapy that becomes action," he adds with a laugh.

At times the group's cooperative dynamic has made the CIW a somewhat unwieldy organization. Members freely admit that with no single leader it is occasionally difficult to work with other community groups, media organizations and even their negotiating partners. Even Benitez, who was a cofounder and has emerged as the public face of the CIW, will insist that any meeting, any interview, be a group affair. This kind of egalitarian worker cooperative has been tried all over the developing world, often to disastrous effect. Other groups that posture on equality of management and organization have, in fact, a "man behind the curtain" orchestrating events. But in Immokalee, the coalition appears to have found a way to make it work. Members say their ability to be communal but still effective comes from the culture of their membership: "These people come from a populist background. They are accustomed to community-based solutions, not ones pinned on hierarchy," says Romeo Ramirez, a staff member from Guatemala. They also point to the membership's ongoing connection to field labor and the fact that no one has become insulated from the daily realities of agricultural work. "There is no leadership not living the problem," says Lucas Benitez.

The CIW gained a victory when they staged a one-week general strike in 1995 to protest a grower who had lowered wages. The grower backed down. Now the CIW began to focus on what the workers called gaining respect. This wasn't an abstract issue. They wanted growers to stop mistreating and harming the laborers on the job.

The giant food service companies that buy tomatoes picked in Immokalee do have policies against cruelty. But the policies apply to animals, not people. Taco Bell's corporate parent makes a big deal of this on their web site:

> As a major purchaser of food products, we have the opportunity, and responsibility, to influence the way animals supplied to us are treated. We take that responsibility very seriously, and we are monitoring our suppliers on an ongoing basis to determine whether our suppliers are using humane procedures for caring for and handling animals they supply to us. As a consequence, it is our goal to only deal with suppliers who promise to maintain our high standards and share our commitment to animal welfare.

What an irony that these companies had very strict policies against animal cruelty but overlooked violent abuse against people. Lucas Benitez recalls that when the coalition was first established, they would receive four to five reports a season of physical violence inflicted on workers by the job foreman. It was one of these incidents in 1996 that Benitez and others credit for galvanizing the community and forging widespread support for the efforts of the CIW. A single act of violence in a tomato field sparked a mass movement.

It began with a simple request for a drink of water. Availability of drinking water for the workers who were out all day under the hot sun was an early demand by the CIW. Still, the *rancheros* didn't always provide it. "Even when they did, it was never kept cool and would get hot after being out in the sun with us," recalls Benitez. One afternoon in 1996, a young immigrant worker asked his boss if he could have some water. The boss refused but the thirsty worker took a drink anyway. What followed was a beating so severe that the worker's shirt was drenched in blood. The worker recovered from his wounds, but to this day the coalition keeps the shirt stashed in a file cabinet in their offices to show visitors and to remind members how bad things used to be. Back in 1996, that shirt became a rallying call for the outraged community. For many it was a violation of their humanity, calling them to act. Holding the bloody shirt above their heads as a talisman, over 500 workers marched to the foreman's house and rallied outside. Benitez says that since that day they have had almost no complaints of violence in the fields.

The bloody shirt rally was just the beginning for Benitez and his fellow workers. Now flush with support from the community, they began campaigning for workers' rights. The first step: documenting a series of workplace abuses that they claimed constituted modern slavery. To date, six of those cases have been successfully prosecuted. In the agricultural industry, they are the only slavery cases in modern American history.

As the CIW grew, it got support from a handful of legal aid representatives, among them a man named Greg Asbed. Asbed had worked in Haiti and knew of Immokalee through contacts among expatriates in the United States, many of whom had fled the Caribbean nation during the first Aristede coup. Some of these refugees wound up working in Immokalee, and through them Asbed learned of the need for legal help. He headed across the Everglades to see what he could do. The timing was excellent. Asbed was voted in as a member and has remained a valued asset to the workers' movement. Like all the staff, Asbed does hard manual work: He picks watermelons in between tomato seasons.

The coalition first achieved national recognition through a six-person, month-long hunger strike held in Immokalee that stretched over Christmas and then into January of 1998. The goal was to pressure growers into a wage increase. The growers refused to meet with the workers. The strike ended only through the intervention of former president Jimmy Carter, who promised to use his human rights center to mediate. Two years later, the coalition followed up with a 236-mile march across Florida. Through these high-profile campaigns they were able to win some concessions and make a name for themselves.

But the growers still refused to raise wages. In 1978, workers were paid forty-five cents for each thirty-two-pound bucket they delivered. By the 1990s, the rate had been reduced to only thirty cents. While most American workers were trying to get pay raises tied to inflation, Immokalee workers' wages were shrinking. Even so, the coalition was never able to get the growers to budge. In every discussion the growers would claim that they were locked into fixed contracts with their customers. That it was a very competitive business. That there was nothing they could do. Eventually, through pressure from the governor, the growers did restore the per bucket rate to the 1978 level. It was a victory but still left the workers earning poverty wages.

After years of dealing with intransigence from the grower community, Benitez and the others knew that they needed to come up with a different plan. Their breakthrough idea came in 2000 from one of their newest members, an immigrant from Oaxaca, Mexico. At one of the coalition's weekly Wednesday night meetings, he brought up the idea of leaping over the growers and the landowners. Why not go straight to the buyers for help? The only problem: The business was so competitive, so secretive, it was very hard to determine just where the tomatoes actually ended up. So, the coalition went on a fact-finding mission. They began combing through industry publications until at last they hit pay dirt: an article in *The Packer* that discussed a contract between an Immokalee grower called Six Ls and Taco Bell. The tomatoes of Immokalee went from the fields surrounding their town to the salsas and chopped tomatoes in chain-restaurant tacos. The coalition reached out to Taco Bell.

Taco Bell executives immediately pointed to the many layers that insulated them from direct involvement. This was largely true: From Immokalee to a Taco Bell outlet there were wholesalers, resellers, packaging plants, shippers—an entire phalanx of intermediaries. What did managers in a boardroom in their corporate headquarters in Irvine, California, know about tomato picking? Mathieu Beaucicot, a soft-spoken fifty-two-year-old Haitian who was an early member of the CIW, remembers bringing a tomato bucket with him to some of the initial meetings with executives to show them what was actually involved in running their global operations. The workers even filled it up, he said, to show them how heavy it was to carry when full. The business people showed sympathy but maintained that it wasn't their place to help.

But the coalition knew that Taco Bell had an Achilles' heel. Their business model relied on publicity and branding. Their target consumers were brand-conscious young people of high school and college age. Benitez believed that the same folks who responded to messages from a talking Chihuahua could surely be won over by a well-crafted outreach campaign that demonstrated the suffering of the workers.

In 2001, the coalition held a small press conference in a parking lot outside the nearest Taco Bell, in Fort Myers, Florida. That was only the beginning. Over the course of several years they staged rallies across the nation, where crowds in the thousands turned out to urge Taco Bell to increase compensation to the pickers.

The coalition called for a national boycott of Taco Bell. How to make that happen? Benitez and the CIW came up with an innovative approach to scaling up. The obvious ally for them was organized labor. But the coalition did not see their fight merely as a labor relations issue. Benitez and his colleagues cast their struggle as nothing less than human rights for all. So instead of labor unions, they reached out to students, religious leaders and community activists. The response to the plight of the Immokalee workers was impressive. At its height the "Boot the Bell" boycott campaign was in place on 300 college campuses and in church and community groups all across the country.

This integration, particularly with student and religious organizations, was key to increasing awareness and ramping up pressure. But the campaign remained very much rooted with the workers of Immokalee. Staff members took turns traveling to rallies and protests to speak, taking time off from the harvest to represent the views of actual workers. This is where, the coalition says, their cooperative structures really paid off the most. Actual workers, fresh from the fields, took turns sharing their own personal views rather than relying on well-rehearsed presentations crafted by spokespeople or figureheads.

There were contacts and discussions with Taco Bell executives, but no breakthroughs. The workers learned that the college campus boycotts had stung the company. The amount the CIW was asking for was tiny for a billion-dollar corporation. But executives made it clear that they feared concessions to the CIW might open the floodgates to a series of other claims from workers up and down their supply chain. Besides, it wasn't entirely clear how to even start to comply with the workers' requests. There was no mechanism in the business to pass along a wage increase from the boardroom all the way down to the field. The industry just wasn't set up that way. If the executives agreed to pay more to the companies that supplied Taco Bell with tomatoes, there was nothing to ensure that these distributors or growers wouldn't simply keep the increase and maintain their existing arrangements with the pickers. That was a point the workers agreed on. Given their difficult relationship with the *rancheros,* they certainly didn't want to see their hard-fought gains vanishing into the grower's pockets.

Lucas Benitez and the CIW members recognized that it wasn't going to be easy for Taco Bell to provide what they wanted. But they weren't going to let them off the hook. They had observed from their years in the fields that from time to time the big corporations did send representatives out for inspections, to make sure they were getting the quality and quantity their contracts stated they would get. To the Coalition of Immokalee Workers it simply didn't make sense: If Taco Bell could send people all the way to the fields to check stock, why couldn't they also send money? So they tailored their demands accordingly.

In addition to checking the actual tomatoes, the inspectors should also verify claims made by the CIW as to how many buckets, pounds and truckloads their members were harvesting. These claims could be for-warded directly to Taco Bell corporate headquarters in California and a check, in line with what amounted to a small raise on a per pound basis, could be sent directly back to the CIW. There was logic to the request, but what the CIW was asking for was revolutionary in the business. If they won, they would short-circuit the entire supply chain, going from the giant corporation at the top right down to the lowest worker.

What was being requested was an increase of only one single cent per pound. But Taco Bell balked. Undaunted, the CIW continued to protest. In 2003, they staged a seventy-person hunger strike right outside corporate headquarters in Irvine, California, lasting ten days. It ended only at the urg-ing of the archbishop of Los Angeles. They stepped up their picketing of board meetings and protests of restaurants, and planned a march to the Louisville, Kentucky, headquarters of Taco Bell's parent company, Yum! Brands. Yum! is the world's largest restaurant chain and CIW members had increasingly realized that the decision-making power was based with them. The group received a big boost in 2003, when their work on exposing slav-ery rings and other instances of exploitation in the agriculture industry won the group, Lucas Benitez and two other members the prestigious Robert F. Kennedy Human Rights Award—the first such award ever given to a group working in the United States.

In the end, Yum! Brands and Taco Bell gave in. The coalition had worn the corporation down. The campus boycott had grown significantly and showed no signs of abating. The negative publicity had been piling up for years. And the CIW was able to convince executives that they actually had an opportunity, not just a liability, stemming from the campaign against them. In giving in to the small demands that the CIW had been so publicly making, Taco Bell had a tremendous potential to enhance the stature of its brand. The coalition understood a basic lesson in fighting a bigger foe: Give them the appearance of a victory, allow them to save face and even benefit from the result.

So, on March 9, 2005, vice president Jonathan Blum stood together with Lucas Benitez and announced that Yum! Brands had reached an agreement with the coalition. The company would immediately begin pay-ing higher wages directly to the workers in the tomato fields. In the end, all it cost Taco Bell was an estimated $100,000 a year, a sum almost inconse-quential for a company that does nearly $2 billion in sales in that same pe-riod. Overnight, Taco Bell went from being a pariah in the eyes of the farm workers and their supporters to becoming one of their champions.

Taco Bell pledged not only to change their practices, but to fight to make their subsidiaries do the same. "We are challenging our tomato sup-pliers to meet those higher standards and will seek to do business with those who do," said Blum, signaling their new position and outlook. In 2007, there was even more good news. Yum! Brands agreed to extend the wage in-crease to all of its restaurant chains, which include Pizza Hut, KFC and Long John Silver's. The victory made headlines all across the country. A ragtag bunch of field workers brought a corporate giant to its knees. And among the migrant labor community all across America, Immokalee be-came known for fighting—and winning.

What Benitez and the others show us is that people who are at the bot-tom of the economic scale actually have tremendous power. That holds true even in this jaded age of big money and big politics. The Coalition of Immokalee Workers began its journey through empowerment, taking small steps that showed farm workers they could achieve change by working to-gether. And the story doesn't stop there. CIW came up with inventive ways to take action and scale up. They created a new image for themselves as they grew. They did not depend on traditional labor unions for support. Instead, they defined their struggle as an effort to gain basic human rights for all Americans. Their broad-based coalition of immigrants, students and reli-gious groups snowballed into a national phenomenon.

There is a lesson here about the power of a movement that leads from within. Outsiders could never have galvanized the hardscrabble tomato pickers. They were suspicious of folks who turned up with lots of promises. Landlords and employers had already cheated them. Better not to trust any-body—unless they had lived with them and worked side by side. What led to the eventual triumph of Lucas Benitez and other leaders of the CIW was the strength of their identity and the close relationship they shared with the problems faced by even the lowest worker. Legitimacy was the key to their success.

Still, what had been won in the fight impacted only those laborers who worked jobs in Immokalee under contract with Taco Bell—only about 3,000 workers in total, a fraction of the town's workforce. The majority of workers got no benefit.

That's when Lucas Benitez and the others realized that the most significant aspect of their battle with Taco Bell was that they had designed a successful template. They had one victory under their belt. Now they could replicate the campaign and take it to the other big buyers of Immokalee tomatoes. Very soon they settled on a new target: McDonald's. Yum! and Taco Bell had been powerful adversaries. But now the coalition was taking on an even bigger company with one of the strongest brands around the globe.

From the start, McDonald's resisted. They used many of the same arguments Yum! Brands had about the supply chain. McDonald's didn't want to acknowledge that there was a successful model already in place and that the amount of the wage increase was essentially insignificant. For years the "Golden Arches" continued to fight. That was until the CIW made plans to descend with great numbers on the fast-food chain's corporate headquarters in Oak Brook, Illinois.

But instead of a protest march, there was a victory rally. McDonald's suddenly gave in. Benitez had been in talks with company representatives at the Carter Center and had negotiated a last minute deal. In a joint press statement, the CIW and McDonald's announced a one-cent-per-pound wage increase and an agreement to improve workplace conditions.

President Jimmy Carter heralded the deal as a call to action: "I encourage others to now follow the lead of McDonald's and Taco Bell to achieve the much needed change throughout the entire Florida-based tomato industry." McDonald's supply chain executive J.C. Gonzalez-Mendez promised to bring more pressure on the growers that supply them: "We've made progress with our suppliers through our existing Florida tomato grower standards, which hold the growers accountable to standards higher than the industry, but that was only the beginning. We believe more needs to be done. McDonald's produce suppliers are required to purchase tomatoes only from those growers that have adopted our standards."

The coalition is not resting on its laurels. Even before its victory with McDonald's, the group set its sights on a new target. Just a few hours' drive across the Everglades, outside the shiny downtown business district of Miami, is the headquarters of Burger King. On November 30, 2007, two thousand people gathered in front of the Miami offices of Goldman Sachs Group, one of three multibillion-dollar finance companies that own a controlling stake in Burger King. (The other two are Texas Pacific Group and Bain Capital.) Then they marched nine miles to the Burger King headquarters to demand that the company pay its tomato pickers an extra penny per pound. Half the protestors were workers; the other half were supporters who came from thirty-seven states across the nation.

Burger King has refused to budge and has even threatened growers who are paying the extra money to workers. Meanwhile, Goldman Sachs Group enjoyed record profits. In 2005, Chairman and CEO Henry "Hank" Paulson Jr. earned $37 million, and in 2006 President Bush tapped him to be treasury secretary.

Benitez and the coalition know they are in for another long struggle, but they've had lots of practice in fighting and winning. They went from empowerment to action, and figured out how to scale up to a huge national campaign. They've won huge victories against some of the biggest food giants in America. It wouldn't be a surprise to see them expand their organization to farm workers across the country. Not so fast, according to Gerardo Reyes. Even though their campaign gave them a global reputation, they plan to stay rooted in their own community. "In order to carry out our work we needed to understand issues like free trade and globalization and multinational corporations. But we always balanced that with the fact that all decisions were taken by Immokalee workers, for Immokalee workers," says Reyes.

Lucas Benitez says that from the start he wanted to erase the image of the tomato pickers as "*Los Olvidados de Immokalee*" (The forgotten ones of

Immokalee). His struggle was all about gaining essential human rights for every worker. Their victory was to overthrow the idea that they were nothing more than work tools like tractors or animals. Mathieu Beaucicot says believing in their own power is why they were able to take on such daunting adversaries without hesitation. "We never accepted the notion of being small. We never accepted crumbs from the table. We insisted on being *at* the table."

PRODUCER'S SNAPSHOT: LUCAS BENITEZ

The first time I met Lucas Benitez, I was preoccupied, as producers often are, with framing a shot. Lucas and I were standing in the Coalition of Immokalee Workers' office, a boxy storefront building located right across the street from where workers catch the buses to and from the fields. Lucas was straightening up, quietly moving some chairs around the room. Their weekly meeting was coming up in a few hours, and the now-empty office would be filled with dozens of workers, tired after a long day in the fields.

My mind was on the geometry of the interview—how to position the camera and the chair where Lucas would be sitting. I wanted to get the warm afternoon sunlight streaming through the windows onto his face and still see in the background the painted mural on the back wall of a man carrying a bag of produce. As I visualized the problem in my head, Lucas asked me something in Spanish. All I heard was *"Donde?"* I answered in English, looking around the room, "Hmmm, I'm not quite sure yet." He quietly laughed and stifled a smile, clearly not wanting to embarrass me. And then he said in English, "I'm sorry. I asked you where you were from."

When you first meet Lucas, you might think he's not "leader" material. He is quiet and reserved. He doesn't dominate the conversation. When he speaks up, he is direct and to the point. His face is wise—but youthful. He is the polar opposite of the traditional Latino boss, the *cacique*. When I asked to interview him, he wanted me to speak with one of the other workers as well. The CIW is set up like a cooperative, and Lucas was pushing other workers to get in the media. He didn't want to be the only spokesperson.

Then I saw Lucas in front of a crowd, and I knew immediately why he has become the coalition's go-to guy. He comes alive. It happened that evening, when Lucas stood in front of a group of workers who had just worked thirteen backbreaking hours picking tomatoes. At the meeting, Lucas was a different person. He spoke forcefully, even shouting at times. He told jokes and got the workers laughing and cheering. Today, Lucas had planned a skit about wages. For field workers in the tomato fields, the pay had not increased in 25 years. They brought in a grocery cart filled with bags of food. Lucas pointed at the food and said, "Years ago, we could fill this grocery cart with food on what we make." Then he started taking groceries out of the cart. "But today, on the same amount of money, we can only buy half as much. The cost of the food has gone up, but not our wages!" It was a simple visual demonstration—but Lucas got his point across. The workers understood they were getting less and less.

How did Lucas become the leader he is today? What is the inner power that points some people to speak out, protest, stand up and fight? I began to understand when I sat down with Lucas and did an extended interview. I realized that Lucas Benitez has a profound belief in the goodness of humanity. He has a great sense of hope that people will do the right thing when they're given the choice. At the end of the interview, I asked Lucas why he thought Taco Bell came around, what made them change their mind. He replied, "All corporate executives are human."

THE PRODUCER: KARLA MURTHY came to broadcast journalism seven years ago, changing course from a successful career as a graphic designer and art director. She both shoots and produces her stories. In 2006 her report on Lucas Benitez and the boycott of Taco Bell was nominated for a Business Emmy award.

4

CORPORATE CRUELTY

KATIE REDFORD

WHAT SHE'S DONE:
Redford has scored huge victories in
holding U.S. corporations responsible for
human rights violations around the world.

LOCAL HERO HIGHLIGHT:
She started her fight while still in law
school and came up with innovative legal
approaches to make corporations behave.

GRASSROOTS ACTIVISM CAN BE MICROSCOPICALLY LOCAL, INTENDED TO benefit a single neighborhood. Or it can be global, with the aim of improving the lives of people half a world away. The cause Katie Redford championed was separated by eleven time zones from the wealthy community of Wellesley, Massachusetts, where she grew up. She shared no cultural, linguistic, ethnic or historic bonds with the people she defended. But what they all had in common was the bond of humanity, and that was enough.

When Katie Redford takes on a challenge, she aims to win. She's tough and competitive. In school, Katie Redford was a jock. She loved baseball. In high school she was active in competitive swimming, diving and track. At Colgate University, in upstate New York, she excelled in rugby. Today, her lanky frame, long blond hair and earthy charm may not fit the image of a rugby player, but a certain toughness in her gaze is enough to convince you that the jock instinct remains alive and well.

After she finished college, Redford pointed her sights at law school. First, though, she wanted to travel, see some of the world and go out of the classroom to get real-life experience. So she took two years off before starting at the University of Virginia's law school.

Katie didn't head for Tuscany or Provence. She wanted a challenge and chose to teach English at one of the most remote locations in the world. In 1991, Redford arrived in Tak, Thailand. The town was near the border with Burma and was the main administrative center for a region that was host to a massive refugee community, people who had fled their homes in Burma for freedom across the river in Thailand. Katie had never been out of the developed world. Her education in global human rights was immediate and intense. She loved Thai culture and Thai food, but the plight of the Burmese people drew her in. She began volunteering within the Burmese community, doing social work. During her summer break from teaching, she lived and worked in a Burmese refugee camp.

Burma, or Myanmar as it is officially called by the generals who rule it, is without question a rogue nation. In 2005, Secretary of State Condoleezza Rice called the military junta "one of the worst regimes in the world." Earlier in the year she'd appointed Burma to a second-string "Axis of Evil" that she called "Outposts of Tyranny," along with Cuba, Zimbabwe and Belarus. Myanmar has long scored poorly on the State Department's human rights reports. The regime's most notorious outrage was the arrest and subsequent eighteen-year detention of democracy activist and Nobel laureate Aung San Suu Kyi. She won a landslide election in 1990, but the country's paranoid generals, who had come to power in 1988 in a bloody coup, immediately nullified the vote. She never assumed office, and the country has been ruled with a pathological brutality ever since. The tools of governance include torture, rape, murder, forced labor and wholesale community relocation.

Burma's generals operate in their own world—as odd as it is cruel. On the advice of a fortuneteller, they switched the direction of road traffic from British left side to Continental right side. They've ignored the pleas of the international community to open up, free Aung San Suu Kyi and stop victimizing their own people. In a further act of defiance, the generals recently decided to move their capital city to a location hundreds of miles inland. The historic capital, coastal Rangoon, was seen as too vulnerable to meddling warships that might show up. So the impoverished country is now engaged in building a new capital city in the jungle.

War and rebellion are not new to Burma and did not begin in opposition to the 1988 coup. Ethnic minorities have been fighting the central government since independence was granted by the British shortly after the Second World War. But the generals swung into action against the ragtag rebels with astonishing ferocity. They adopted a scorched-earth approach, razing villages suspected of giving support to the rebels. Millions fled across the border with Thailand.

Burmese refugee camps sprouted on the Thai side of the border between the two countries. These are not the temporary camps you see in
other parts of the world, like Darfur, or in the Congo. In those places, you
see makeshift communities sheltering people in long rows of tents. The tent
cities are designed to be temporary. The hope is that things will settle down
so the refugees can return to their home communities. Not so in the
Burmese refugee camps. Many of the camps have the feeling of permanence. They resemble small cities, with sturdy wooden structures and their
own small economy of shops and businesses. It is clear that no one is expecting the political situation to allow anyone to go home for a long time.

It was in this climate that Katie Redford found her life's calling. The
summer before she began law school she lived in one of the camps with a
refugee family. She saw that the benevolence of the aid organizations had
kept these refugee communities fed, clothed and healthy for the most part.
But Redford could not avoid seeing the desperation of the refugees. If they
went back home to Burma, persecution was assured; death was likely. But
they were unable to rebuild their lives in Thailand. The Thai government,
fearful of creating an immigrant problem, refused to give Burmese refugees
citizenship or even the right to buy land. So the refugees lived in purgatory.

As Redford worked in the camp, she heard tales of savage abuse by the
Burmese military. Women told her of how they'd been raped; men spoke of
being pressed into forced labor. New refugees kept streaming in with new
horrifying stories of abuse.

The war was never far away. In fact, it was a physical reality in the
Burmese camps. They were situated very, very close to the border. Some of
the camps even extended into disputed territory claimed by the Burmese
government. If they had been constructed today and not nearly two decades
ago, international aid experts would have taken the standard precaution of
placing the camps well back from danger. But the Burmese camps had
grown up haphazardly. The front lines of ongoing battles pushed closer and
closer. Redford remembered hearing the blasts of bombs and the staccato of
small arms fire. Sometimes the huts would tremble from nearby explosions.
Nearby camps were even invaded for a short time by Burmese forces, trig-

gering official protests from Bangkok and a reinforcement of Thai troops along the border.

Redford was hooked. The young woman who had grown up in the suburban comfort of Wellesley, Massachusetts, was determined to do whatever she could to help the Burmese people. After Redford started law school, she returned to the camp during a summer break. She got to know a prodemocracy activist and human rights investigator named Ka Hsaw Wa, who had fled Burma and begun systematically documenting the abuses of the Burmese military. She had been looking for someone to smuggle her inside the country to meet with people there and help document their plight. Ka Hsaw Wa agreed to help her. Together they crossed into a region of Burma that at the time was held by a coalition of rebel forces. It was far from safe, but Redford was in good hands.

Their trip took them into the dense jungles of eastern Burma. It was a war zone where motley rebel groups were attempting to hold off the onslaught of the Burmese army. The front lines changed every day. Redford and Ka Hsaw Wa managed to steer clear of the fighting, but everywhere they went the destruction of the war was evident. They met throngs of people who were living life on the run, constantly on guard to stay one step ahead of the military. Their homes had been destroyed. Their meager possessions, the stores of food, were gone. They had only the clothes on their backs. They implored Redford to remember them and find a way to help them.

Redford vowed she would take up their cause. She had discovered a path forward for her life. And as unlikely as it sounds, she also found true love. She and Ka Hsaw Wa became close friends during those illicit trips in the Burmese jungle. Later, romance blossomed and they were married in 1996. Today they have two children, aged ten and six. The struggle Redford had started as an outsider had become intensely personal.

But what could someone like Redford really do, even armed with a law degree and the resources of U.S. citizenship? Despite protests, international sanctions and declarations at the United Nations Security Council, nothing seemed to ever get through to the generals. Redford homed in on the involvement of U.S. corporations in Burma. There had already been a divestment campaign similar to the one used against the apartheid regime in South Africa. Activists had had some success in Burma. Harvard and Stanford universities canceled contracts with Pepsi because of its work there and eventually the soft drinks manufacturer pulled out. Arco, Texaco and Reebok all abandoned operations or investments there. But one large American corporation remained in Burma, on the ground: Unocal, the oil and gas producer based in southern California.

While Redford was making her trips to the Burmese camps, Unocal was pouring money into a project with the Burmese military government. They had a $1 billion joint venture to build a 250-mile pipeline that stretched from coastal waters across the middle of Burma. Its purpose was to carry natural gas tapped offshore to power plants across the border in Thailand. During the time Redford spent undercover in Burma with Ka Hsaw Wa, she heard many stories of abuses committed in connection with the construction of the pipeline. The Burmese regime was burning villages and dislocating entire communities that stood in the way of the pipeline's path. The military was forcing local populations to help build roads and helipads. It was a form of slavery—at the point of a gun. Many of the villagers were called "pipeline porters," but they worked directly for the military, carrying supplies for army troops attached to the pipeline project. Any resistance was met with a brutal response. In one horrific example that Redford heard about, the wife of a man who had escaped a forced labor project was interrogated and beaten by security forces. When she wouldn't give them information, she and the baby she was nursing were kicked into a blazing fire. The woman survived with horrible scars, but her baby perished from the flames.

This story and many like it galvanized Redford's resolve to act. Redford began documenting abuses along the pipeline route. But how could the evidence be used to get Unocal out of Burma? Unocal had already ignored protests and calls for divestment. Crafting a legal strategy against Unocal seemed impossible. Many laws that govern U.S. corporations in America don't apply outside U.S. borders. Here in the United States, the system of laws places boundaries around corporate activities. You can't employ children in an American factory—it's illegal. You can't dump PCBs into the nearest river—it's illegal.

Outside the United States, the picture is entirely different. American corporations doing business overseas aren't bound by U.S. labor laws and environmental regulations. You've heard of the "long arm of the law?" Many of the carefully crafted regulations that keep a lid on corporate misbehavior go only as far as our country's borders.

Redford's inspiration for a new approach came in the classroom: a second-year international law seminar. Her professor introduced the class to something called the Alien Tort Claims Act. The law had been enacted by the very first Congress back in 1789 as a measure to protect against pirates and to ensure safe passage of diplomats at sea. Specifically, the act allowed foreign nationals to sue in U.S. courts against a civic wrong that constituted a violation of the "law of nations." It had been signed into law by George Washington.

For almost two centuries, the law had been virtually unused. Redford's professor brought it up because it had become a tool in international law to seek justice for victims of human rights violations. The renaissance of the Alien Tort Claims Act began in 1979. The family of a seventeen-year-old boy who had been tortured to death years before by a police inspector in Paraguay discovered the perpetrator living with impunity in Brooklyn, New York. The court found that the case met all the criteria of the nearly two-hundred-year-old act. The plaintiffs were foreign nationals and the torture and killing of their relative constituted a civil wrong that violated the "law of nations" (the term was interpreted to refer to what are today known commonly as crimes against humanity). In subsequent years the Alien Tort Claims Act was used to sue for genocide, war crimes, summary execution and cruel, inhuman and degrading treatment.

Redford started to see possibilities in the ancient law that might be applicable to what she had witnessed going on with the pipeline project in Burma. But there was a hitch. In all cases in which the Alien Tort Claims Act had been successfully employed, it had been used against individuals and government agents. But could it be used against a corporation? Redford embarked on an independent study in her third year to tease out her idea. She wrote a paper laying out the case. Why couldn't Unocal be sued by Burmese victims for the inhumane treatment they had received as a result of the work on the pipeline?

Redford's paper, "Corporate Accountability for Human Rights Abuses Under the Alien Tort Claims Act: Unocal in Burma, a Case Study," broke new ground. Using the act against a corporation rather than an individual was uncharted waters. Redford got an A- on the paper. But she also got a word of advice from her professor. As Redford told *NOW with Bill Moyers* in 2004, he didn't want her getting her hopes up. "At the end he said: 'Good job, you've done your research, well written, but I hate to tell you this will never happen. It's impossible. It's unconstitutional, and it's not gonna go any farther than this paper,'" Redford recalled.

From the legal perspective, there was one critical question: How was Unocal to be held responsible for crimes committed by the Burmese army? Unocal employees hadn't displaced anyone. Its workers hadn't raped or enslaved any Burmese citizens. It came down to the question of complicity. Who was liable and who was to blame?

Global energy companies end up working in remote locations—wherever they can find oil and natural gas. Getting to these resources necessarily puts the companies in close contact with local populations—often with troubling results. As Vice President Dick Cheney said, "The good Lord didn't see fit to put oil and gas only where there are democratically elected regimes friendly to the United States." In fact, many of the most richly endowed places on earth are ruled by downright nasty folks. Think of oil-rich Sudan, which has been inflicting a form of genocide on part of its own population.

Local governments have the upper hand, because they control the resources. They often force multinational corporations to enter into joint venture agreements. These agreements commonly require local contractors for technical support and government troops for security. The agreements bind the companies to the behavior of the host country and occasionally put these companies in the center of local political conflicts. At worst, the foreign company's equipment might be physically used to commit atrocities. This is what happened in Nigeria where local security forces reportedly used a Chevron helicopter to raze a village in which protestors were living. But even when there is nothing so clear and dramatic linking a crime to the foreign investor, there is the simple security relationship that exists.

The arguments companies often use to justify putting up with a host government's bad behavior just didn't hold water for Redford. The multinational companies are much more powerful than they let on, she says. "It's completely disingenuous for the companies to say: 'Oh, we have no way to negotiate around that.' Or, 'We would have lost the contract.' Give me a break. Corporations are convincing nations to override their *constitutions* in their contracts," Redford says. "But it sounds good. You say 'You poor oil company, you're a victim.'"

To invest in Burma, Unocal had to employ the Burmese Army for protection. They claimed there was no alternative. Troops were essentially on the Unocal payroll. The way Redford read the law, this relationship was enough to qualify Unocal for an action using the Alien Tort Claims Act. Redford made the Unocal matter her first priority once she finished law school and passed the bar. Right away she resumed documenting abuses, exploring her legal options and gauging the willingness of prospective plaintiffs to sue. It wasn't long before she was ready to bring a case.

Katie Redford, law student, had decided to take on one of the biggest corporations in the world. Her legal strategy had never been used to win a case. Her professor had told her the approach would fail. But Redford believed she could make a difference. For her, this was the moment of empowerment. Redford had already learned first hand and in enormous detail about the abuses being committed against the Burmese people. She now wanted to use U.S. courts to make a difference.

The first step was to reach out and create a network of support. Pursuing the case against Unocal would require years of legal work and tens of thousands of dollars. She began to assemble a legal team. An early supporter was the Center for Constitutional Rights (CCR). William Kunstler and other progressive lawyers had formed the CCR back in the 1960s to help with civil rights cases in the American South, and the group now pursued civil liberties cases around the world. CCR got two heavy hitters to work on the case: Judith Chomsky, legal activist and sister-in-law to Noam Chomsky, and Paul Hoffman, the man who had been at the center of several important cases where the Alien Tort Claims Act had been employed. Hoffman is considered the guru of this law.

The team Redford built was formidable. They were good lawyers and good litigators who knew this would probably not bring in a big fee. The group was eager to apply the Alien Tort Claims Act in a novel way, to bring justice to the suffering. The team began to hone a closely argued legal brief making the case. Redford and Ka Hsaw Wa drew up a list of plaintiffs against Unocal—individual villagers who had suffered abuse because of the pipeline construction. Because of the danger that the villagers would be tracked down and killed by the Burmese government, they remained anonymous in the legal filing. They were called John Doe I, Jane Doe I, Baby Doe I, and so on. One of the Does was the woman who had been kicked into the fire by security forces and endured the loss of her baby.

The case, which became known as *Doe* v. *Unocal,* made headlines when it was filed in 1996, mostly for the maverick way it was attempting to use the old law. Just getting the U.S. District Court in Los Angeles to agree to hear the case was a big deal. Many legal analysts quickly lined up with Redford's law professor, doubting the courts would allow it to go very far. Indeed, right away, the battle had more to do with the applicability of the law and the question of jurisdiction than the actual violations that had occurred in Burma. Redford mounted a two-front attack. In Washington a team of lawyers fought the battle of jurisdiction and applicability of the Alien Tort Claims Act. In Thailand and Burma Ka Hsaw Wa worked with other lawyers, building up the evidence and testimony of the actual case. Redford herself bounced between the two duties, running the overall operation.

Doe v. *Unocal* took over Katie Redford's life. She formed EarthRights International, a nonprofit organization, as a way to raise money and support the massive effort against Unocal. From the beginning, Redford's vision was global. She wanted to win against Unocal, and she wanted to use the law to help others around the world. In a 2003 profile of Redford in the *Boston Globe* a co-worker remarked: "Katie was outraged by the injustices and naïve enough to think that she could take them on." Naïve? Maybe. But Redford was determined to make a difference.

Unocal's response from the start was that it had not known what the Burmese Army had been up to and that it was innocent of any charge of complicity in anything they had done. Back in 2004 when *NOW with Bill Moyers* first told the story of Redford and the Unocal case, they interviewed Unocal's lawyer Daniel Petrocelli. Petrocelli had been propelled to fame as the lawyer representing the Goldman family in the O. J. Simpson civil case, but now he was on Unocal's team. The case was still in the courts and Petrocelli was defiant: "You can't be charged with liability simply because the Burmese military has a bad reputation." Unocal was simply there for business, he said. They had created jobs and initiated some social programs in local communities. Besides, what could they really do? "Unocal doesn't control the Burmese military. And Unocal can't stop the Burmese military from doing what they're going to do in that country. No more than the American government can," said Petrocelli.

Doe v. *Unocal* began working its way through the U.S. federal court system in California. The Unocal argument of knowing nothing, controlling nothing, met with a skeptical reception. In hearings, the court zeroed in on Unocal's involvement and questioned their claims of innocence. Particular focus was given to the helipads next to the pipeline route. The Burmese Army had used forced labor to construct them. The following is an excerpt from the transcript of a hearing in a San Francisco courtroom, when the judge was considering a motion by Unocal to dismiss the case.

JUDGE: Tell me first what the helipads are for.

UNOCAL ATTORNEY: For landing helicopters.

JUDGE: To construct the pipeline. To help construct the pipeline.

UNOCAL ATTORNEY: . . . They're there for any purpose that the government wanted to use them.

JUDGE: I know, but why would you build the helipad, you know, in a
   remote location right next to the pipeline right of way?
UNOCAL ATTORNEY: Well, the location where the pipeline's going
   through . . .
JUDGE: You have to draw these inferences in favor of the opponent
   to your motion.

This was but one of dozens of legal skirmishes. The big battle in *Doe* v.
Unocal was whether the case had any rightful place in a U.S. courtroom.
Here Unocal had a whole host of allies. There was a tremendous amount at
stake for the entire international business community. A victory for the
plaintiff would have severe impact on any corporation doing business in any
nation where human rights were being trampled (and there are many,
sadly). Corporate America started to pay attention once the case had picked
up steam and had survived initial jurisdictional challenges. Very powerful
forces were brought into play on Unocal's side. The concern was that if U-
nocal lost, the floodgates would open to all sorts of litigation against U.S.
corporations doing business overseas. This debate still rages today. A recent
op-ed in the conservative *Washington Times* says Alien Tort Claims Act
cases "needlessly clog our courts" and called lawyers who use the act "Alien
Ambulance-Chasers."

   The Bush administration was worried too. *Doe* v. *Unocal* went against
its probusiness philosophy. At least in theory, the Department of Justice
should have backed Redford and her team since the Alien Tort Claims
Act was on the books as an actual law of the United States. But DOJ opposed the lawsuit. There was a notion within the Justice Department that
the old, creaky Alien Tort Claims Act was not enough to trigger a lawsuit.
They contended that a specific authorization from Congress was required
for this.

   Legal analysts trace this line of thought back to an influential article
that appeared in the *Fordham Law Review* in 1997, the year after Redford
and her team filed suit against Unocal. The author—none other than Katie
Redford's old professor, Jack Goldsmith. He had given her an A- on the

paper but told her it would never fly. Now he was framing the main legal argument against Redford's case. In 2002, Goldsmith joined the Bush administration, first at the Department of Defense, then at the Department of Justice. Today he teaches at Harvard Law School and is a visiting scholar with the conservative American Enterprise Institute.

The White House came up with lots of objections to the Alien Tort Claims Act. One was based on the notion that the president, and only the president, has the legal authority to determine America's foreign policy. Invoking the Alien Tort Claims Act, the argument went, was equivalent to challenging White House power. Government officials complained that the act stood in the way of good relations with other countries, and by extension threatened national security. At one point they even brought out the biggest cudgel in their arsenal: that the Alien Tort Claims Act impaired their ability to prosecute the "war on terror."

The government filed an *amicus curiae* (friend of the court) brief to try to persuade the court to drop *Doe* v. *Unocal*. The irony was that Redford's position in the lawsuit was essentially in line with State Department policy toward Burma. Foggy Bottom had long criticized the Burmese government regime. But as the first landmark case, which would set significant precedent if it won, it still attracted the ire of the State Department and the White House.

Years went by as the legal battle over *Doe* v. *Unocal* wound through the courts. In 2000, opponents were successful at getting the Unocal case dismissed in U.S. District Court. But Redford managed to get the Ninth Circuit Court of Appeals—the one in San Francisco frequently accused of liberal judicial activism—to reverse the decision and put the case back on track.

Then came an unexpected development, one that threatened to undermine the very basis of the Alien Tort Claims Act, upon which Redford's entire case stood. The highest court in the land was going to have a chance to weigh in on the legal debate that had been raging over the applicability of the act. A separate case based on the Alien Tort Claims Act reached the U.S. Supreme Court in the 2003–2004 docket. The case was called *Sosa* v.

Alvarez-Machain. It had been brought by a Mexican citizen, Dr. Alvarez-Machain, who claimed that the U.S. Drug Enforcement Agency had approved plans to illegally abduct him in Mexico and bring him to the Unites States to face charges. *Sosa* v. *Alvarez-Machain* was based on the same law Redford was using, the Alien Tort Claims Act, although the lawsuit was aimed at the U.S. government and not a corporation. On the last day of its term, the Supreme Court rejected Alvarez-Machain's claim. But now it gets interesting. David Souter, writing the primary opinion, said the Mexican doctor's claim did not satisfy the requirements of the law. But Souter explicitly supported the Alien Tort Claims Act as law of the land and still in force.

That was good news for Redford and her team. And there was more good news. Souter left the door open for new cases. In his opinion, Justice Souter cautioned that the law had only a narrow window of applicability in modern times. But he went on to say: "Judicial power should be exercised on the understanding that the door is still ajar subject to vigilant doorkeeping. . . . For two centuries we have affirmed that the domestic law of the United States recognizes the law of nations."

Doe v. *Unocal* had survived. Not only that—indications were that it was doing well in the U.S. Court of Appeals for the Ninth Circuit. Perhaps reading tea leaves, Unocal caved in. They settled *Doe* v. *Unocal* instead of risking a costly and uncertain legal battle. The company made no admission of guilt but did write a huge check to the plaintiffs in order to head off a judicial decision that might have resulted in an even bigger payment.

The out-of-court settlement was a landmark event. It was a huge victory in the battle for accountability for corporate crimes committed overseas. "John Doe I," the lead plaintiff, and the thirteen members of his co-class were reportedly awarded $30 million. A significant portion of the money was designated to a fund to develop the region, provide human rights training and assist those displaced by the Burmese regime's brutality. One of the plaintiffs told EarthRights, "Most of all I wanted the world to know what Unocal did. Now you know."

Redford's lawsuit didn't bring down the Burmese government. And it didn't stop construction of the natural gas pipeline. Today the generals sit in their new capital city, counting their share of the profits from the 525 million cubic feet of natural gas that gets sent to Thailand every day. In the summer of 2007, at least some of that money went toward the brutal suppression of peaceful protests, resulting in widespread beatings and hundreds of arrests. There were several people known to have been killed, and with all information tightly controlled by the military regime, human rights activists fear the real number of fatalities could be in the hundreds.

But Redford's victory sent shock waves through the global business community. The message went out to corporate executives that consorting with dictators can be disastrous—and illegal. Redford has forged a tool that activists, lawyers and citizens rights groups everywhere can use to force accountability on those who would seek to profit from the misery of others. Today you will find reference to *Doe* v. *Unocal* in textbooks at both business and law schools. And it goes beyond the classroom. "The fact that every oil company today now has a social responsibility statement, has codes of conduct . . . that they hire consultants. That's a concrete indication that at least they're pretending to take it seriously," says Redford. Since *Doe* v. *Unocal,* the Alien Tort Claims Act has been used to target corporations from Pfizer to Ford to Citigroup.

Redford doesn't have a problem with these big corporations making money. She acknowledges that corporations are the engine for the American economy and for much of the world. It's the single-minded pursuit of profit at the expense of everything else that's the problem. Toxic dumping and abuse of workers might increase the profit margin. But even if it's profitable, it's morally wrong.

Redford hopes that the victory in *Doe* v. *Unocal* will help foster a different mentality within the international business community. One that values the big picture, not just the pursuit of short-term profits. "I truly believe that in the long run, and things like oil pipelines are over thirty-year periods, respect for human rights is good for business. And you need to operate in a way that the local population is going to welcome you," says Redford. She is hopeful that with each legal victory, executives get the picture and factor human rights into their business plans. But until this becomes accepted as what she calls "just good financial sense," there are more cases to be brought.

Redford knows that the law often favors those with the ability to pay for it. She has seen how it was used to shelter corporations and maintain, rather than halt, wrongdoing. What Redford realized, from the time she was still in law school, was that with creativity the law could be a powerful ally for everyone, not just the rich and powerful. Through dedication and clever application, it could be used to seek justice for some of the most vulnerable victims on the planet, those in faraway places who have been subjected to the worst crimes against humanity: genocide, torture and slavery. And she saw a way to use the law of the Unites States to effectively hold some of the most rich and powerful corporate entities accountable for complicity in these crimes.

Katie Redford, EarthRights International and their colleagues and co-counsel have taken up battles around the world. In Nigeria they have filed suit against Chevron, based on the use of their boats and helicopters in attacks against villagers. They have a lawsuit against Shell in the case of activist Ken Saro-Wiwa, who was executed by the Nigerian military in 1995. Shell is being sued for complicity in the torture and killings of several activists, including the hanging of Saro-Wiwa. The lawsuit charts new ground for Redford because neither the plaintiffs nor the defendants are U.S. entities.

EarthRights International also recently announced a case filed on behalf of Colombian peasants against Chiquita, the banana company. The charge is that Chiquita hired and armed paramilitary groups who conducted brutal raids on villages and killed labor organizers. EarthRights International lawyers are confident that the lawsuits based on the Alien Tort Claims Act will help force better behavior by U.S. corporations all over the world.

And they have branched out to break new legal ground. In April 2007, they filed suit on behalf of the indigenous peoples of Peru's Amazon basin. The case alleges California-based Occidental Petroleum devastated the waters and lands of Peru's Achuar people. The legal basis for the lawsuit is unusual. EarthRights International is applying a legal doctrine called toxic tort—which has rarely been used outside the U.S.—to an environmental disaster in the remote jungles of the Amazon. Redford believes, as with the Alien Claims Tort Act, that the toxic-tort law can be stretched to cover this new application.

EarthRights International has grown. In its first year of operation, 1995, a grant of $30,000 got it started. Now the annual budget is around $1.5 million. The group has added staff lawyers like Marco Simons, who is in charge of the Occidental Petroleum case in the Amazon. He was inspired to get into this line of work after hearing Redford speak when he was still an undergraduate at Harvard. In addition to its headquarters in Washington, EarthRights International has a big office in Chiang Mai, Thailand. The Thai office runs educational and advocacy programs for Burmese refugees and focuses on human rights investigations, documentation and fact-finding throughout Southeast Asia.

Redford is modest about her journey. She says she's shocked that what started out as a school assignment has turned into a well-respected strategy for corporate accountability. But she had the courage to believe that she could make a difference. Her story shows that civic engagement can work on a global scale. With her help, Burmese villagers sued a corporate giant and won millions. Redford took an obscure law and fashioned it into a tool for holding giant American corporations responsible for their actions around the world.

"This is a huge long journey that is probably going to carry on long after any of us are around," says Redford. "We are part of a long road to justice that maybe started in 1948 with the Nuremberg Trials and the modern development of international human rights law. And it's a very young field and it's a long way to go."

PRODUCER'S SNAPSHOT: KATIE REDFORD

I arrive at the EarthRights International office in Washington, located on the fourth floor of a nondescript K Street monolith. I am here alone, filming an update on EarthRights founder Katie Redford and her groundbreaking lawsuit against oil giant Unocal in Burma. I'm not sure what I will find. Our original report on Redford had been broadcast years earlier, produced by a different team. This is my first chance to meet her. What will this mighty crusader be like? She'd taken on one of the largest and most powerful corporations in the world and won. She came up with the legal strategy while in law school, and now the strategy is being taught in law schools.

I ring the bell outside the office door and wait. Nothing. I try the knob and find it unlocked. There's a man standing just inside, reading something intently, not looking up as I lug my camera equipment past. "Um, do you work here?" I finally interrupt. It turns out to be Rick Herz, one of Katie's partners in law, lead counsel on an EarthRights lawsuit against the oil giant Chevron. "Yeah, go on in!" Rick says, waving me through, no questions asked.

EarthRights International's offices are buzzing. There are stacks of documents on the desks, and people crisscrossing the small space. Katie and her husband Ka Hsaw Wa are both on the phone. They got back to Washington yesterday after spending several weeks in Thailand. Marco Simons, EarthRights legal director, greets me as he whizzes by, headed for the fax machine. He's off to Geneva tomorrow. Art and mementos from around the world cover the walls. There are brightly painted murals, an Asian tapestry, photographs of lawyers, teachers and activists, plus numerous awards that Katie and Ka Hsaw Wa have won over the years. The display is a visual testament to the mission and passion that drive this organization.

I still need to confirm an interview with Katie for the following day, and assume she must at least have an assistant, given her demanding schedule. When I ask Rick Herz who that might be, he just laughs and says, "Talk to Katie herself!"

There are no luxuries for the attorneys here. You won't find the lavish buffets, personal assistants, gleaming board rooms or exorbitant salaries that so many of their law school classmates enjoy at the big-name law firms. The EarthRights International lawyers have given all of this up to follow a very different path. Their work might not pay much, but its importance is beyond measure. At the end of the day, they go home knowing that what they're doing is saving lives and righting wrongs. This tiny group has fundamentally transformed the way American business is done overseas.

I begin filming. I want to make a visual sequence about the EarthRights lawyers. All the staff is focused on their tasks, and my moving around doesn't distract them. Katie is working at her computer as I set up the tripod and aim the camera at her through the office door. When she looks up, she is warm and friendly. "Is there any coffee left? I don't care if it's stale!" she says, bounding across the office. Even though she is exhausted from her trip from Southeast Asia, she is calm, confident and laughing. She carries the burden of her work lightly.

Katie's office is full of images of the people she's helped all over the world. There are photos of her children. But there is also the large poster of her beloved baseball team, the Boston Red Sox, who were the underdogs for so many years. On her desk is Tupperware containing a lunch brought from home. She pins her long brown hair up with a ballpoint pen and apologizes for a mess in the corner. Katie Redford is authentic. She's a real person who doesn't put on airs or act like a big-shot lawyer. It's a reminder that some of our greatest heroes aren't in glossy magazines or on TV. They keep their heads down. They work hard and honestly and without fanfare.

Katie and her staff finally find a moment to sit down together and talk. I hover around, sticking my camera over their shoulders and in their faces. They discuss sensitive budget issues, ignoring me the whole time. They have a lot to worry about: Nigerians whose lives and villages have been destroyed, Burmese refugees victimized by a brutal military regime, Amazonians whose ecosystems are being devastated.

Katie says she hopes someday she won't have to do this job—that one day there won't be any more victims to defend, any more corporate criminals to fight. Right now, there is still plenty to do. The meeting ends and they all go back to work.

THE PRODUCER: MEGAN THOMPSON is one of *NOW*'s newest video journalists. She both shoots and produces stories for the broadcast. Previously, Thompson was a congressional aide on Capitol Hill for four years, then worked with a women's cooperative in Ghana, West Africa. While studying journalism and documentary film at NYU, Thompson directed, filmed and edited a documentary film about women in agriculture ("Ladies of the Land"), which won a Student Academy Award and a Gracie Allen Award.

5

HELPING THE CHILDREN

JOHN WALSH

WHAT HE'S DONE:
Walsh has put foster care kids on an express
track for quick help and a better future.

LOCAL HERO HIGHLIGHT:
Working within a dysfunctional system, he
has created a revolution from the inside.

WHEN JOHN WALSH DECIDED TO TACKLE THE ENORMOUS PROBLEM OF helping children in foster care, he knew the system was broken. Walsh created a solution. He now heads up an agency that has revolutionized the treatment of foster care children by rocketing them through the courts and getting their cases resolved quickly.

One man's tenacity has created a better life for hundreds of children. But there is more to tell about John Walsh. Walsh worked inside the system, back when it was broken, and he still works on the inside. Anyone with a job in a dysfunctional bureaucracy knows how tempting it is to quit and walk away. Walsh the civic activist believed he could empower the people inside the system to work better, to place the children first. He figured out a way to fix the system from within.

Walsh was raised in Cleveland, Ohio, part of an embracing family, one of four children. The whole family was very involved in the Catholic church. Walsh served as an altar boy. He has always been close to his family, particularly with his identical twin brother, Jim. The two went to high school together, formed a band together, and went to Florida State University together.

John Walsh's career as a crusading lawyer almost didn't happen. His father was an attorney, but Walsh steered toward a different career. At Florida State he majored in media communications. His plan was to work in film or television production. But an internship in Miami at a company that made television commercials convinced him that the glitzy life wasn't all it was cracked up to be. Walsh took a fresh look at his father's profession and decided to become a lawyer.

Right out of law school in 1989, Walsh starting working on critical matters involving children. He went to work for Florida's big state agency, the Department of Children and Families, representing the state in cases involving child abuse. For Walsh, it started out as just a job. But over the years something started to change within him. It began with a growing frustration with the slow and often ineffective system. There was little money available to solve the problems of children. Every day Walsh witnessed incompetence and missed opportunities.

Walsh decided to try working as an advocate outside the system to see if that would be a better way to help troubled children. In 1997 he joined the Legal Aid Society of Palm Beach County as a lawyer for their Juvenile Advocacy Program. Walsh's job was to represent children who had serious or habitual run-ins with the law. Many had been in foster care. Walsh found children in real need of help. He soon noticed something exceptional in his meetings with the children. As he was leaving, some of them would tell him they loved him. Walsh was shocked. For him, it was a sign that these troubled kids were absolutely desperate for affection. "When you realize that these kids have no one in their lives, that they're telling *me* they love me. That really drives home the seriousness of the situation," says Walsh. "I didn't want anyone to ever have to tell their lawyer they love him because they don't have anyone else." Walsh stopped thinking of what he was doing as a job. It became a mission.

Through his work with kids, Walsh realized the state of Florida was failing to help the vulnerable children entrusted to its care. The state was left holding the bag when families failed their children. Parents did unspeakable things. They shot up with drugs with their children underfoot. They abused their children sexually. They abandoned them on street corners, in parking lots. The government's responsibility was to take care of the children and quickly find a better life for them. But the system was failing, and as a result, the children were suffering.

Walsh came to understand from the inside how deeply flawed the system was. When children were at risk living with their parents, the state wasn't doing a good job of intervening. And its system of placing kids into foster care homes was a mess. There weren't enough investigators to make sure that the foster homes were taking good care of the children. The results were tragic. Between 1989 and 1997, a total of 648 children died from abuse while in the foster care system in Florida, according to an investigation by the *Tampa Tribune*. And there was the heartbreaking story of Bradley McGee, a two-year-old boy who was returned to his biological mother. Government workers had been warned that the mother was abusive and unfit. Sixty-six days later, Bradley's mother and stepfather became enraged that Bradley was not toilet trained. They held Bradley's head underwater in the toilet and then beat him to death.

How do you even begin to fix a system that is so badly flawed? Walsh knew the biggest problem was a lack of resources. Florida has no state income tax. Low taxes mean little money for social services. And even though the state has successfully marketed itself as upscale and hip, a vacation paradise, there are many areas of terrible poverty and blight.

Case in point: Palm Beach County. It's one of the largest counties in the state, and the contrasts of wealth and poverty are extreme. Cross the bridge that connects the mainland to the narrow barrier island called Palm Beach, and stretching down the avenue are mansions with fancy gates and stately rows of royal palm trees. But go inland a few miles from the coast, and you'll find derelict trailer parks and shacks that tilt against each other. With poverty sometimes come drug addiction and violence. The city of West Palm Beach has a murder rate that is three times the national average, on par with Oakland or Atlanta.

However, to the credit of the area's legislators and board of commissioners, Palm Beach County took action to help the most vulnerable. They made a decision back in 1986 to establish a dedicated children's services organization. Florida's social services are so underfunded that it is up to each individual county—not the state—to set up such an office. Of the sixty-seven counties in the state, only eleven have established agencies for children's services.

The first step was getting voters to pay for it. Palm Beach County voters agreed to an annual contribution of a little over fifty cents for every $1,000 of assessed real estate value to fund children's services. These days this arrangement gives the organization over $95 million a year to operate.

Children's Services Council of Palm Beach County helps kids in lots of ways, including prenatal care and after-school programs. Council officials knew of Walsh's work and were impressed with his dedication and effectiveness. When they approached Walsh to see if he had any ideas as to how to help kids who were in the foster care system, he jumped. Walsh knew exactly what needed to be done. He'd been pondering that very question for years.

With many of the troubled kids he'd encountered there was one theme that had become a common denominator: time spent in foster care. The years a child spends in foster care, he says, are like being in prison. Even when a child is placed in a foster home with caring, responsible foster parents, Walsh believes the dislocation, lack of permanence and uncertainty can lead to a level of anxiety similar to that produced by life in jail. He compares life in foster care to Chinese water torture, with each drop of time in state care chipping away at the sanity of young minds.

And Walsh had a simple solution. He wanted kids out of foster care and into a better place—fast. The goal was a permanent parental-like environment that provided stability and safety. He is utterly convinced that the system is so toxic that no amount of counseling or therapy will help. "It's putting Band-aids on a bullet wound," says Walsh. He knew he would be fighting the system to get kids out of foster care quickly. He had seen judges, lawyers and investigators drag out the process. "These people sometimes want everything to be perfect, but it doesn't have to be. You don't have to be able to give every child their own bedroom to make a healthy home. You just have to solve the problem that caused them to be removed and get them out of the system."

In 2001 the Foster Children's Project got its start, funded by the Children's Services Council with John Walsh at the helm. It was a brilliant and innovative approach to civic activism. Walsh would be working to solve an urgent problem, from inside the belly of the beast. The group began with six lawyers, helping very young children. With success, it has grown. The annual budget is now nearly $2 million, and Walsh's group represents kids from birth to twelve years old. In addition to lawyers and legal aides, the

Foster Children's Project recently added three social workers to their staff. The aim is to understand the full complexity of the children's lives.

The single-minded goal of Walsh and his colleagues is speed. As long as it is safe to do so, they want to shorten cases for kids taken from their parents. They want quicker, permanent placements for the children. Walsh backs up his approach with simple economics. It costs $68,000 a year to keep a child in juvenile detention, which is often a breeding ground for career criminals. Making the system work is cheaper than producing thousands of young adults with poor education, no career skills and no family support network.

So what is life like for Walsh on a typical day? There are small steps forward and a couple of gut punches. On a bright Wednesday afternoon, Walsh walks from his offices to the county's juvenile court building in West Palm Beach. At the courthouse, Walsh stops again and again to chat with a stream of lawyers, judges, bailiffs and clerks. An attorney for the state, who at times is Walsh's bitter adversary inside the courtroom, asks for detailed advice on a foster care case involving an undocumented alien. Walsh is in his element. For him it's not about policy or personal opinion. It's about giving a voice to the most weak and vulnerable.

The third floor of the modern court building is where Walsh does much of his work, arguing cases in the courtroom. But he spends a lot of time in the wide, windowed hallways outside, where people involved with the cases congregate before and after hearings. Sometimes he may be chatting with a judge, sometimes he's strategizing with foster parents, sometimes he's gearing up for a fight with his opposing counsel, probing them for their arguments and tactics. Only very rarely do the children Walsh represents actually come to join him in court. They are usually at school. Walsh doesn't want to drag them away from their classrooms and make them wait, sometimes for hours, for an action that usually lasts only a few minutes. But when something requires the children to be there, like an appearance to testify, Walsh actually relishes it. He feels it helps the kids to see the judge and watch the proceedings. It demystifies the whole experience and shows them that real people, adults, *are* working on their behalf.

This day, Walsh is in court for two reasons. The first is a routine appearance to accept new cases. This is how it starts out: children whose lives have just been changed. They were removed from their homes the previous day or even in the middle of the night. Some days the Foster Children's Project may be given as many as seven new children to represent.

Sometimes there are resources that can make a difference. There are children who have close family members who step up to help. Grandparents, uncles or aunts may offer to take in the child. A family connection is always a good solution. If that's available, Walsh's project leaves the case to be resolved through regular channels. Walsh wants to reserve the resources of his project to take on the difficult cases, the kids twelve and under who don't have a family member to take them in.

At Wednesday's hearings, Walsh and his associates get three new cases. It's a highly charged setting. The parents are frequently in the courtroom, and their children are being taken away from them. The courtroom atmosphere is often punctuated with outbursts—either shouts or sobs.

In this day's cases, drug use comes up again and again. One involves a ten-year-old boy who had begun to act out sexually with other children. Child protective investigators discovered that both his parents were using drugs in the home. In another case, two very young children, ages two and four, had been taken by their mother to a crack house so that she could get a fix. In the courtroom, bailiffs have to keep the parents apart, since the mother had a restraining order taken out on the father after episodes of domestic violence. Each is escorted separately in and out of the courtroom.

Walsh's fixation on the devastating effects of foster care is evident in another case. The mother had been a foster child. Child protective investigators found her living on the streets with her own newborn who will now be removed from her and will be sent to foster care. It is a heartbreaking cycle to witness.

Each hearing is a chronicle of terrible treatment of young, helpless children. Walsh is on the side of the children, passionately engaged in finding them a better future. A less measured person might reach over the table and throttle parents who act so irresponsibly. But Walsh's demeanor throughout is calm, logical, even-keeled. He maintains his equilibrium as family tragedies play out in front of him.

Walsh is determined to help out the children in his care at every step of the way. That's evident at a hearing on this day to consider an emergency motion he has filed on behalf of a girl named Ashley.* Ashley, who is now fourteen, is about to graduate from junior high. She's had a tough childhood. Her mom was a drug user and moved the kids around, on the run from authorities. Ashley's two younger siblings had been removed from her mother's care and were already being represented by the Foster Children's Project. Ashley herself had been left to live with a family friend in Martin County, just north of Palm Beach. She had been there for about six months. She'd enrolled in the local junior high school and was doing remarkably well, with a grade point average of 3.71.

Walsh is impressed. Children he sees rarely do well in school. For Ashley it was already the fourth school she'd attended that year. She'd made friends even in the short time at her new school and is very much looking forward to attending her formal graduation ceremony in two weeks. As with all of the cases Walsh takes on, he has had a lot of personal interaction with Ashley. He knows how much her junior high school graduation means to her.

But just weeks before commencement, Ashley's life has hit a major snag. A child protective investigator made a site visit to Ashley's home and came away with serious concerns regarding its suitability. The custodian was a single male and was hosting a fourteen-year-old girl. Ashley was doing well there, and there was no indication that the man was mistreating her. Walsh felt that the investigator's moral code was challenged by the arrangement and this discomfort alone guided her decision.

The investigator had decided to remove Ashley from the home and transfer her to what she deemed a safer environment. But the only place available to house the teen was an institutional group home in the Orlando area, hours

---

* The young girl's name has been altered because of privacy concerns.

away. And while Ashley would be able to complete her junior high school studies there and receive her degree, she would have no way to attend the graduation ceremony she had so been looking forward to in Martin County.

Walsh, who was assigned to the case after Ashley's removal, has requested for the emergency hearing to ask the judge to return Ashley to the custodian's home so she can graduate in her school there. He thinks it could be a vital turning point in Ashley's life. "It's so rare to see a child who has been through what she has been through do so well. And with constant discouragement, from her home life and now from her academic life, you really run the risk of turning her achievement into a mere blip." Walsh, who has seen so much lost opportunity, so much suffering, truly sees Ashley's graduation as a make-or-break moment in her life.

For John Walsh, it's all about the details, and finding speedy ways of resolving them. Sometimes it's a junior high graduation. Sometimes it's distance. If there's a chance a child might be reunited with family members, Walsh's priority is finding foster care nearby. That way, there can be supervised parent-child interaction. "For reunification, visitation is key and distance kills it," says Walsh. Sometimes children from Palm Beach are placed as far away as Tallahassee, more than 400 miles across the state, because there isn't any closer location.

Walsh doesn't look at the parents as the enemy, even if they've done bad things with their children. "Every once in a while you do encounter evil, but most of the time you just see people who are troubled, even pathetic," he says. If they can clean up their lives, get off drugs, taking back their children is a good solution. Overall, about 60 percent of the cases that come through the Foster Children's Project end up in reunification. Walsh sometimes develops close relationships with the parents. But he also says he has had to "flip" on parents and become their worst enemy if he determines reunification is not going to be an option. The children always remain his primary concern.

If children are not going to be reunited with their parents, the next step is to move forward with adoption. Here, the Foster Children's Project plays an equally important role, making sure proceedings are not held up by red tape, or by the typical backlog encountered in an overburdened court system.

He characterizes much of what he and his coworkers do in this phase as "cajoling, nudging and badgering" to speed things up. The goal is to speed the case through the system and get the kids out of state or foster care.

John Walsh counts on a member of his own family for help in making this happen. His twin brother, Jim, also became a lawyer specializing in advocacy for children, and also made the leap to work at the Foster Children's Project. Today they occupy adjoining offices and serve as codirectors. It often happens that someone over at juvenile court will get the two of them mixed up. Once, an angry parent who had just been arguing in court with John hurled a nasty insult at a very confused Jim in the courthouse lobby.

John and Jim still play bass and lead guitar—in a singer/songwriter band they formed after law school. The band's name, Thursday's Child, serves as a metaphor for the aspirations of their day job. "Thursday's child has far to go," says the old nursery rhyme. The band has been a fixture on the coffeehouse scene from Palm Beach down to Miami and is now starting to tour the country. When you learn that the Walsh brothers are hipsters by night, their daytime style—the loud ties, the shaggy hair—makes sense. But the relaxed style hides a fierce determination of purpose.

Walsh's aim is to get every case completed in twelve months, from removal to resolution. If everything goes smoothly, his lawyers are able to wrap them up in six months. Even with all the resources of the Foster Children's Project, some cases will drag on to two years, but these are cases that would have otherwise taken four years to resolve. And even when a case does go through to adoption, it doesn't get easier. Florida's adoption system, says Walsh, is broken. It's a mishmash of privatized and subcontracted agencies that compete with each other rather than cooperating.

Walsh's activism inside government has produced dramatic results. Since 2001 Walsh and the Foster Children's Project have been able to help represent 800 children from assignment to resolution. Before Walsh came on the scene, it took the government twenty months to complete the cases of preschool kids, and over three years to handle the cases of children between six and ten. Walsh and his team have cut the case time in half or more, to an average of ten months. They have salvaged many young lives.

NOW on PBS first met Walsh in 2005, doing research on a different story. The program learned that Walsh was in favor of opening up adoption to gay couples, and included an interview with him in their report on the issue.

Walsh wanted to permit gay couples to adopt children—not for the sake of "gay rights," he says, but for the sake of the children. His logic was based on simple arithmetic. Allowing gay couples to adopt could get more kids out of foster care. And adoption, for Walsh, is always a better option than foster care. An adoptive home is a "forever" home, not a temporary one. Most gay couples turn out to be great parents, says Walsh. The state is never, ever, a great parent.

The law against gay adoption was pushed through in Florida thirty years ago, backed by evangelical Christians. They argued the Bible condemns homosexuality. Walsh says the lesson of the Bible is quite different. He's a devout Catholic, a former altar boy, married with four kids of his own. The way Walsh reads the Bible, it's about helping the most vulnerable. "Whoever welcomes one of these little children in my name, welcomes me," Walsh finds in the Gospel. "And Jesus didn't say, 'you have to be heterosexual.'"

The gay community and Walsh discovered they had common goals. Walsh took an important step as a civic activist: He enlarged his movement to help troubled children. The building of unlikely alliances can attract attention, support and strength. By tying in with the gay rights movement, Walsh expanded his support base.

The proposed legislation to allow gay adoption failed to pass in the legislative session in Tallahassee. But Walsh is undeterred. He vows to keep at it. Still, he doesn't let advocacy of gay adoption get in the way of his day job—his intense focus on the children under his care.

Which brings us back to that Wednesday afternoon. Walsh is determined to help Ashley, the fourteen-year-old who is likely to miss her junior high school graduation. Walsh paces outside courtroom 3A. He's waiting for the emergency hearing he's requested, and it keeps being delayed. He can't believe Ashley was removed from her foster home in the first place.

He's still astonished that the system can be so overcautious that it actually penalizes some of the people it is supposed to protect.

A last minute influx of juvenile criminals cases has threatened to push back Ashley's emergency hearing. Walsh knows the judge is about to go on vacation. A hearing on this Wednesday is Ashley's only chance. He agrees to abbreviate the presentation, by dropping some of the five witnesses he has brought in to testify to the suitability of Ashley's custodian.

Walsh gets his hearing. It is immediately clear that the judge is not in the mood to reopen Ashley's removal from her custodian's home. He refuses even to listen to any of the witnesses. He is not swayed by Ashley's express wish to attend her graduation ceremony. He is only concerned, as an emergency matter, to make sure Ashley gets credit for junior high school. Walsh had come in to fight for Ashley to be rewarded for her hard work in school. He knows from experience that a child's self-esteem is a precious commodity. He firmly believes that Ashley's very future is at stake with this decision. But the judge reduces the entire issue to one question: "Will she be able to go on to the next grade?" Walsh is forced to respond in the affirmative.

The hearing is over. Walsh has failed. He and the five witnesses he had summoned gather in the hallway and vent. Ashley's court-appointed guardian *ad litem* (for the case) is there and is furious as well. An injustice has been done to this young woman. They are angry at the judge. They are angry at the child protective investigator who caused Ashley's removal from her custodian, kicking off the whole situation. Then the investigator emerges from the courtroom and is set upon by Ashley's supporters. Walsh joins in with his trademark measured manner. They accuse her of jeopardizing the young girl's future and argue that she has let her personal opinions cloud her investigative judgment. The investigator stands her ground. There are no easy answers here.

Walking back to Foster Children's Project's office, Walsh grows more upset with each passing step. Each block, he passes through a different step of those well-known stages of grief. Between the courthouse and Banyan Boulevard he just can't believe the judge wouldn't listen to his arguments.

From Banyan to Clematis Street he rages about the investigator letting her personal moral code threaten Ashley's future. From Clematis to Datura Street he begins to question his decision to permit an abbreviated hearing. From Datura to Evernia he wonders aloud why he even bothers. And from Evernia to the office door, a form of acceptance has set in. It doesn't last long, however. Within minutes of arriving at his desk, he summons in a paralegal and asks her to immediately begin preparing motions to depose every single member of Child Protective Investigations involved with Ashley's case, all the way to the director. It seems too late to find a way to get Ashley into her cap and gown. Walsh now wants to give investigators a kick in the pants to get their goals in line with his—moving vulnerable kids quickly through the system.

There are setbacks, like Ashley's. But there are many, many successes. Recognition for the group's work has been pouring in. In 2003 Representative Robert Wexler nominated the Foster Children's Project for the "Congressional Angel in Adoption Award." They won and both Walsh twins attended a banquet in Washington, D.C., dining with Mohammed Ali and Bruce Willis.

But there is a larger measure of success. Other counties in Florida, and indeed across the nation, are adopting the approach Walsh pioneered in West Palm Beach. Hillsborough County, Florida, which encompasses Tampa, recently set up its own Children's Law Center. Broward County, which includes Fort Lauderdale, recently asked John and Jim to help them start a pilot program modeled on the Foster Children's Project. They are planning to hire staff lawyers soon. And a representative from a similar program in Orange County, California, recently flew in to Florida to consult with Walsh about his project. This is all about scaling up a successful grassroots project. Walsh's work at reforming from the inside has become a model. As more locations adopt the approach, a "virtuous cycle" is created. More children are helped; more people talk about it; more places pick up the system.

What's the lesson for people who want to make a difference in their communities? John Walsh proves that there are ways of fixing a broken system from within. From the outside, advocates for foster care and adoption kept yelling, "It's broken!" Walsh knew the government bureaucracy was broken, but he believed the system could be made to work. What was missing was people and resources inside the system fighting on behalf of the children for the best and fastest result. Walsh got government resources to create that missing piece. And with success came attention from other localities who want their system to work better.

And Walsh keeps pushing for new ways to help the children. He recently helped found a local Palm Beach chapter of the Heart Gallery, a non-profit where portraits of foster children are shown in exhibition-like settings. The aim is to encourage adoption, particularly of the older, harder to place children. Their first show was held in summer 2007 in the ritzy shopping area along Worth Avenue. The images brought together those with the greatest need and those with the greatest means.

Occasionally, Walsh gets treated to a real surprise. In a job where he is constantly confronted with the worst of human nature, he lives for these occasional glimpses of the good he is doing. After the bruising courtroom setback over Ashley's graduation, Walsh picked himself up, dusted himself off and got back to work. He hounded officials, threatening them with depositions. He worked the phones relentlessly. In the end, Ashley did make it back in time to walk with her class and graduate from her junior high school. Her custodian, the family friend, is now her permanent guardian. Ashley has started high school and is earning straight A's.

Walsh, who never expected to become a lawyer, let alone a child advocate, sums up his life in his typically modest fashion: "The cool thing about being a lawyer for these kids is that most of what you do is just talking to them, giving them advice, explaining what happened to them and making sure they know there is someone out there who is looking out for them."

PRODUCER'S SNAPSHOT: JOHN WALSH

Before I finally spoke with John Walsh, I kept hearing about him. Everyone I called in Palm Beach County for information about foster care said he was *the man*. Judge Ronald Alvarez, a family court judge, told me that Walsh and his twin brother, Jim, had revolutionized the foster care system for the kids who came through his courtroom. Maxine Williams, a legal aid attorney representing children, said Walsh was hands down the best source.

So I called Walsh. Repeatedly. A legal aid attorney, he had started the Foster Children's Project in West Palm Beach in 2001 and cut the average time kids spent in the system from two years to one. The shorter the time in the system, studies have found, the fewer problems children have later in life. But Walsh didn't call me back. Later I learned that he was too busy actually *doing* his job to care about media coverage of it.

Finally, Walsh called me from his cell phone on his way home from work. He was passionate and a fast talker. The issue I was researching was why gay couples in Florida could be foster parents but not adoptive ones. Walsh, a man who had dedicated the past sixteen years of his life to finding permanent homes for foster children, said this issue was maddening. Why eliminate prospective families when there were so many children in need of permanent homes? For the sake of permanency, children could be removed from nurturing foster homes with good-hearted people because those people happened to be gay. The ban prevented what was sometimes the only good outcome for kids.

Several other states were considering ballot initiatives or legislative proposals to limit gay people from adopting. The issue was being driven by the religious right as a way to get conservative voters to the polls. But Walsh, a Catholic and former altar boy, knew his Bible and was having none of it. The Bible says that homosexuality is a sin, he admitted, but the good book also says that the greatest sin of all is arrogance. How arrogant is it, he asked, for the religious right to sit in judgment of homosexuals—to tell us they should not be allowed to adopt, not be allowed to raise an orphan? Walsh went on preaching: "The Bible says there is no greater calling than caring for widows and orphans, and yet we sit in judgment?"

I was writing furiously. I had expected Walsh to counter the religious arguments by citing facts about how many children were in need of permanent families (300 in his county in Florida alone). I wasn't expecting him to be able to fight religious fire with religious fire. Before I hung up, I knew we had to interview him.

When I finally met John in person, I was intrigued. For one, he was younger and hipper than I imagined. He and Jim played in a rock band, I learned. He had four children, but was only 42, which seemed young to me. What motivated him, I wondered? Religion? Family? He is Catholic, his wife a born-again Christian. He gave me an example of how their faiths bring them together. They had gone out for dinner to celebrate their anniversary one year. At the time, they already had two children but they were aware that there were Chinese girls in need of homes. They said to each other, according to John, "We have room at our table, why not?" And that was it. They adopted their third child, a daughter, from China.

In the interview, John Walsh did not disappoint me. Over the years, I've learned that the camera crew, people who have rolled tape on hundreds of interviews and who have seen and heard it all, are a good barometer. They were transfixed. Walsh talked about what it was like for foster children to live with the constant fear that the next knock at the door could take them away from their home. We all had chills. By the time he showed us photos of children who were searching for permanent homes and families to love them, everyone in the room was considering adopting.

I've met a few people like John in my day, people who are devoted to making change, who are so smart and so talented that they could do anything they wanted in the corporate world. I'm always curious to learn what makes them tick. Walsh is one of those special people who are genuinely answering a calling. As a journalist and as a citizen, I'm grateful for John Walsh and others like him, who are passionate in their commitment to fight for those who can't fight for themselves.

THE PRODUCER: BRENDA BRESLAUER has produced dozens of investigative reports for *NOW*. Previously, she worked in the ABC News investigative unit for five years and NBC News for eight. Breslauer has received the IRE Award, the National Headliner Award, the Overseas Press Club Award and an Emmy for Outstanding Investigative Journalism for her post-9/11 reporting overseas.

6

A LITERARY MOVEMENT

RUEBEN MARTINEZ

WHAT HE'S DONE:
Martinez has put 2 million Spanish-language books into the hands of schoolkids and adults.

LOCAL HERO HIGHLIGHT:
He earned a living cutting hair, then transformed his barbershop into a bookstore and community center.

ALL HIS LIFE RUEBEN MARTINEZ HAS LOVED TO READ. HE SET OUT TO share his passion with others, and his movement is changing America. Why? Because this country's burgeoning Latino population consists of people who work hard but read poorly. At the eighth grade level, Latino students score significantly lower on national reading tests than their white or Asian peers. Latinos drop out of school at a rate that is twice as high as for blacks and four times as high as for whites. And Latinos who enroll in college are far less likely to graduate than whites.

Rueben Martinez created a movement for reading and literacy among Latinos that has touched thousands of lives. Along the way, he faced daunting personal obstacles. How did he overcome an impoverished childhood and a career as a factory worker? What was the lightning bolt that galvanized him when he was already in his mid-fifties? And how in blazes did he nurture his literacy movement from a tiny barbershop?

Martinez was born in 1940 in a small town in the Arizona desert called Miami. The town, like its better-known neighbor, Globe, had been put on the map by massive copper mines established nearby in the late eighteen-hundreds. Mining is what brought Martinez's family here from Sonora in northern Mexico in the late 1930s, but Rueben never saw a future for himself under the ground. At home, an abusive situation made him long for a way out of the desert. His father left the family when Rueben was still very young. His mother remarried, but Rueben didn't get along well with his stepfather, a rough man who abused him and his family again and again. At the time Rueben had no inclination to explore the man's motivations. Looking back, Martinez now realizes that his stepfather had felt challenged by Rueben's emerging intellect.

Rueben found solace in reading from an early age, but it wasn't easy. He had to pester his teachers to lend him books. He would sneak off to read whatever they provided because he couldn't take the books home. His stepfather was illiterate and wouldn't allow books in the house—once, when he discovered a few, he threw them in the fireplace. During this period Rueben read and reread the Bible, the one book it was easy to get his hands on. Martinez also likes to tell the story of how he would steal out of the house in the early morning, before anyone else was awake. He would go over to the driveway of his neighbor's house and quickly scan the headlines of the newspaper.

It wasn't long after he turned seventeen that Martinez decided he'd had enough of life in Arizona. He and a group of friends dreamed of seeing the ocean, which they'd only glimpsed in films. They had heard there were jobs and the chance to make a new life in California. One of them had a beat-up car, so they hopped in and headed west. Martinez first settled in Long Beach and then later moved to East Los Angeles. He found a job at the massive Bethlehem Steel plant in Maywood, working in the heat of the blast furnace but earning a decent wage. He settled down, married and began to raise a family.

Martinez tried to keep up with reading, but it was difficult. Shortly after he got to California, he enrolled in a political science class at Santa Ana College, thirty miles away from his home. He didn't have a car and it took him three buses and two full hours each way to make it to class. His friends confronted him with the foolishness of wasting that much time on buses. Not foolish at all, Martinez told them: It was on the buses that he got all his reading done.

The work at the steel mill was hard, but Martinez had good job security. By the standards of his community, he was a success. He had a stable income and a good family. But as the years went by, Martinez found he wasn't satisfied. He decided he'd had enough of the heat of the furnace and tried out a series of other jobs in southern California. He was looking for a fit, a comfort zone, and nothing seemed to be right. He moved south from East Los Angeles to the town of Santa Ana in Orange County and did very well for a while working for the Ford Motor Company. It was the sort of job he needed to be able to send his kids through college, one that earned him good money. Martinez says his heart just wasn't in it, that it felt like being in prison. He tried to quit several times, but his bosses kept enticing him to stay with offers of new cars and promotions.

Martinez had achieved professional success and a good salary, but it still didn't feel right. He knew he had to follow his own compass, so he quit at Ford. It was time to try something entirely different. He's fond of saying that he was drawn to cutting hair because of how impressed he was with the clean white jackets he saw barbers wear. During the years he'd toiled in the heat and soot of the steel mill, he'd always envied the impeccable appearance of his barbers. He'd even taken time back then to attend barber school and already had his license. With his savings he opened a small barbershop in downtown Santa Ana. The shop prospered.

It was now the late 1970s. Martinez had much to be proud of: He was a self-made man and had achieved a comfortable life. His stepfather had been illiterate; he himself had only gotten through high school; and now he was well on his way to putting his three children through university.

Along the way Martinez never lost his love affair with reading. He'd noticed in the years he'd lived in East Los Angeles that few of his Chicano neighbors ever sat down to enjoy a book. In fact, many in the community were functionally illiterate. And the kids had big problems too. The dropout rate from school was as high as 50 percent. And even the kids who went to class rarely read books at home. Martinez wanted his community to know the same joy he experienced in expanding his mind with literature. And he knew that reading opened new doors, to better jobs and a better life. The failure of the school system—and parents—to teach Hispanic kids to read had a profound impact on the future of the entire community. If he could come up with a revolutionary system to give Latino kids (and their parents) the keys to betterment through the world of books, he'd give the entire community the ability to lift itself up.

Martinez made the decision to take his lifelong passion and extend it from his own personal needs to serving his greater community. So what if he was middle-aged? He was ready to leap into the world of grassroots advocacy. The success he was about to achieve is testament to the fact that it is never too late to start on the road to civic engagement.

By the time Martinez began cutting hair, he'd amassed a decent collection of books. He shifted a lot of it to the shop—after all, what was a barbershop without reading materials? It might have been the only barbershop in California with Tolstoy, Dostoevsky and Hemingway instead of *Sports Illustrated* and *Newsweek*. The highbrow stuff started to catch on. But many of his clients did not read English. So Martinez began making runs down across the border to Tijuana, Mexico, to pick up books in Spanish—for his own needs and also to have around at the barbershop. And then he set out advocating literacy to his clients—one haircut at a time. At first it was all very casual. People would glance through the titles while waiting for the barber chair. They'd often start talking about a book with Rueben and other customers. Rueben charged for the haircut but lent out the book for free, asking the borrower to bring it back on the next visit for a haircut.

The idea caught on—so well, in fact, that Rueben began to find his library was rapidly depleted. More and more books were borrowed and it appeared to be hard for people to remember to bring them in when they were back for their next haircut. That's when Rueben began to get into the book business proper, stocking the corner of his barbershop with an array of titles he thought people would like to buy and perhaps more importantly, titles he thought people *should* read. In an interview with *NOW on PBS* in 2004, Rueben said: "We started out with just a few books, two books to five to ten to twenty-five. And then we placed that big, giant order of a hundred books, laid them in the barbershop. And I didn't want to sell them. I wanted to keep them all."

By 1993, his zeal for running the bookstore part of his business took over from his love of cutting hair and he made the decision to put down the scissors and razor and sell books full time. And so Libreria Martinez was born.

From the very beginning, Martinez adopted an unusual approach to running the bookstore. He wanted to break even, but he also had social goals that were paramount. He planted one leg firmly in the world of business, the other in the nonprofit world of charity and education. He'd already attracted attention for being the barber with the bookstore who always pushed members of the Latino community to read. Now he was variously referred to as an educator, entrepreneur, philanthropist, motivational speaker and even "reading missionary."

The Spanish-speaking community of the United States is estimated at around 30 million. The United States has the fifth largest Spanish speaking population on earth. You'd think there would be plenty of books in Spanish for sale. Yet Martinez found it so hard to find books in Spanish that for many years he continued to drive to Mexico in order to stock his library. It was puzzling. Great literature was being written in the Spanish language, celebrating the cultures of Spain and the Americas, but the American Latino population was being cut off from its own social heritage. Martinez the businessman saw this as an opportunity, especially in southern California. But it was mostly Martinez the community leader who had decided to take action. Martinez, the avid reader, wanted to open wide the minds of the Latino population by cultivating a love of literature. It was that simple. Rueben was clear that the social and community goals came first. He told *NOW on PBS*, "Libreria Martinez defines its mission as more than commercial success. It is, rather, to develop a community of readers thereby improving the performance of children in schools, enriching families, instilling pride in the cultural roots and traditions of Latinos, and celebrating the successes of learners."

For Hispanic authors doing book tours, Santa Ana, California, is not a natural first choice for a visit. It's not known as a center of Latino culture. But Rueben's enthusiasm is contagious. Martinez remembers chasing down that first handful of writers: "When we first started the book store I used to call them. And they used to say, 'Well, who are you?'" Isabel Allende was one of his early triumphs. "When she came into the barbershop bookstore, she said 'Is this it?' And I said, 'This is it.' Because I only had two bookshelves. I had art. And I had the barber chair. And I said, 'This is it.' And she looked around like this. And she said, 'I like it.' And we had a good time. But we also had one of the biggest audiences that ever came to see an author in the city of Santa Ana. We had quite a few people, about 3,000, in a little shop that was 386 square feet."

Other big names followed. Carlos Fuentes, considered Mexico's leading intellectual and writer, held a rare book signing at Libreria Martinez. Well-known Latino authors who have stopped by include Sandra Cisneros, Jorge Ramos and Laura Esquivel. Allende has returned three more times for readings. They were all there to promote their books, of course, but Rueben had cleverly drafted them into his cause. Soon, the attention they brought the Libreria Martinez paid off in the ability to reach more people in the community. Martinez is unabashed about what he calls his guerrilla marketing techniques. He leverages his bookstore's assets to serve the core mission, just like any good entrepreneur would. It is yet another lesson Rueben the businessman and Rueben the literacy advocate teaches about effective activism tactics.

Word of the little barbershop bookstore in Santa Ana spread with each high-profile reading and soon he was filling the small room to capacity. Sometimes people even had to line up outside and wait their turn to get in. Martinez hoped his big idea was not going to stay confined to a single barbershop and eventually found he needed more space for bigger crowds, and more importantly, more space for more bookshelves. So in 1999, Libreria Martinez moved to bigger digs across town, to its current location on Main Street.

On prominent display in the bookstore is Luis Rodriguez's novel *Music of the Mill.* Martinez is fond of pointing out the book to visitors and sharing its story. The novel is based on the years Rodriguez spent working at the same Bethlehem Steel mill where Martinez long labored. It is just the sort of book Martinez would have in the store anyway, and he has had Rodriguez in for readings and signings. But for Rueben it's personal as well. He delights in the way *Music of the Mill* shows the astonishing connectivity of life: two Chicanos bound first in the forge, then later in literature.

Martinez is well aware that books alone can't fix the failure of the education system to adequately serve the Hispanic population. The solutions aren't simple. There's the outcry over whether immigrants, legal and illegal, are soaking up a disproportionate share of the tax dollars that go to education and health care. And there's the shadow economy in the United States of over 10 million people without legal papers, who work for a pittance. Martinez has avidly followed the issues about ethnicity and immigration for decades. But when he became an activist, he made a decision to avoid the conventional debate entirely. He just stuck to books. He discovered that once you made them available, made them accessible, they did a pretty good job of selling themselves. And his approach worked.

In fact, everything seemed to be working: Lots of visitors came to the bookstore, and there were frequent community events featuring books and learning. But a financial crisis was brewing. Fast forward to 2004, for a lesson in the hard knocks of grassroots activism. Sometimes the difference between success and failure comes down to a simple question of sacrifice and resolve.

In mid-September 2004, sixty-four-year-old Rueben Martinez woke up on the old couch that sat along the wall of his office. The wall above the couch was covered with awards in his name, along with framed newspaper clippings about his social and educational contributions to his community. On each side of the sofa where he'd just spent the night were tables with trophies, some glistening metal, others made from clear Lucite.

The bookstore was in dire financial straights. There was simply not enough income from book sales to cover the rent, the salaries of the workers and make a profit. Rueben hated the thought of firing employees or packing up and moving to a smaller location, so he embarked on his own personal savings plan. Now divorced, he moved out of his apartment and placed his belongings in a storage unit. He began living in the shop, sleeping on the office couch and washing in the bookstore's bathroom. He'd stopped paying for his own health insurance. His own kids, now fully grown and quite successful, had offered to take him in. It was a father's pride that kept him on the couch. But now, even this sacrifice wasn't enough. He was six months behind on the rent for the store. Business was decent, but nowhere near enough to keep it afloat.

For Martinez, this was his darkest moment. He had taken a great risk walking away from a lucrative career to become a barber and then a bookseller, and it had led him to the verge of ruin. He was nearly destitute. Many people would have thrown in the towel, but not Rueben Martinez. It had become the dream of his lifetime, and he didn't want to let go.

Then, on that day—September 19, 2004—something remarkable happened. In the small office at the back of the bookstore that had become his bedroom, the phone rang. The caller began by imploring Martinez not to hang up the phone. And what he said next completely changed Martinez's world and that of the Hispanic literary community he has long championed. It was an offer of a half million dollars, completely out of the blue, and with no strings attached.

For over twenty-five years, the John D. and Catherine T. MacArthur Foundation has sponsored a grant called the MacArthur Fellows Program. Most people refer to these casually as the "genius grants," as they are usually awarded to people who have exhibited a high level of intellectual or artistic achievement. There are no application forms. No essay writing is needed. In fact, direct applications are not accepted at all. Instead candidates are selected by a hand-picked and anonymous group of nominators. Then the program begins a process of careful yet secret investigation into the various merits of those who have been nominated. The process is not unlike a background check for a job at the FBI or CIA: Staff members descend on the community, watch the "target," interview the target's associates in strict confidence and build up a profile. For this award, there are only three criteria: creativity, a track record of success and the promise that the grant will further enable their creative process to make significant contributions to society. Grants are always in the amount of $500,000 and there are never any requirements of any kind—no speeches, no evaluations, no defined obligations. To date more than 700 individuals have been bestowed the honor, including Thomas Pynchon, Susan Sontag and Jared Diamond.

To this day Martinez doesn't know who put his name forward for the "genius grant." He says unequivocally that without the MacArthur money, Libreria Martinez would have ceased to exist. Nobody had any idea, not his staff, not the local media and certainly not the MacArthur representatives who had been making surreptitious visits to the bookstore to assess its effect on the community, how close Martinez was to losing his dream. The very first thing he did with his money was to catch up on his rent. The rest he salted away, to earn interest so he would never face losing his bookstore again.

Today Libreria Martinez carries on as if its flirtation with ruin had never occurred. The store runs about the length of a basketball court along Main Street and is filled with brightly colored rows of bookshelves punctuated with small areas where customers can sit and read. Cheery Latin acoustic guitar fills the space.

Rueben has realized that while he had been able to make a big difference by providing reading materials for the adult Hispanic population, there was more he needed to do. He has begun new programs for younger members of the community—to get them books, teach reading skills and cultivate the love of reading. He learned an important lesson for anyone interested in civic activism and community betterment: Empowerment begins with the young. Lift them up with the tools for success, and you will make the entire community better.

Much of Rueben Martinez's success comes from his outgoing personality and bright, hopeful demeanor. On a recent Saturday morning talk at a leadership conference for local high school students, Rueben, the keynote speaker, had an easy rapport with the audience. He had come in designer jeans, black leather boots and an immaculately pressed white *guayabera*. The kids loved him. And Rueben's personality is a big part of the bookstore experience. Someone may come in the store to browse, but soon Martinez starts up a conversation. He wants to know what they like to read and where they go to get books. Is this their first visit to Libreria Martinez? How did they hear about the store? How far had they come?

Martinez now has an annex to the bookstore, a large space in the building next door. He named it "Libros para Ninos" (Books for Kids). It is where children's events and the bigger adult readings take place. Once again the simple barbershop that had become a bookstore is becoming something more. "We have a lot of teachers that send students here to us because they don't have the time to sit down and tutor them. So they send them to us because they know that these young students are exceptionally smart and they're afraid that they might drop out of school. We just take the time to listen to them. Sometimes they tell us more than they tell their parents. I share stories about myself growing up. And they listen. Today, young people want to listen to stories," says Martinez.

The Libreria annex holds programs for children from toddlers all the way through high school. Sometimes it's just story hour. Sometimes the local school system comes in and uses the time to teach about things like nutrition while the kids are reading. When Rueben hosts groups of older kids, teenagers, it's usually less about the books and more about life skills and the need to stay in school. He knows how to talk to the kids, knows what is important to them. When schools are too far away to get the kids all the way to the bookstore, Martinez hops in his car and drives to them, taking the Libreria Martinez experience on the road.

Martinez also tries to make the bookstore a source of inspiration and betterment for his own employees. He pays a decent wage, but that's not all. In order to work at the store, employees must be enrolled in some form of education. And Rueben hires members of the community he thinks need a helping hand—he delights in telling the story of a young Mexican woman he hired who brought her first paycheck home to show her family. He says they proudly passed it all around the dinner table so that each member could get a look.

Quite a few years have passed since Martinez outgrew being a barber and bookseller and became a civic activist in his own right. These days he spends more and more time away from the store. He is in great demand as a public speaker. The man from the little mining town in Arizona was shocked to find himself addressing crowds at the Sorbonne in Paris and at Oxford University in England. Every spring, he finds his weekends booked up with graduations all across the country, and especially in California. His engagements range from California State universities to small high schools in the desert. He also has a weekly kids' book show on a local television channel, and a book review segment on the Univision TV news program *Noticias Solo A Las Once* called "El Libro de la Semana con Rueben Martinez" (The Book of the Week with Rueben Martinez).

But no matter what the venue, no matter what age or background or cause he is addressing, Martinez never loses sight of his roots in books, the passion that gave him a lifetime of enrichment: "Reading is going to take you to your future. We need to read the words. . . . We need to be around them. We need to have books at home. Because books give you life."

Rueben still keeps his barber chair in the office in the back of the bookstore (the same room he lived in back in 2004). In fact, the barber chair is the most prominent feature of the room, sitting dead center and facing a mirror that runs the length of the back wall. Apart from the absence of hair clippings on the floor, you might very well think the room is still in use as a barbershop. The banquette under the mirror still holds jars filled with combs soaking in blue solution. An electric razor, still plugged in, hangs on a hook on the wall. Martinez keeps a smock draped across the chair. On the seat cushion is a beat up book on barbering that he's had for many, many years. The room contains a powerful story for school groups who have come for a reading or a lecture. Rueben brings them there to tell them the inspirational story of the barber turned bookseller. His message: Dreams do come true.

Rueben's bookstore business is now bringing in enough money to support itself. But he knows that storefront bookstores across the country are threatened. Libreria Martinez is no exception. Big, powerful competitors are taking a bite out of his bottom line. He has watched as small bookshops have closed up everywhere. Amazon sells titles in Spanish, and the big chain stores like Barnes & Noble and Borders are adding Spanish-language sections to their existing megastores. He takes a measure of satisfaction in the growing market for Spanish-language books. That's what he's been working for all along.

Rueben has responded with a strategy to build his business for the future. Last year, Rueben turned the children's annex into a nonprofit organization. The tax abatements and benefits will help it survive. As for the bookstore, Rueben is working on making his offerings available online, like his competitors. And he negotiated a joint venture with Hudson Books, the newsagent and bookseller that runs hundreds of concessions at airports and train stations across North America. Martinez became a partner in their three stores at the John Wayne/Orange County International Airport. He has already started doing a brisk trade in Spanish books there for the many Hispanic passengers who use the terminal. Hudson Books also knows it is onto something good: They are looking into using Rueben's fame to market Spanish-language collections at other airports, including Chicago.

The improbable arc of Rueben Martinez's life holds a key lesson about how to create change at the grassroots level. Success for Rueben came through empowerment. Books and reading enabled him to envision a future beyond a mining town, beyond a steel mill, beyond a sales floor, beyond a barber's chair. Rueben Martinez became empowered to follow his life's calling. And he applied the same approach of empowerment to transform his community. Others might petition the government to improve the schools. Martinez often speaks at schools and he is an advocate for more resources devoted to education in minority communities. But his literacy movement works on a different principle. He wants to empower others. He wants Latinos to get charged up with the power of words so that they will become passionate advocates for their own future and the future of their children. He knows through personal experience that transformation only happens when you believe in your own possibilities so strongly that you are willing to toss away what little you have in order to grasp something better.

At an age when many people would have retired, Rueben Martinez presides over the counter at the bookstore, dispensing advice and helping to plan community activities. On a recent day a family came in looking for a birthday present for their father (it has to be in Spanish, says the son, because "he's a migrant"); an employee of a state children's services group came in because their offices didn't have any books in Spanish for kids; a professor from California State University, Fullerton, came in to see what new works from Latino authors might have arrived. And the store continues to serve as a platform for Rueben's one-man mission to reach out and touch an entire population. Rueben is hopeful that the public speaking he does and the new project with Hudson Books will help bring his literacy advocacy to the national level. And there's another project that he is itching to do—write an autobiography. He wants to give inspiration to others by chronicling his struggle to educate himself as the son of impoverished miners in the Arizona desert.

But the store and the barber chair in the back office keep him grounded in the grassroots sensibilities that have been key to his success. Standing in his office, giving the official tour of the barber chair, the trophies, the news clippings, Martinez stops to pick up a copy of Tolstoy's *Spiritual Writings*. He says he's been deeply moved by the book, written on the other side of the world, over a century ago. "You see, that's what reading does: It's timeless," reflects Martinez. "Words are forever. They may have been written hundreds of years ago but it's the same language that we have today."

PRODUCER'S SNAPSHOT: RUEBEN MARTINEZ

Santa Ana, California, ten minutes from Disneyland, is a working-class community with a tough exterior. We come upon Libreria Martinez on the nondescript, four-lane road that leads into the center of town. It sits among not-so-bustling fast-food joints, banks, and strip malls. But when we enter, Martinez and his store have a special aura that makes them both jump out of the landscape.

It's not a big place, but it is chock-full of character and great literature. On the walls there are photos of Allende and Fuentes, colorful local artwork, and pictures of wide-eyed children at book readings. Libreria Martinez has become a city landmark, an institution of learning and a lifeline of culture for a community whose needs are often ignored, even in a place like Santa Ana, which has the most Latinos per capita of any large city in America. It's a home for the mind that enables both children and adults to broaden the imagination and come closer to meeting their full potential. That's why it feels like a special place.

Rueben Martinez immediately makes me feel like Libreria is my home. After talking with him on the phone before our visit, I knew I would be meeting southern California's number-one pied piper of reading. In person, he has even more energy than I anticipated. He takes us back and forth, from one corner to the other, recommending titles, recounting visits from famous authors, tough school kids, and gratified parents. He confides that he himself is a hard-core reading addict. He wakes up reading, goes to bed reading, and often can't help himself from stealing fifteen to twenty minutes to read during the workday, leaving his employees to wonder where he could have gone. If we had taken his advice, we might have sent our camera crew home and read ten books right then and there.

Martinez wants to create "a revolution of readers." He often uses fiery language to describe what he is doing. "We need to eat more words," he says. "We need to digest them!" He understands the challenge is daunting: nothing less than the intellectual awakening of his community. It is a battle to overcome a lack of opportunity and the stereotypes that come with it. Just because many people in his community earn their paychecks with their hands, Martinez says, doesn't mean they don't have a love for learning. What they need is a means for that love to thrive. Martinez cultivated his own love of learning with very little help from the small mining town where he grew up. He saw many people lose out on their potential because they had no place to nurture it. With Libreria Martinez, he is determined to reverse that course and help people find the joy of learning, just like he did.

At the end of our tour of the shop, Martinez takes us to the back room. We are unprepared for what we see—a barber chair. Quite a bizarre thing to have in a bookstore, but a wonderful symbol of what Americans can do when they stumble onto a great idea and have the courage to follow it through. We all took a seat in the chair, of course. Martinez pantomimed his old moves with a pair of scissors, laughing and joking. He reminds us that the boundless enthusiasm and dedication of people like him make the American dream an inevitability—both for the individual *and* the community. We only need to clone Rueben several thousand times. Or just try to be more like him each day.

THE PRODUCER: DAN LOGAN joined *NOW* right out of college. His first job was answering phones and making photocopies. Seven years later, he's worked his way up to field producer. His report on an innovative health care system in east Africa was awarded a National Business Emmy in 2007.

7

AGITATE! AGITATE! AGITATE!

ROBERT MOSES

WHAT HE'S DONE:

Moses has helped tens of thousands of poor
and minority schoolkids prepare for
twenty-first century jobs.

LOCAL HERO HIGHLIGHT:

His program doesn't just teach kids, it
empowers them to make a difference in
their lives and in the world.

W E ALL CELEBRATE THE FACT THAT AMERICA IS A LAND OF OPPORTU-
nity. But how do we handle the abundant evidence that the
opportunity to succeed is very unevenly distributed in this nation? If you really believe in equal opportunity, how hard are you willing to
work to make it happen?

Robert Moses has spent over fifty years fighting to gain equal opportunity for all. He started out in the struggle for civil rights, and now he's
working to fix the education system. Over twenty years ago he founded the
Algebra Project, which has turbocharged math education for tens of thousands of young people. All along, he's had extraordinary faith that the people who are most in need will rise up to become the agents of their own
transformation. In education, Moses believes the students themselves will
make change happen. That's the key goal, according to the group's mission
statement: The Algebra Project "uses mathematics as an organizing tool to
ensure quality public school education for every child in America."

Bob Moses, the man we're talking about here, isn't the builder and ar-
chitect who had such an impact on the growth of New York City. Robert
Moses is African American, born and raised in Harlem, New York. Growing up in the 1930s, Moses was a good student right from the start. He
earned admission to the prestigious Stuyvesant public high school in New
York City by passing a competitive exam and on graduation got a scholar-
ship to attend Hamilton College in upstate New York. From there, he went
immediately to graduate school at Harvard, earning a master's degree in
philosophy.

In his academic path, Moses benefited from the changes sweeping
through America in the aftermath of the Second World War. He was able

to advance in ways that hadn't been open to earlier generations of African Americans. However, Moses remained an outsider in a largely white society. The same pattern held true for his first teaching job. He was hired at Horace Mann, one of New York City's elite private schools. He threw himself into teaching, but almost immediately his attention was drawn elsewhere, to the dramatic events unfolding in the civil rights struggle. He was captivated by the newspaper pictures showing the growing protest movement in the South. "I was looking at these images and the students really looked like I felt inside," Moses recalled.

Moses was restless teaching the children of the privileged. He made the fateful decision to see for himself what the protest movement was all about. During his spring break in 1960, Moses went to stay with a relative in Hampton, Virginia, and joined the picket lines and protests. He found it was a liberating experience: For so long he'd been careful not to rock the boat, as he lived within a world that largely excluded him. His life was framed by racism and prejudice, but he had said nothing. All the while he had carried what he describes as an inner turmoil. Now he had an outlet for all the feelings he harbored. "It is what I felt participating in my first demonstration in Newport News, Virginia—release," writes Moses in his autobiography, *Radical Equations: Civil Rights from Mississippi to the Algebra Project.* He returned, reluctantly, to finish the school year in New York. But he went up to Harlem in his time off and began volunteering at offices of the Southern Christian Leadership Conference—Dr. Martin Luther King Jr.'s group.

When summer arrived, Moses asked to be assigned to work somewhere in the South. He wanted to get closer to the action. While volunteering at King's offices in Atlanta, Moses learned of a fledgling organization called the Student Nonviolent Coordinating Committee (SNCC). He found out that they needed people to travel around the South from Atlanta to New Orleans to help with recruitment and fact-finding. Moses signed up. It was his first venture into the Deep South and it changed his life.

That fall, Moses was back in New York, teaching at Horace Mann. He could only follow the movement from a distance. In May 1961 the first

Freedom Riders climbed aboard a bus in Washington, D.C., bound for New Orleans. The group of blacks and whites was testing the implementation of the 1960 Supreme Court decision *Boynton* v. *Virginia,* which declared that segregation on interstate transport was illegal. In the south, Riders were harassed and arrested, but SNCC and other groups organized more Freedom Rides. SNCC also ramped up its voter registration work, and that summer, when Moses was asked to lead a voter registration effort down in Mississippi, he jumped at the chance. This time there would be no turning back for Moses as he left the privileged halls of Horace Mann for the last time. It was tough work, going door to door in the summer heat, trying to convince frightened people to drive to their county seat and sign up to vote in the face of hostility and intimidation from the white community. And once he started to have a degree of success, it got even worse. He was arrested, thrown in jail, beaten by angry whites on the street. Once, the car he was traveling in was ambushed by machine-gun fire. Although thirteen bullets penetrated the car, all managed to miss Moses. The driver, who was hit, survived. But other activists were not so lucky. One of Moses' allies, Herbert Lee, a farmer and member of a local Mississippi chapter of the NAACP, was shot one night outside a cotton gin. Lee's body lay there for hours because white people, including police and medical personnel, refused to touch the corpse. Finally a black coroner was located to transport Herbert Lee's earthly remains to the funeral home. The shooter, a state legislator, was never charged with the crime.

The overt brutality of southern whites fighting the civil rights movement stunned Moses. He was undergoing a great awakening, something that would stay with him throughout his entire life. What was most shocking was the complete disenfranchisement of African Americans. The social and political geography of the South was like a foreign country. "I had no idea," says Moses. "Even though I'd been through all these colleges and universities, that there was a whole congressional district that had an overwhelming black majority and had never been able to elect a representative . . . I had no concept, really, of the history of the country in Mississippi and the Deep South, so I had no concept of the life of sharecroppers, of a whole people trapped in this kind of feudalistic system."

This would become the guiding theme of Moses's life. It was a question of empowerment. He draws an analogy between the Deep South and Europe in the Middle Ages. For Moses, the connection is feudalism: the socioeconomic system where a social stratification marks levels of entitlement in society. For Moses, American blacks in the 1960s represented serfs, the lowest tier who were never allowed to own land and labored as de facto slaves for landowners. To him the solution to raising the sharecropper up from his condition was political empowerment: the right to vote and the audacity to have a voice. All else would follow.

The efforts of Moses and his colleagues went far beyond assisting these sharecroppers in attaining and guaranteeing their right to vote. Their goal was to empower the folks in Mississippi to rise up and take action on their own. "The issue was, are you going to be able to create in this oppressed, targeted population this demand for political access?" says Moses.

The key here was organizing, and organizing takes time and patience. Moses and the others had to gain the trust of local community groups. They couldn't just go from protest to protest, they had to "dig in," as Moses puts it. The organizers had to really work with the community, even if that meant going family by family and living on rural farms. It can be frustrating, but it is where Moses excelled. "Organizing work really has a very different kind of rhythm. Well, it was a rhythm that suited me. What you're living on is the energy in the people that you're working with. So you're taken into families, you become part of their lifestyle." It wasn't long before Moses and his fellow organizers were able to make real bonds with the community. Soon they were viewed as family, protected and nurtured. This was the victory to Moses. As he writes in his autobiography, "Inside this 'family' was the true place where the movement's moral authority was anchored."

This approach was radical within the civil rights movement. Moses and his fellow activists were placing the power of the movement in the hands of the uneducated, illiterate, oppressed rural poor. He described it to *NOW on PBS* as an "earned insurgency." Organizers had to earn the right to ask people to take risks to improve their lives. "There's no reason for sharecroppers to risk their lives and their livelihoods, to go down with us to register to vote unless they could trust us," he said. "We had to earn their respect." Moses and the cadre of young people who worked with him earned respect by facing down hostile whites and brutal treatment by police. And they earned respect by sticking around—getting to know people, and giving support and encouragement month after month.

Then Moses took a giant turn in his life. In 1965, he left the whirlwind of organizing and activism in the South and eventually ended up in Tanzania, working as a schoolteacher. What happened? There were profound changes in the leadership and direction of the civil rights movement. The Freedom Summer of 1964 became a test for the limits of nonviolent activism. During a massive voter registration drive that summer, three civil rights workers were killed. And there was another setback on the political front: SNCC fought to have a voice at the Democratic National Convention but was excluded. It was a heavy blow to those who thought the way to bring change was to work through the mainstream. Moses says SNCC faced an "inability to regroup." Schisms appeared. Moses's cherished model of decentralized, grassroots organizing lost favor, and the organization moved toward a top-down model of change. And there was the hot button issue of race. SNCC had been formed on the idea that blacks and whites should work hand in hand for change. But now a new black nationalism was emerging within the group. Moses left by the end of 1965 and Stokely Carmichael assumed leadership of SNCC in the spring of 1966, riding the wave of anger generated by the Watts riots. Under Carmichael, SNCC became a highly centralized organization that championed Black Power.

In Tanzania, Moses and his wife had a very different life, a much quieter one. They lived in a home right across the street from the schoolhouse where they both worked. "We were never more than a stone's throw away from that house," says Moses. Over in Tanzania, his neighbors didn't know who Moses was or what he had done. He says it allowed them to start up a family in a supportive and calm environment. And Moses found he now enjoyed teaching. It was another form of empowerment—giving students the tools, and the vision, to change their lives.

In 1976, Moses decided it was time to resume life back in the United States. He returned to Harvard University to continue his doctorate studies in philosophy. He settled down with his family in Cambridge, Massachusetts. It was there, in 1982, that Robert Moses's next life as a social activist and organizer was born. One day the phone rang, and, like Rueben Martinez, everything changed for Robert Moses. His MacArthur Foundation "genius grant" was largely in recognition for the work he had done as a civil rights organizer. As is always the case with these grants, there were no requirements that Moses do anything specific with money. But the gift of a half million dollars was just the catalyst required for Moses to embark on his next career as an activist.

His renewed activism started close to home, with the schooling of his oldest daughter, Maisha. Moses, a teacher long before he became an activist, was always on hand for extra help with tutoring and always took a keen interest in what his kids were studying. Maisha was entering the eighth grade and Moses had been working with her on math. She was ready to start algebra, but Moses learned that the school Maisha attended wasn't offering it. That was a big problem for Moses.

One of the things he and his wife had felt strongly about upon returning to the United States was sending their children to public schools. But they also wanted to make sure the public schools were adequate. The situation with the algebra class sent up a red flag for Moses. Maisha's school system offered algebra as part of the high school curriculum, but Moses believed that was way too late. He stepped in and began a special tutoring program for his daughter in algebra. What started as a father helping his daughter with her homework grew bigger and bigger over the next twenty-five years.

So why was it so important to Moses that his daughter be able to get started on algebra in middle school? It came down to the purpose of education in a changing world. When Moses had worked in the South, the most important skills to pass on to sharecroppers were reading and writing. Now Moses felt strongly that for the next generation it was math literacy that had become fundamental.

While Moses was away living the simple life in Africa, profound changes in technology had altered the way people lived their lives in America. And all signs pointed to the fact that this trend was only going to amplify. It came as a shock to Moses. It turned all his ideas about serfdom and feudalism and access—those key theories he'd made when working with sharecroppers in the South—upside down. "I had no idea about the technological revolution," Moses told *NOW with Bill Moyers* in 2002. "I had no idea that the nature of work was going to change from work where you're using machines to assist physical work to where you're using computers to assist knowledge work."

This new dynamic, which is sometimes described as the shift from an industrial economy to an information economy, requires a whole different approach to education. Moses believed there was a need for increased focus on math literacy as the key to economic survival. "We could get away with it when we had the industrial technology and really all we needed was that people could function at the post office for their mathematics. But computer-based technology is something different. And it really requires a different level of mathematical foundation for the kids."

Keep in mind that when Moses started this campaign for math literacy, it was still long before the era of personal computers, instant messaging and the Internet. All those changes only serve to make Moses seem even more prophetic. And Moses's quest was much deeper than giving kids the skills to send e-mail and use Google. He was looking for key skills to leverage empowerment.

As Moses sees it, there's a link between the civil rights struggle and his movement for math literacy. Here's his reasoning: The civil rights movement revolved around the question of citizenship. The central issue was the right to vote and fully participate in a democratic society, something that had been promised in the United States Constitution but had never been universally delivered. At its core, the movement was about making sure that all Americans were citizens. Moses started with that core concept—citizenship—and in pushing for math literacy, he says, that same core concept is central. Without an equal opportunity for a quality education that includes math skills, Americans are being excluded from citizenship in the brave new world of high technology. These educational skills have become a prerequisite for participation in today's democratic process.

In the past, you could get by without these skills, but today you cannot. And it goes beyond constitutionality and democracy. It also impacts survival. "In the knowledge economy," Moses says, "educational access is necessary for economic access. If you don't have access to these educational structures and you're poor, then you're not going to have access to legitimate economic structures."

What Moses learned was that the serfdom he had seen imposed on black sharecroppers in the South had been updated for the late twentieth century and had been relocated to American inner cities. Without basic math skills and the education built on those skills, poor urban youth had no access to many of the kinds of jobs available in contemporary society. The future for these kids was very bleak. "You're not talking about a stable population that has access to an economic arrangement that can support families . . . we are just feeding the criminal justice system," says Moses.

Moses identified the failure to provide algebra education through the public school system as one of the main factors keeping poor kids locked in systems of this new urban feudalism. It was the threshold, the breaking point between possibility and failure in a student's education. His analysis was that simple arithmetic was fine for the industrial age. But for the information age, algebra was a necessity. Algebra is all about abstract computation, using variables and equations. The modern world of quickly changing bits of information requires the ability to do abstract calculation, Moses believed. "We need a populace that can think and figure out how to problem solve," says Moses, "That 'X1 plus *delta* X equals X2' allows you to use abstract symbolic representation to cover any multitude of particular cases. It allows you to handle concepts."

Moses explained this in an interview, using the example of a school district in south Florida to which he has been traveling from his home in Massachusetts to work for the last few years: "If you look at Miami-Dade

College right here, it's the open enrollment college for the city of Miami. But 60 to 80 percent of the students who graduated from high school and get into Miami-Dade . . . have to remediate math. Not only do they have to remediate it, they have three levels of remediation: either basic arithmetic, or elementary algebra, or what is called algebra 2. So you test into one of those levels of remediation. If you test into the lowest level, you have to go through all three before you can take your first math course for college credit." And, Moses says, he sees the same situation elsewhere: "It's not just Miami. It's all over the country. I was in Denver. It's the same thing at Metro State. I was in California, in LA. It's the same thing at Cal State, LA."

Moses is quick to point out that math literacy is not a battle he is waging on behalf of just one race. He sees the problem as more a function of poverty than skin color. "I was up in a school about thirty miles south of Ithaca in rural New York. And I'm sitting in a room with thirty students they brought together, all white, with their teachers and administrators. And they're telling me that 20 percent of the kids won't graduate."

In some ways, Moses says, math literacy is even more difficult to achieve than basic civil rights. Although he and his colleagues faced bullets and beatings in the 1960s, they always had federal legislative backup—at least in theory: "It's different for the right to vote," says Moses. "We had 1870, the Fifteenth Amendment, which says there's a constitutional right to vote. The argument now is there's nothing in the Constitution that says that anybody has the right to an education."

This lack of commitment to seeing education as an investment and a national resource is something that surprised Moses when he returned from living in the third world. In Tanzania, where Moses taught, only a small percentage of children went to high school. But they were treated as a national treasure, says Moses, because everyone knew that they would be the ones who would one day run their country. There was a strong understanding that education was an important investment in all the people's future. Moses says this is something he finds sorely lacking back home. "The question is why do we tolerate this? Why do we allow this to go on? Why should we tolerate this in this country at this point? It doesn't make sense as a strategy for the country," says Moses.

Moses is worried that the failure of math literacy across the country represents a serious danger to society. He points to the fact that a majority of students receiving master's degrees in math and science in many schools in America come from overseas. We have avoided a crisis by importing expertise from outside our borders, but Moses doesn't see this as a long-term solution in an increasingly competitive and globalizing world.

The solution that Moses came up with is called the Algebra Project. It would eventually be active in as many as twenty-three school districts in thirteen states and engage 10,000 children a year. But the Algebra Project got off to a rather low-key start. Moses began tutoring his daughter Maisha and three other students in a corner of a classroom. He says that he started off more as a "parent-organizer" than a teacher. The venture was a success and the children immediately benefited when they advanced into high school. It was a huge leg up for them, so it wasn't surprising that word quickly spread among parents. Soon there was a movement afoot to get the program officially recognized by the school committee of the city of Cambridge. The Algebra Project incubated there for several years.

As Moses worked with students, he refined and standardized his approach. Games and math puzzles, even origami, became part of the toolkit. He drew up teaching materials and developed courses so that when the time came, the Algebra Project could grow in other places. To do this, Moses relied on the nest egg he'd received from the MacArthur Foundation. What some might have seen as a gift, Moses turned into an investment.

Eventually, though, the money ran out. Moses had by then made enough of a name for the program that he was able to bring in new funding through grants and donations. By the start of the 1990s, the Algebra Project was ready to grow. And it grew like wildfire. In 1991, it expanded to Chicago, Milwaukee, Louisville and Oakland (where Moses's daughter Maisha would eventually move to help out, a source of great pride for her father). The next school year Algebra Project programs opened in San Francisco, Los Angeles and Indianapolis. Soon it would come to New Orleans and New York. Moses and his team opened up what they called their Southern Initiative and set up programs in the Carolinas and Alabama.

Then came Mississippi. A return for Moses to the state where he'd risked his life to help sharecroppers was all but guaranteed. The education system in that state was in a shambles. According to Moses, more than 60 percent of eighth graders were scoring below the absolute lowest level for math proficiency. In some parts of the state, such as down in the delta, the poorest part, only half of the high school students went on to graduate. Ironically, one of the biggest victories of the civil rights movements, school desegregation, had been largely reversed through the trend of whites fleeing the public school system. Moses followed the call of duty back to Mississippi for the second time. In fact, he decided to take personal responsibility for this chapter and teach there himself. The need was just so great.

Successes built up quickly. A year after the program came to West Tallahatchie County, Mississippi, a school district that was 94 percent black and very poor, students scored at or above state levels on standardized tests for the first time. By 1998, after four years with the Algebra Project, the district managed to get itself off the state's list of schools placed on probation for poor performance. Another big victory was in a rural town in North Carolina. When the Algebra Project arrived in the school district in 1994, it was ranked at the absolute bottom of the state's 119 school districts. But in only three years the percent of students considered to be proficient in math jumped twenty points, from a dismal 34 percent to 54 percent.*

As the Mississippi program ramped up, Moses split his time between his home in Cambridge, Massachusetts, and Lanier High School in Jackson, Mississippi. The return to Mississippi was rich in symbolism. Moses, who had fought so hard to get its African American residents the right to vote, was back two decades later helping to give essential schooling to their grandchildren, some of the poorest kids in America. He says, "It was

---

* Robert P. Moses and Charles E. Cobb, Jr., *Radical Equations: Civil Rights from Mississippi to the Algebra Project* (Boston: Beacon Press, 2001), 143–144, 153, 164.

sharecroppers, the people at the very bottom of the society in Mississippi, who struggled for the right to vote. And in some sense, they're the metaphor for their grandchildren and great grandchildren. And we need to work with them to honor the work that the sharecroppers did to get that right to vote."

Moses made empowerment a basic part of the Algebra Project. He wanted students to learn math skills, but he also wanted them to adopt what he called a "culture of change." The idea was to create a broad movement determined to change the system. Just like during civil rights, empowering people to be agents of change was the eventual endgame for Moses. He recalls the similarities of the two struggles: "When you went down in the 1960s to organize people, you said, 'Well, we need to organize the sharecroppers to make a demand for themselves.' And right now you're saying, 'Who's being affected in the situation?' And it's the students." Moses says the solution is the same: "We need to organize these students to make a demand for themselves."

How do you get students to be social activists? Moses says kids all too often buy into the status quo that brands them as having little potential. The solution Moses came up with is called the Young People's Project. It was designed as an after-school program for young kids with Algebra Project graduates as mentors. The goal is to teach math but also to empower students as a group and create a culture that encourages peers to become involved and make greater demands of the system. He doesn't expect immediate results. Moses, the visionary, speaks of a time frame that runs in decades. He's already put in half a century. He expects the same of the young people he's working with now. Moses knows more than anyone that social organizing cannot be rushed.

But already there are victories for Moses's empowerment strategy. Case in point: in 2006 in Baltimore, Maryland, where a branch of the Algebra Project has been working with inner city schools for a number of years. Students from the program began to ask critical questions about why conditions at their school were so desperate. They learned that the state of Maryland had been underfunding the Baltimore school system by millions of dollars each year—money that could have been used for computers, books and even basic infrastructure.

The students staged a series of high-profile protests, demanding reforms. Their activism made headlines. The protestors also received the attention of the local court system, which has demanded an accounting for the money. The protest effort, which uses the slogan—and catchy rap song—"No Education, No Life," still continues today. The activism of the Baltimore students embodies the twin struggles of Moses's life: civil rights and education reform.

The story of Robert Moses and the Algebra Project is one of those ongoing stories that *NOW* has been privileged to follow over the years. The most recent piece about the Algebra Project appeared on *NOW on PBS* in 2007, detailing the situation in Baltimore and traveling to Miami, where Moses had been running the project in a tough elementary school in the middle of the city's Little Haiti neighborhood.

In the last five years the project has grown and begun to incorporate other subjects, including reading and writing. Adding the new topics is based on the premise that language is power, and is essential for education and for efforts to reform the system.

Moses has even bigger ideas going forward. The goal is to get the country to think seriously about doing something about the education system, not just math and not just at the poorest of public schools. Moses wants to open a national discourse to get more resources put into education. He believes America's place in the world is at risk. "We've been talking to people in different places all over the country," he says. "You need school people. You need community-based people. You need university people. And you also need foundation people. You need people who have resources."

Through all the years and three successive careers, Moses has always believed that the least among us has the power to change, to transform, to be empowered. In running the Algebra Project, he's faced critics who have said the kids themselves aren't up for it, that they don't want change. "The current conversation is, well, the kids can't do it. And the reason they can't do it is because they're dysfunctional, or they don't care, they're not motivated, or their parents aren't, their communities aren't," says Moses. It's essentially the same thing people used to tell him in Mississippi at the beginning of his struggle there, says Moses. "The argument was the same. Every newspaper reporter would come up to me and say, 'Well, Bob, isn't the problem with your people that they're apathetic? That's why.' So that argument disappeared when they presented themselves by the hundreds trying to register to vote."

Moses is now in his seventies. He won't live to see the day that every child in America gets a decent education and leaves school an active citizen. But he has faith that kids like the student activists in Baltimore will take up the challenge. That's how empowerment works, says Moses: the new generation gains the drive and the vision to move the country forward.

PRODUCER'S SNAPSHOT: ROBERT MOSES

Most people know about the civil rights movements from film reels and History Channel documentaries. Scenes of police officers with fire hoses, brave students sitting in a whites-only restaurant and angry mobs fighting the National Guard to keep a lone little girl out of a school building are images that slip into one's mind whenever that time is invoked. I had done my best to understand that turbulent period. As a black woman, I was proud of what had been accomplished. I studied it in college, imagining it as an age to which I, a self-appointed revolutionary (at least in my mind), truly belonged.

Suddenly, I had a reason to be excited. I had been assigned to cover a story on Robert Moses, a legendary civil rights activist. In the 1960s, Robert Moses was a leader of the Student Nonviolent Coordinating Committee (SNCC), formed by young people who helped organize southern black sharecroppers to vote. I first learned of Robert Moses in my high school history class, through a film that left me with lingering questions about the time, the struggle and the consequences. I had always hoped to meet one of these radical characters looming in my audio-visual memory. Now I was about to step into the path of Bob Moses himself.

Moses is a compact, reddish-brown man with a silver beard and a ring of short curly hair wrapped around his head. The man presents a striking contrast to his younger version as seen in the old film clips. On this day, he has organized a meeting for the parents of high school students he is teaching in Miami, Florida. The informational session will answer the parents' questions and concerns about letting their "babies" live away from home. The students will be attending an upcoming residential academic program that Moses and his colleagues have created. Yet, with Moses at the helm, the "informational session" becomes a strategy conference, a dialogue among peers about how the summer would unfold. Moses is leading the group, but it's hard to tell who's in charge.

Moses sits in the midst of the rapid discussion, melding quietly into a crowd of fast-talking, lively adults and teenagers. They are discussing the summer's daily schedule and although the group had started with a blank sheet of poster paper, the sheet is now covered with notes. "We don't have enough time for homework," a girl interjects at one point. "We need to do homework!" Everyone in the room responds to the comment at once, one parent stepping up to direct the flow of conversation. Moses sits back and listens, occasionally asking questions of the group, confirming what they agree upon before it is written down, but rarely stepping in to direct the flow of conversation. I watch, fascinated, as the children and parents of Miami's low-income community, so often described as "inactive" and "complacent," create the daily agenda for a college-based curriculum.

I was surprised, but Moses wasn't. He believes firmly, with an unwavering faith, in the promise and potential of the communities in which he works. Moses argues that people in disadvantaged communities don't need solutions imposed on them. What they require are merely the tools to make solutions work. I thought I was going to meet a fiery 1960s radical. Instead, I encountered a person who makes change happen by empowering the entire community.

A few weeks later, I was sitting face to face with Moses, camera rolling and my questions ready. I was going to get the chance to ask this legend any question I wanted about a time that seemed familiar and yet was still draped in mystery. As we talked, Moses the revolutionary began to emerge. Slowly, but passionately, he told me about his plans to help transform American education and how it all began. Our discussion ranged from theory to the classroom, from Tanzania to Mississippi. He described the Algebra Project, which makes math fun and accessible for students while giving them responsibility for their own learning as peer leaders and teachers.

One thing comes across quite clearly. Moses believes that the biggest problem in America is the failure to give every child a quality education. Kids are not learning enough in schools to contribute meaningfully to their communities as adults. It adds up to a failure that carries an enormous cost for society. Drastic change is needed. He is certain change will come at the hands of his students, the people who are the most disadvantaged in the system as it stands.

Moses saw such transformation happen firsthand in the 1960s when sharecroppers learned to read in order to pass the literacy tests that kept them from voting. Then he witnessed this transformation again, when those same sharecroppers self-organized, took to the streets and demanded the right to vote. He recognizes the same potential in the kids he works with every day. He knows that they carry within themselves the seeds of revolution.

After the interview, as the crew cleaned up, Moses and I helped ourselves to some coffee. Questions still lingered in my mind. Before I left, I hoped to talk not to Moses the radical or Moses the visionary, but to Moses the person. I asked about his friends from the 1960s. I gently posed a question about how the movement had strained the romantic relationships of the activists involved. It was a dangerous subject. Moses's first marriage was to another activist and the relationship had ultimately ended in divorce.

He took off his glasses, rubbed his eyes, and thought for a moment. "Some did okay," he said deliberately, citing a few exemplary couples and then trailing off. I watched him carefully, imagining the scenes running through his mind—the tears, the blood, the frustration he witnessed so long ago. What was he remembering that would never show up on the TV sequences I knew so well? He conceded that the movement had, in fact, taken its toll on the young people like himself who had so famously laid their lives on the line for the sake of freedom. Is that why he fled to Tanzania after the momentum of the movement died down? Was he still mourning the loss of King, Goodman, Cheney and Evers?

In the end, I got my interview and met a civil rights hero. I learned a lot about Moses's program, his scholarly endeavors and his students. I have no doubt that his legacy of cultivating leaders "on the ground" will continue, and I've met some of the kids that demonstrate what he has already accomplished. But there are some questions that never get answered. And that leaves me right back where I started—amidst my black and white, two-dimensional recollections of a time full of color that is still much too real to forget.

THE PRODUCER: KHADIJAH WHITE worked as a teaching fellow in New York City prior to joining the staff of NOW as an assistant producer. She pitched pieces, researched stories, and helped produce broadcast reports. She is currently a PhD candidate at the Annenberg School for Communication at the University of Pennsylvania.

8

TELL ME THE TRUTH!

PEGGY BURYJ

WHAT SHE'S DONE:
Thanks to Buryj, the U.S. Army is doing a better job of investigating and reporting on military deaths on the battlefield.

LOCAL HERO HIGHLIGHT:
She learned that the army had been untruthful about her son's death in Iraq and waged an epic struggle to find out what really happened.

PEGGY BURYJ IS PROUD TO CALL HERSELF A PATRIOT. SHE BELIEVES IN THE greatness of America, she says—its astonishing rise to economic and political power in the world, and the promise of even greater things to come.

You wouldn't choose Peggy Buryj as a likely candidate to mount a ferocious campaign against the U.S. Army. Buryj voted for George W. Bush—both times. She supported the invasions of Afghanistan and Iraq. The walls of her home are covered with pictures of her son, Jesse, in uniform, and plaques and medals awarded to him for his service in the U.S. and Iraq.

Peggy Buryj took on the U.S. Army because she came to believe that high-ranking officers were doing something that was deeply unpatriotic. They were lying to her. They were hiding the truth about how her son died while fighting in Iraq. So this working mom from the Midwest began a battle to find out what really happened to Jesse Buryj. She made common cause with other families to demand a transformation of how the army handled its investigation and reporting of casualties. The army refused. But that wasn't going to stop Peggy Buryj.

She says she'll never forget the moment her life changed. It was a spring morning in 2004. Her husband, Steve, had come home from his night shift. Buryj had the day off from work. They were doing house cleaning as they waited for the arrival of a carpeting company to put in a new upstairs carpet. The doorbell rang. She looked through the glass-paned door and saw an army soldier in formal dress. She knew instantly that Jesse had been killed. She refused to open the door. She was unable to speak. She heard screaming, and then realized it was her own voice. She saw Jesse's wife, Amber, standing with the soldier. "Peggy, he's gone," she said. Amber, age twenty, was now a widow. Buryj had lost her son.

What followed was a time for mourning, for Peggy, Steve, Amber and indeed for their entire community. Peggy took comfort in the power of the U.S. military, all it stood for and all that Jesse had fought for. She would soon learn just how powerful and how implacable the army could be. Peggy Buryj was to become a leader in one of America's biggest battles—for the truth about exactly how our soldiers have died in battle.

The Buryj's hometown of Canton, Ohio, has an immediate association for many people: the Pro Football Hall of Fame sits to the north of town right off the interstate. And indeed the region is crazy for the sport. Some high school games might attract up to 25,000 fans and Canton's McKinley High School Bulldogs have won three state championships and one national title. It is a proud city, though not necessarily a pretty place. Still, the neighborhoods of small houses close together on small parcels of land ooze a feeling of community fellowship. This is a town where you know the people who live on your street. Not many new faces move in and only a few more ever leave.

Jesse's death, and the beginning of Buryj's battle for the truth, occurred at a time of turmoil in the local political scene. Jesse Buryj was killed in May 2004. The tide of opinion in Canton and the surrounding area was beginning to turn against the war in Iraq. Stark County had always been a loyal Republican stronghold. It had sent a GOP representative to the U.S. House of Representatives since 1951 and had gone Republican for governor and senator for several election cycles. Stark County was considered the fulcrum of Ohio politics. One of the county's business leaders, W. R. Timken, described the region to the *New York Times* as a "Maginot line between Republicans and Democrats in the state." But now some of Buryj's neighbors began to reconsider their positions. The war in Iraq was going badly. The local economy was stagnant, even declining. Democrats pointed to the nearby factories that had closed down, their products now made overseas. Hoover, one of the biggest employers in Canton, had been downsizing for years.

Buryj's own political choices stand in stark contrast to the turbulence of the presidential campaign that swirled around her in 2004. Peggy Buryj voted for Bush, just as she had in 2000. She continued to back Bush even though she was, by then, fully embroiled in a battle with the military for accountability over how her son had been killed. She didn't blame the president for her son's death. And her tragedy did not change her views about the campaign in Iraq. She remains convinced that good things will eventually come from the overthrow of Saddam Hussein's regime. She is comforted by the knowledge that Jesse would have accepted the sacrifice he'd made for his country. Her problem was not with the president or with the war in Iraq. It was with the Pentagon.

Jesse was born while Ronald Reagan was president, in 1982. Until he left for the army, his life revolved around family and the small house on Smith Avenue. Jesse was an all-American boy. He loved football, played baritone horn in the school marching band and, just before deploying to Iraq, married his high school sweetheart. It couldn't have been easy growing up with a last name that is pronounced "booty"—the bullies didn't even need an imagination to work with that—but it was perhaps what gave Jesse his trademark sense of humor.

From the third grade, Jesse wanted to be a policeman. Many young kids imagine themselves in a fancy uniform, but Jesse was serious about it. There is still a framed picture in his bedroom of Jesse dressed in the uniform he wore as a member of the Canton City Police Youth Corps. Buryj says that it was his dream that led Jesse to sign up for the military: "He knew he couldn't be a police officer until he was twenty-one, usually twenty-three. So, he was going to join the army and become a military police officer, do his stint in the army and come home and join the police. That's what he wanted."

Jesse joined the army even before his graduation from high school. In the first interview Buryj did with *NOW on PBS* in early 2006, she said she initially tried to convince him not to do it: "I didn't want him to join the army for obvious reasons. I was afraid. Especially after 9/11. I knew we were going to war. We were going to war with somebody and here he is all wanting to join the army. I tried to talk him out of it. 'Jesse, we're going to go to war.' Well, there was no talking him out of it. He knew what he wanted to do. I used to tell him, 'Go have your great adventure, Jess. Go have your adventure and come home.'"

He was assigned to a military police unit in Fort Lewis, Washington. His first deployment was to a security detail at the Pentagon. Later he was sent to Kuwait and from there to Iraq. The invasion had happened a year earlier. The situation on the ground was uncertain but had not yet fallen into the insurgency that raged later. Jesse was thriving. Buryj recalls, "He was proud of everything he did in the military. He did everything the military ever asked him to do. He did it. He was so proud."

Once Jesse had gone overseas, Buryj immersed herself in current events. "I was on Iraqi time, you know," Buryj recalls. "I'd stay up all night watching the news, making sure where all the battles were and anything you heard on the news, any map of Iraq you could get on the computer. I was getting pretty good at reading Arabic. And I tried to educate myself as much as I could as to what was going on over there." It was a difficult period for a mother with a son fighting in Iraq. Every time Buryj heard news that a U.S. soldier had been killed, it stopped her cold. She was always so afraid it would turn out to be Jesse. But, she says, she was helped by the knowledge that Jesse himself had accepted the risk.

As an MP, Jesse was often tasked with manning checkpoints. At this stage of the war, in spring 2004, this was one of the most dangerous jobs for a soldier in Iraq. Jesse's unit was in Karbala, in the mainly Shiite south of the country. At the time, the most violent area in the country was the Sunni Triangle, to the north. But there was still plenty of tension in Karbala. On the night of May 4, Jesse was guarding a traffic circle. U.S. troops had been joined for this duty by a contingent of coalition partners from Poland. Each group had a different section of the circle.

Shortly after midnight, a dump truck broke through the perimeter. The giant truck barreled toward Jesse's position. The driver ignored insistent demands to stop. Rules of engagement mandated that the truck be disabled as quickly as possible. Everyone on the traffic circle began firing at the truck. Jesse, mounted on top of a Humvee, took aim and began to fire round after round at the truck. But all that firepower wasn't enough to stop the massive vehicle. The truck crashed, at high speed, into Jesse's Humvee. The army told Peggy Buryj that Jesse had been thrown from the vehicle and had died of internal injuries.

Jesse's body came home about a week later. On May 15, 2004, much of the city of Canton lined the streets for his funeral procession. It was a sign of hometown pride that even the soggy weather couldn't keep throngs from turning out, flags in hand, to honor their local son. Peggy, Steve, their daughter, Angela, and Jesse's young widow were joined by hundreds of mourners. For the funeral, 250 people packed the small, local Church of God. TV monitors were set up so that the overflow crowd in the basement and outside could see the service. Buryj received special permission to bury Jesse in the small cemetery of the Catholic church, across town, because it was on the route of the Pro Football Hall of Fame Grand Parade. From when he was still in diapers, Jesse had loved watching that parade. Later, he even got to march in it. Now, each year, the marchers would pass by his headstone.

Buryj was devastated. Her life had revolved around Jesse. The two had shared a very special and close bond. She told herself that Jesse had died doing something he truly believed in. With the support of the community and her husband, Buryj looked for the strength to go forward. Then, two months after Jesse's death, his widow, Amber, sent Buryj a copy of the death certificate. Buryj opened it and read it. Her blood went ice cold. Cause of death was listed: "Penetrating gunshot wound to the back." Buryj had buried her son believing he had died after he was hit by a truck. Now she was reading that he'd been shot. She began questioning everything she'd been told. At that moment everything else that had been going on in Buryj's life stopped. This would be her darkest moment, with the pain of her family tragedy now clouded by confusion and utter shock. Empowerment happens in many ways. For Buryj, it was involuntary—she needed the truth.

Buryj's closest friends had questions: "What good would it do to find out the exact details of Jesse's death?" Several times she was told, "It's not going to bring him back." Buryj knew that. She also felt strongly that Jesse would not have lasting peace until she unraveled all the details. "Maybe some other mothers could say, 'Well it didn't matter how he died.' Well, it does. It's important. It's a part of history. It's a part of my son's life, how he died. And they're not going to take that away from him," says Buryj. The army had posthumously awarded Jesse a purple heart and a bronze star, and that was a comfort to Buryj. She says the awards were "the last gift he gave us." But she needed to know how her son had died.

She'd never faced a challenge like this before. She had to get information from a massive bureaucracy that wielded enormous power. She knew that the U.S. military did not always respond well to outside scrutiny. In fact, Buryj didn't know how to begin. So she reached out for more information. "In July, I start making phone calls. I'm calling everybody I could possibly call that I could think of. I even called like the Red Cross. Could you help me here? Anybody, help me! How do I find out more information?"

Buryj went to the army and asked for more details about her son's death. She had learned that the autopsy report was critical. The army refused to give it to her. "If Jesse was killed here at home, I could go to the police station and say, could you please give me a copy of this—the police report. I could go to the coroner and get a copy of the autopsy," says Buryj. But that's not how it worked for Jesse. "Everything went through the military. I have a son that's dead. That was shot. I don't know who shot him, how he was shot. I know nothing other than the fact that my son's dead. That's pretty much it."

One of the main problems Buryj faced right away was the army's "next of kin" procedure, which placed Jesse's widow, Amber, as the primary point of contact for any communication from casualty services. Buryj knew Amber well, but their relationship had been deteriorating even before Jesse had been sent overseas. As Buryj fought to get more information about Jesse, Amber started her life over, dating and eventually re-marrying. Jesse's widow, now with a new husband, became a less reliable information conduit. Buryj knew she was going to have to get what she needed on her own, but she had a big obstacle in her way because she was not next of kin.

An investigation by *NOW on PBS* found that the casualty notification process of the U.S. military was a huge source of difficulty that families have faced when dealing with the loss of a child in war. In many cases the family might not even be in contact with the spouse or might not have good relations. Many key documents, like the death certificate and the autopsy, are given to the spouse only, not to the parents. And when the military conducts a death briefing, it is to the spouse, not the parents.

Buryj's efforts to inform herself began to pay off. She learned the arcane details of army procedure. And she learned about the Freedom of Information Act. FOIA is a tool frequently used by individuals, journalists and interest groups to obtain government documents and information that are not readily circulated. Congress enacted FOIA in 1966 and in the years that followed, the law has become an indispensable tool for creating a more open and transparent government. When a government official says, "I can't tell you that information," you can respond with a FOIA request. It has become so commonplace in the media profession that the acronym has transformed into a verb. But FOIA-ing is not easy. You need to know how to craft the request using required terms and, most importantly, you need to know specifically what you are asking for.

Buryj had heard of FOIA. She knew that it was something the newspapers used. But she didn't have any idea where to start. Her daughter, Angela, helped and, after calling around, managed to find someone at Fort Campbell in Kentucky who sent sample letters that showed them how to write a FOIA request. Buryj's first mission was to get that autopsy report. (Amber, who would have been able to get it easily, was not interested, so Buryj had to try the FOIA route.) It might seem shocking that a mother of a twenty-one-year-old soldier killed in Iraq had to use FOIA to get the autopsy report, but that was how it went for Buryj. And just because FOIA is effective doesn't mean it is fast. Not only did Buryj have to make the request, she also had to follow up again and again.

Buryj didn't want to sit around and wait. She wanted to use every resource at her disposal. She discovered that in the summer of 2004, only months away from the presidential elections, she had a special aura as the mother of a fallen soldier. Politicians would take her calls. Busy campaign officials would find time to meet and talk. And then the Bush campaign reached out to her. Bush's political handlers had no idea of the circumstances of Jesse's death and Buryj's emerging battle with the army. They called up and asked Buryj and her husband to meet with the president on a campaign stop in Canton. Buryj saw it as a sign from God: "I took an index card and wrote down all my information and all Jesse's information, because I knew if I, indeed, got to meet him, I was going to say, 'Please help me find out what happened to my son.' And, that happened." President Bush did say he would help. He told Buryj, "Sometimes it just takes a phone call from the president."

And it appeared that Bush did make that call, because soon Buryj got a call from Lieutenant Colonel Kevin Logan. She had gotten through to the very top. At the time Logan was the commander of casualty affairs. But even this special access wasn't enough to resolve things. From October, when she had first heard from Logan, until February 2005, Buryj was still unable to get Jesse's autopsy report. Every time she called there was another reason given for the delay: the election, the holidays, paperwork and so on. Finally, nine months after Jesse had been killed in Karbala, Buryj got the autopsy report. And once again, there was new and disturbing information. The report said Jesse had been killed by friendly fire. He'd been shot three times, two times in the legs and once in the back. The shot fired into Jesse's back, from behind, had killed him.

Buryj couldn't believe what she was reading. She'd fought so long to get answers and had found only more questions. She called Lieutenant Colonel Logan and demanded the truth. He tried to calm her down and promised she would receive a complete death briefing in April. He said the army was completing a careful investigation that would have accurate results. He dismissed the autopsy report as unreliable. So Peggy Buryj waited.

In April 2005—almost a year after Jesse's death—a team from the army came to her home and made a full presentation of the investigation. The team's conclusions were similar to the autopsy report. According to the investigators, the troops that ringed the traffic circle all opened fire trying to stop the dump truck. Jesse had been killed in the crossfire. The shots had come from a member of the coalition—"friendly fire." The presenters said the fatal shot was suspected to have come from the Polish sector. They were careful to tell her, "Suspected does not mean proven."

Buryj had a better picture of the truth but not everything. Why couldn't they establish for certain who had fired the shot that killed her son? Why had the weapons used that night not been collected? Why had full ballistics tests not been carried out? Where was the Polish investigation as to what happened that night? She began to realize that politics were involved. Coalition partners were not exactly easy to come by for this Iraq intervention. The United States was afraid to alienate the partners they had. It would have been awkward to open a full investigation of the behavior of the Polish troops at the checkpoint. Buryj saw that Jesse had fallen victim to international politics. But while politics might have stopped the army asking questions, it wasn't going to stop Buryj.

She called the Polish embassy in Washington, D.C., explained the situation and sent documents. The diplomats promised to check with Polish military officials. Months went by. Finally Buryj got a call from the Polish embassy. The Polish army denied any involvement in Jesse's death.

Buryj had hit some dead ends in her search for the truth. The story had been changing so much and there was so much conflicting information that Buryj didn't know what to believe anymore. "I understand the 'fog of war.' I understand 'friendly fire,'" says Buryj. "I don't understand almost a year of not knowing what happened to my son. And then getting the final report. And after looking at it and digesting it, and trying to understand it. There's still no answers there. There's more questions in that final report than there are any answers to my son's death."

Peggy Buryj was not alone in her frustration. Many military families had gotten a runaround from the U.S. military as they struggled to get a full and accurate story of a soldier's death. Buryj had been following what happened to former NFL star Pat Tillman. In April 2004 he had been killed under mysterious circumstances in Afghanistan. His parents had nightmarish problems getting the truth. The army kept changing its story.

Even though Pat Tillman was famous, and his death got enormous media coverage, his parents were still kept in the dark. In fact, new evidence emerged that suggested army officers had intentionally tried to conceal that Tillman had been killed by friendly fire. The alleged motive: to preserve morale in the war effort. Buryj began to wonder if the same thing was happening to her.

As *NOW on PBS* investigated the story of military families struggling to learn the truth about what happened to their loved ones overseas, a common thread emerged. The U.S. Army had serious problems with investigations of suspicious deaths. Just as bad, the army was doing a poor job of notifying and communicating with the families of the slain soldiers. In case after case, the pattern was the same: bad information, then new information that was different but just as unreliable. Was it incompetence? Or a cover-up?

NOW on PBS spent time with another mother, Karen Meredith of Mountain View, California. The army gave an inaccurate account of how her son, Ken Ballard, had been killed in 2004. Ballard had been in Najaf, in a tough firefight with members of the Mahdi army, the Shiite group led by cleric Muqtada al-Sadr. Ballard, a veteran tank commander, did more than fight hard. That night in Najaf he saved the lives of many of his comrades. The army issued him a posthumous bronze star for valor. Still, it took Meredith almost two years to get the details of what exactly had happened to her son. Her fight even led her to confront the secretary of the army. After much effort, Meredith learned that her son had not been killed in battle. He'd been riding atop his tank when a tree branch hit his machine gun, mounted next to him. The gun discharged, killing him instantly.

Back in Canton, Buryj was afraid she'd reached the end of the line. She did not have the answers she longed for. After the formal death briefing, the army told her Jesse's case was closed. There was going to be no further investigation, no ballistic tests and no bothering the Polish military or the Polish government. Desperate, she called Josh White, the *Washington Post* reporter who had been covering the Tillman story. Initially she only planned to ask him for contact information for Tillman's mother, but she ended up explaining all that she had been through. Buryj felt she had no choice but to turn to the media. She'd avoided this approach for more than a year. She'd done all she could to work with the army, rather than embarrass it, but she'd hit a wall. The front-page investigation that followed got Buryj the attention she was looking for. Now politicians, antiwar activists and representatives of the global media knew her name and her story.

It also pushed Buryj's quest from a personal one to a public matter. Sometimes going to the media and sharing your story about an injustice that has happened to you is part of the journey to become a civic activist. In Buryj's case, she did not set out to bring attention to the systemic deficiencies of the army's casualty notification process. She just wanted truth and justice for Jesse. She had crossed a line but the gamble quickly paid off. "I talked to the media. The media talked to the senator. The senator talked to the secretary of the army. And now there's supposedly a new investigation into Jesse's death," Buryj told *NOW on PBS* back in early 2006.

Indeed, there was a new investigation of Jesse's death, launched by the army. And the media attention that Buryj provoked led to another astonishing development. One night, a soldier who had served with Jesse in Karbala, Iraq, showed up on Buryj's doorstep with shocking news. "He came here, came to my home. Sat here in my living room. And told me that the Polish had absolutely nothing to do with Jesse's death," recalls Buryj. "He was not there when the incident occurred. But he was at the briefings and the meetings that took place. He was there when the confession was made as to who shot Jesse. He was there when statements were coerced and the reports were falsified. And he said the Polish were a complete scapegoat. They had nothing to do with Jesse's death." He told her it had been an accident, not an intentional shooting. The news turned Buryj's world upside down, all over again.

Buryj wanted to bring this account to the army investigator who was reopening the investigation of Jesse's death. But the soldier was hesitant to go on the record. He had left the army but was still afraid of repercussions for talking. Buryj says military officials told her that they suspected the soldier had an "ax to grind" with his former unit and the matter was dropped.

The army's second investigation wrapped up in late 2006. The results were delivered personally to the Buryj home by the army's inspector general. The army continued to claim that as best as they could determine, Jesse had died as a result of fire from the Polish sector. But the bullet that had killed him had been improperly destroyed so there would always be a degree of uncertainty. They admitted that the investigation into Jesse's death had been disastrous and apologized. The Polish military released a statement subsequently reiterating their denial. As far as the army was concerned the matter was closed. For Buryj, many questions lingered.

But at the same time there was a very positive outcome. The activism of Peggy Buryj and others like Karen Meredith and the Tillman family paid off. The army announced fundamental changes in policy. A first wave of changes was pushed through in early 2006. The army overhauled its notification procedures. Communication with the families was improved and broadened. The army expanded casualty assistance to parents, even in the event that they are not the officially designated next of kin. That would have saved Buryj a lot of trouble in the early stages of her investigation into Jesse's death.

The army also moved to make casualty reports more accurate. They instituted a change that requires unit commanders in the field to certify the content of casualty reports. The purpose is to avoid mistakes being passed along.

Why did the army make these sweeping changes? Officials pointed to the incidents of mishandling the casualty process that had occurred. So the credit goes to the families who insisted on the truth. Their battle made them citizen activists, and they had a lasting and important impact on the U.S. Army.

Later in 2006, the army carried out a comprehensive review of 810 casualty reports. It was an unprecedented audit that accounted for almost 40 percent of all deaths up to that time. By the end of the year they had discovered seven instances where families had been misinformed about the death of their loved ones, including the cases of Jesse Buryj, Pat Tillman and Karen Meredith's son, Ken Ballard. Recently, the continuing investigation into Tillman's death had resulted in the censure of a retired three-star general, the former head of U.S. Special Operations Command. The army found that he had provided misleading information about Tillman's death.

The story of Peggy Buryj carries lessons for us all. She refused to make her opponent, the U.S. Army, into her enemy. When she met with officers and soldiers, she made sure they knew that she loved the army. She told them how proud she was that her son Jesse had chosen to enter the military and go to Iraq. She knew that the organization she was trying to change was not her nemesis. Buryj embraced the troops and she embraced her president. She just needed things to be done in a different way. In a better way.

"Embrace your opponent"—easy to say, but not an easy path. There were moments of outrage and long dark periods of frustration. Buryj knew she was being treated unfairly, and that wasn't right for the mother of a young man who'd made the ultimate sacrifice. "My attitude was, any information you could have given me should have been given to me at my feet on a silver platter," says Buryj. "I should not have had to beg, scream, cry, call politicians, play the political game. I shouldn't have to be going to the media. My gosh."

For Peggy Buryj, the personal became political. Buryj's single-minded determination to resolve what happened to her own son, Jesse, ended up helping to change policy throughout the entire U.S. military. Now, Buryj didn't set out with the intention of changing the military. She says her goals were always immediate and personal—she needed the truth in order for Jesse's soul to rest in peace. But she discovered in order to learn about Jesse, she had to push the army to change the way it did business. Today the army is far more accountable to the families of the fallen, and Peggy Buryj played a large role in making that happen.

Today, Peggy and Steve Buryj's home in Canton looks much like it did when Jesse lived there and dreamed of getting a job with the local police department. Upstairs, Jesse's bedroom remains exactly as he left it. There's a picture on the wall of Jesse with his prom date, Amber, who would become his wife. Another snapshot shows him with the high school marching band. Downstairs in the living room, Jesse's father, Steve, sits in his easy chair in front of the TV. He's decompressing after his night shift working at Diamond Network Polymers. Steve has a quiet anger at everything that he and his wife have been through. He can't maintain faith in the president and his mission in the Middle East the way Peggy can. Steve wants the truth about his son just as his wife does. As he speaks, outrage at the process bubbles underneath. You get the sense that he allows Peggy to assume the brunt of the fight for Jesse because if he dived in, he would explode.

Buryj has not stopped waging her battle for the truth. She carved off a section of their dining room and turned it into her office. A portrait of Jesse looks down from the wall as she works. Almost every day, she sits at the computer, chain-smoking and poring over leads on the Internet. The flicker of the monitor reflects off of her thick glasses, framed by her short blond hair. She checks out new information using e-mail and the phone. When the process threatens to overwhelm her, she takes the short drive to Jesse's grave. His headstone was designed to incorporate Jesse's high school mascot, a bulldog, and emblems of the military honors he'd been awarded. On the back someone has stuck on the logo of the Dave Matthews Band, Jesse's favorite. It is a peaceful spot, far enough up the hill to be away from the noise of the traffic on busy Cleveland Avenue but still close enough to catch the lilting music of the marching band that passes every August.

"I never thought in the United States of America that this would happen. My son was a good soldier. He was a good human being. I've been a good soldier. I've been nothing but supportive of the war and my president since this happened," Buryj told *NOW on PBS* back in 2006. For a moment, bitterness passes across her face like a shadow, toward those responsible for the war that took her son's life. But only for a moment.

"You just can't ship him home to me in a box and not tell me what happened to him. He's my son," says Buryj. "Jesse cannot have peace and I will not have peace until I know I have made every effort to find out what happened to him. Does that mean I'm going to find out? No. But, I cannot go to my son's grave and stand there and say, 'I have not fought a good fight for you, Jesse.' I cannot. I can't just let it go."

REPORTER'S SNAPSHOT: PEGGY BURYJ

The reporter in me knew that Mary Tillman was not the only one. She was not the only mother who would be lied to by the U.S. military about the circumstances of her child's death.

By nature as a journalist, I don't trust institutions. But even I was taken aback at the twisted image put out by the U.S. military about who Pat Tillman was and how he had died. I started digging, and found that Pat Tillman was not your typical "all-American" football star. He was an independent thinker. He read Noam Chomsky and he questioned the war in Iraq. The ugly truth began to come out about how Tillman was killed by friendly fire. The cover-up had been elaborate. The military was lying to one family about how one soldier died. I knew there had to be more.

I held onto this story idea for months and months. When I left CNN to become Senior Correspondent for *NOW on PBS,* I knew that this was one of the investigative pieces that our audience would care about. Sources told me of case after case in which the military was keeping the truth from soldiers' families. Military families pointed me to Peggy Buryj to learn more.

Peggy Buryj had come to understand that to get attention paid to her fight for the truth, she herself was going to have to speak up. She had gotten some attention from local and national media. Though she was uncomfortable being in the spotlight, Peggy knew she had to open herself up to being scrutinized by reporters. She knew the reporters would not all be friendly. She took the chance because she needed the truth.

Peggy Buryj told me on the phone the first time we spoke that she was a Republican who had voted for President Bush and who supported the idea of going to war with Iraq. I wanted to know more about her decision to question the truthfulness of one of the most powerful institutions in our nation. "You are prepared to challenge the highest ranks of the military?" I asked. She surprised me. "Rank is something that just stinks to me, Maria. Rank means nothing to me anymore. I just want the truth," she said quietly. She sounded determined, but her voice trembled just a bit as the words came out.

I spend a lot of time preparing myself when I am going to meet the mother of a fallen soldier. I have the utmost of respect for these moms. They are still mourning their child's death and yet they find the ability to push back against formidable institutions of power. And then they allow us into their lives. I know that every time I meet one of these moms I will come away a changed person. I will repeat their story to the moms I meet at my kid's school, to moms I meet on airplanes or standing in line for a cup of coffee. I will tell their story to my own mother and sister. I tell their story on TV because I am a journalist. I repeat their story to others because I too am an American mom raising my kids in a time of war.

Peggy Buryj is alone when we meet her for the interview. Her husband and daughter aren't around. They support Peggy's fight to learn the truth about Jesse, but they have no desire to be around a TV crew. Peggy hugs me and thanks me for coming. I tell her I need to change clothes and fix my make-up. (The things a TV reporter must do. Radio can be so much easier!) Peggy leads me to a small room behind the kitchen and leaves me alone. I lay my clothes on the bed. Maybe Jesse had once slept in this bed, played as a kid in the small backyard I see from the window. I take a deep breath. This is going to be a hard interview.

Afterward, Peggy takes me upstairs to Jesse's old room. It is a shrine to a handsome young man who will never again pound up the stairs, crank up the radio, sleep in the bed. Jesse was a jokester, Peggy tells me. "He made me laugh with his silly jokes and puns," she says, and for a moment her face lights up with the memories. Then the sadness and anger return to her features.

Nothing about Peggy Buryj's life makes you think she would ever want to take on her own government. But what I learned from Peggy and the other moms like her—Mary Tillman, Karen Meredith—is that they know what it means to be an American citizen. They understand their absolute right to question the institutions that rule them. They understand that citizenship and the Constitution are the great equalizers in our country. No one is better or worth more than another citizen. And we all have an equal right to the truth.

When I return home, I share Peggy and Jesse's story with my own son and daughter. As we talk, the war stops being invisible for my family. And the rights and responsibilities of being a citizen become real to my kids. They learn that being an American means following in the footsteps of Peggy Buryj. It means taking up a challenge Peggy handed to me in her humble home in Ohio—to seek the truth and never stop pushing until you get it. What more inspiration does a reporter need? None. Just the story of Jesse and Peggy Buryj.

THE REPORTER: MARIA HINOJOSA is an award-winning journalist and author who joined *NOW on PBS* in 2005 as Senior Correspondent. Prior to joining the show, Maria was the urban affairs correspondent at CNN. For six years, she was a New York–based correspondent for NPR, and she continues to host the weekly NPR program Latino USA. Hinojosa's books are *Raising Raul: Adventures Raising Myself and My Son;* and *CREWS: Gang Members Talk to Maria Hinojosa.*

9

A LOUD WHISTLE

BUNNY GREENHOUSE

WHAT SHE'S DONE:
Greenhouse helped bring accountability and transparency to a giant government agency, the U.S. Army Corps of Engineers.

LOCAL HERO HIGHLIGHT:
As a top civilian inside the agency, she became a whistle-blower and waged a personal battle, refusing to back down or quit.

L ET'S SAY YOU WORK FOR A GIGANTIC INSTITUTION—A CORPORATION, OR A branch of the U.S. government. Bit by bit you advance in your career. You make a comfortable salary, and you're building a retirement nest egg. Then comes the day that you discover something terribly wrong is going on. Do you make a big stink and endanger your job? Or do you just look the other way, knowing that the organization will resist any change and that if you speak out, you'll likely end up as road-kill?

Bunnatine Greenhouse, who insists everyone call her Bunny, never set out to become one of the country's most famous whistle-blowers. Her story is all about transforming an institution from within. How did one person help reform a government bureaucracy with over 35,000 employees?

That Bunny Greenhouse had become the top civilian procurement official at the U.S. Army Corps of Engineers—the first women and the first African American to do so—is part of the story. Greenhouse grew up in a poor family in Rayville, Louisiana, in the 1950s. Segregation was in full force. There was not a lot of opportunity for those living on the wrong side of the tracks. Her father made it only to the first grade, her mother, to the sixth. Still, they never let lack of money or education stop them from creating a household that valued achievement and banished complacency. Greenhouse says her mother "would not let 'not having' set a pattern for her children." In addition to Greenhouse's own accomplishments, two of her siblings went on to teach at the university level. Her younger brother, Elvin Hayes, left Rayville to become an NBA star and member of the Basketball Hall of Fame.

Greenhouse looks back at her childhood and says the discipline they all learned at home had a lasting influence. A tree that grew in her backyard played a special role. If Greenhouse violated one of the rules, she was sent out to the tree and had to choose a branch, which her parents used on her backside. It was called the "switch tree." All the children had run-ins with the switch tree. A sure ticket to the tree was telling a lie. In the Hayes household there was no such thing as a white lie. "My mother always said lying is in the intention, not the content," says Greenhouse. Nor was it acceptable to remain silent in the face of an untruth. This would play a significant role in the choices Greenhouse made years later at the U.S. Army Corps of Engineers. It all goes back to the honesty and integrity she learned from her mother, Greenhouse says. "Once you have that ingrained in you, you can't stray."

Bunny Greenhouse thrived in the love and discipline of the Hayes household. She was valedictorian in high school. She went on to do her undergraduate degree in math—in only three years and *magna cum laude*—at Southern University in Baton Rouge, Louisiana, one of the most famous of the historically black colleges and universities. With her degree in hand, Greenhouse worked as a schoolteacher here and there, eventually making her way back home to Rayville. It was the 1960s, a time of turmoil in the Deep South. Greenhouse became the first African American teacher at the newly integrated high school. It was a "first" in a life that would have a lot of firsts.

Greenhouse threw herself completely into her job. That would become a hallmark of how she worked. "That's Bunny Greenhouse, you know. If I'm teaching, I'm teaching as if my life depended upon it. I feel that any failure is my fault for a student," Greenhouse told *NOW on PBS*. She was a great believer in education—eventually, she would earn three separate master's degrees.

How did Greenhouse get from teaching and academia into the world of military procurement? It came about through the man she fell in love with. Two weeks before she graduated college, she married Aloysius Greenhouse, who became a career officer in the U.S. Army, charged with equipping the troops. He even wrote an essay on "Acquisition Streamlining" for the Army War College. Al Greenhouse's job required frequent moves (the years

Bunny was teaching in Louisiana, Al was serving three tough tours, one in Korea, two in Vietnam). Bunny moved along with her husband in his postwar military career and took teaching positions where she could. But as the years went by, she got more interested in the complex logistics of contracting and procurement. Bunny's first job in contracting was an internship with the army at Fort Hood.

It was in 1997 that Lieutenant General Joe Ballard, then Commander of the U.S. Army Corps of Engineers, brought Greenhouse on board. By that time she'd built up an impressive resume in contracting, both in the army but also for Dynalectron (later DynCorp) and the Dallas-Fort Worth Airport Board. Ballard named her to the plum job of Principal Assistant Responsible for Contracting (PARC), a position that made her the highest ranked contracting civilian in the corps and was the protocol equivalent of the rank of one-star general. Greenhouse was also the corps' competition advocate, a position that made her responsible for approving and signing all procurements and contracts over $10 million. In her time at the corps, she would oversee over $23 *billion* worth of contracts. Ballard tapped Greenhouse because he knew of her integrity and frankness. As she testified before Congress in September 2005: "I was selected not only because I was by far the most qualified, but also because General Ballard was searching for a new head of contracting who would have the fortitude to confront a longstanding 'good ol' boys' network of commanders who routinely engaged in casual and clubby contracting practices."

Ballard, a fellow Louisianan and Southern University graduate, was a career U.S. Army Corpsman. He received his commission right out of college and worked and lived all around the world as an officer, engineer and soldier. Bill Clinton named him the forty-ninth commander of the corps in 1996. He was the first African American to head the institution in its history. Ballard took on the role of reformer at the corps and dedicated his managerial efforts to bringing in private sector business practices to modernize the way the corps conducted itself. In an interview for an internal corps publication in 1998, Ballard used a vivid image to describe what he was trying to accomplish: "To visualize the changes in the corps, think of waves crashing on the shore. Each wave is a new sound business practice, and each successive wave is just a little larger. Some gigantic waves are building, so I'm very optimistic."

Bunny Greenhouse was one of the gigantic waves Ballard had in mind. Right from the start she dove into the job with the same passion she had brought to school teaching in Rayville, Louisiana, so many years before: "[I was] very, very passionate about what I was there to do," Greenhouse told *NOW on PBS* in 2005, "I lived and breathed that. I felt that my life depended on it." It might seem strange that someone could be so energized about something as mundane as contracting, but, as she would say, that's Bunny Greenhouse. She says it was "a wonderful mission to get up in the morning for." Maybe it had something to do with the fact that she saw her service at the corps, indeed the service of all people involved in military contracting, as a patriotic duty: "We look at the job that we do as a real privilege, to be able to serve. We are not out there with the war fighters. We are not out there on the front line. But every time we have a successful procurement, we feel that we are adding value to that war fighter and giving him the protection that he needs."

Greenhouse did make waves. Her appearance alone was enough to send shock waves through the stodgy institution. She is tall, imposing and immaculately turned out. Her job, in supporting the corps' transition to sound business practices, was to install a system of integrity and fairness in the process of doling out big infrastructure contracts, both for the U.S. military and for the civilian projects. Greenhouse was also supposed to make sure every contractor that wanted a chance at corps work got consideration based on the merits of what they could bring to the job, rather than on any connections they had.

Sounds reasonable, right? But Greenhouse's approach was alien to the way the corps had done business for decades. There was a well-oiled system of contracts going to a select group of contractors who were buddies with officials of the corps or Department of Defense. Over the years, the corps had gotten a terrible reputation for this sort of sweetheart contracting. That was what Greenhouse says she was brought in to fight.

Sometimes the preexisting practices verged on outright fraud. During Greenhouse's tenure, officials were disciplined because of a scandal involving the manipulation of a study to justify contracts worth millions for construction on the Mississippi and Illinois Rivers.

The "casual and clubby contracting practices" were not only bad business practice, they were against the law. The Federal Acquisition Regulations (FAR), the guiding principles for any government contract or purchase, are designed to prevent corruption or undue influence. One of the aims of FAR is to promote the use of small and minority-owned businesses in order to diversify contracts and encourage innovation. But the overall goal is to spend the taxpayers' money as efficiently as possible. It was Greenhouse's job to make sure that this was being done.

The FAR approach requires efficiency and impartiality. But the real world of military contracts has always been complicated and opaque. And it's not just at the Army Corps of Engineers. Some people call it the "iron triangle": vendors (industry) and consumers (the Pentagon and government agencies) get into cozy relationships that can freeze out the general public. Congress, which provides the money, forms the third leg of the iron triangle. Key members of Congress vote for sweetheart deals because industry cleverly places portions of big contracts in their districts, so their votes to approve giant appropriations bills can be cast as helping out their local constituencies.

This is made more difficult by Washington's revolving doors. The very same people who have worked on one side of the iron triangle often take a lucrative leap and end up on another. Although government jobs don't pay very well, the work requires aptitude that is equal to or often exceeds that needed for lucrative private sector positions. So an unspoken compromise has been reached. Veteran civil servants have productive and helpful careers, and then they leave the government to take up cushy positions in the private sector. There, the expertise they developed in government service can reap enormous financial benefits for private industry. Their contacts and security clearances are a gold mine.

In Washington, this has become universal. CIA and FBI officers retire to become management consultants specializing in corporate risk. Defense

Department officials leave the Pentagon to work for weapons contractors. And elected officials step down to become lobbyists. Most of this is legal. But it can become political arbitrage, even outright corruption. Hundreds of billions of dollars in government contracts are at stake. The public interest loses out when a company gets a contract from insider ties and not because it is the best qualified or has the most competitive bid.

One Washington, D.C., private equity firm, the Carlyle Group, has become the poster child for revolving-door relationships. Among the folks that have had management or advisory positions are former president George H. W. Bush, former secretary of defense Frank Carlucci and former secretary of state James Baker. Critics say the Carlyle Group has leveraged the unparalleled connections of those former leaders to secure lucrative government contracts. The fund has also had a series of former leaders of foreign countries as advisors (at one time the bin Ladens were investors in a Carlyle fund, giving conspiracy theorists a field day). Although Carlyle has had investments as benign and diverse as Dunkin' Donuts and Hertz, much of the hand-wringing concerns their vast aerospace and defense holdings.

And there's another company that gets people worked up along the same lines: Halliburton. During the Clinton years, Dick Cheney was in exile from power (remember, he had been secretary of defense under George H. W. Bush). During much of that time he was CEO of the energy services firm. When the vice president took office in 2000, he retired from Halliburton with a severance package worth millions. Then came the Iraq War, backed so strongly by the vice president. The invasion and its aftermath resulted in a windfall for Halliburton and its subsidiaries. That fact does not change, whether you fall in the camp that suspects sleazy connections, or if you believe that Halliburton got the contracts because it is one of the only firms with the capacity to take on jobs of the risk and magnitude that Iraq represents.

Much of the controversy surrounding Halliburton is focused on a subsidiary called KBR. Formerly known as Kellogg, Brown & Root, it is a massive construction and engineering firm that has secured huge contracts in Iraq (KBR was spun off from Halliburton in 2007). Not only is it heavily involved in a series of reconstruction activities, it also supplies manpower and services to support the U.S. military in Iraq, from cooking meals to digging latrines. With operations that include oil services, reconstruction, and private military services, all at the same time, KBR has become an obvious target for opponents of the "military industrial complex."

And that's what brings us back to Bunny Greenhouse. It was a KBR contract that got all the fuss started at the Army Corps of Engineers. This came after she had been at the corps for six years. Her mentor, Lieutenant General Ballard, had left in 2000 and had been replaced by a commander with a very different style. Lieutenant General Robert Flowers, a second-generation army man, was a soldier's soldier. According to Bunny Greenhouse, Flowers did not take the same approach to reform that Ballard had. She says the change in leadership resulted in "ever increasing pressure to return to the old ways." She says she faced hostility from the "good ol' boys" within the corps, and she believes some of that was due to her gender and race. It was this climate, says Greenhouse, that forced her to lodge an Equal Employment Opportunity Office complaint in 2002 in order to document the situation. But soon, those factors would be the least of her troubles.

In six years of attacking the old ways, Greenhouse had made quite a name for herself at the corps. She was a stickler for rules. She questioned everything. It got to the point, she says, that officers came up with a devious strategy to avoid her relentless scrutiny. Greenhouse was only responsible for oversight of contracts worth more than $10 million. So the officers carved up procurement deals into small portions. "If someone at the corps wanted to get something past Bunny Greenhouse," she said, "All they had to do was break it up into parts worth less than $10 million." By 2003, this had become commonplace at the corps, according to Greenhouse.

But then came a massive contract that coincided with the onset of the U.S. invasion of Iraq. It was worth billions—much too big to slice up and do an end run around Greenhouse. The contract in question was called Restore Iraqi Oil (RIO). During the first Gulf War, Iraqi President Saddam Hussein had surprised the world by setting alight hundreds of Kuwait's oil wells as his troops retreated from the country, chased out by Allied forces. The result was a huge mess. Specialty fire crews had to be identified, trained, supplied and flown in with tons of equipment. There had never been so many big oil fires at the same time. To make matters even worse, the departing Iraqis had placed mines around many of the wells. The fires raged for months before they were all extinguished, causing an environmental disaster and the destruction of millions of barrels of valuable oil.

U.S. authorities wanted to be ready in the event that Saddam repeated his tactics within Iraq. And they wanted a plan even before troops hit the ground and crossed into Iraqi territory. So KBR had been brought in to do a study for the corps as to what would be needed to have a strategy in place and a recovery force ready. Greenhouse told *NOW on PBS* that KBR had been paid close to $2 million to draw up the plan. So far, so good. KBR had already been used many times before in this way. These sorts of contracts were awarded by the corps, and run under the Logistics Civil Augmentation Program (LOGCAP), the official program the military has for managing its use of private sector entities.

It started to get fishy for Greenhouse when she learned that KBR had turned up as a bidder on the RIO contract. It was a huge red flag for her. KBR had drawn up the plan for RIO. They knew exactly what was needed for the project and exactly what to say in order to get the job. They would have even known the dollar amounts they would be permitted to charge. This was one of the cardinal sins of the contracting world. Under normal circumstances, says Greenhouse, the contractor tasked with coming up with the plan is never allowed to work on the follow-up contract.

But these were not normal times. It had been several years since the Army Corps of Engineers had been back on a war footing. In wartime, goals like "sound business practice" begin to take a back seat to what is best for the troops on the ground. And if you are a soldier yourself, like many in the top leadership of the corps, putting the troops first is all about taking care of your own. But, according to Greenhouse, civilians like her are in the corps for an important reason. "That's where you have the level headedness of the civilians, the contracting people who are sitting in their offices determining what strategy can be and making sure that we use the rules and regulations to the highest ability that we can. There are some times that we have to make those exceptions to our rules. But we don't want to get into a culture that we can't do the best that we can. We are not in the war zone. We are back here trying to make sure that we make the best trade-off and the best business decisions that we possibly can."

The situation with KBR bidding on a contract that they themselves had crafted only got worse when it was revealed to Greenhouse that they were the *only* bidders on the deal. Greenhouse saw this as a deal breaker. Her co-workers were adamant that they had no choice as they had to get the RIO deal in place as soon as possible. They didn't have time to round up other bidders. KBR was ready to go. Greenhouse eventually went along with it, with the caveat that it be treated as a bridge contract, a short one-year stopgap deal that would get them through the critical going-to-war period and allow them space to get an acceptable contract in place. "I am not averse to no-bid contracts when they're absolutely necessary," she said. Greenhouse was even prepared to extend the contract in the event that after one year they still found themselves in trouble: "Any prudent individual, sitting at our desks, with the stroke of a pen could've extended that contract for another year if that were necessary."

Then the contract showed up on Greenhouse's desk for final approval. It was as if her objections had never even been raised. All she saw were the original terms of the RIO deal: a two-year contract with KBR with three one-year extension options. KBR was getting what amounted to a gigantic five-year deal, with no outside competition to worry about. Greenhouse was floored. There weren't many avenues left to her to raise objections. "I had already raised it to the office of the secretary of defense. I had already raised it to the secretary of the army," Greenhouse said. She had gone all the way to the top, but her concerns had been ignored.

Greenhouse was faced with one of the biggest decisions of her life: to sign or not. She knew the war was imminent. She felt an obligation to do whatever it took to make the effort go as smoothly as possible. So she signed. In careful script above the signature line, she wrote: "I caution that extending this sole source effort beyond a one-year period could convey an invalid perception that there is not strong intent for a limited competition." She says she handwrote these comments on the official document because she was afraid a separate memo highlighting her concerns would "inexplicably be lost." But despite her comments on the document, and her repeated complaints, the RIO contract was awarded as a no-bid contract to KBR. Greenhouse lost that battle but was determined to keep doing her job to the best of her abilities.

It might have ended there. The war started, troops took Baghdad, and Saddam did not set the country's oil installations ablaze. Still, the oil industry was in a shambles. Partly, this was due to a dozen years of economic sanctions and controls that kept the regime from acquiring technology to modernize or maintain oil production. A country that had been pumping more than 3 million barrels per day before the first Gulf War was now working at less than half that capacity. Even though there were no fires to put out, there was still much for KBR to do—especially given that war proponents in the administration had often stated that Iraq's oil wealth would pay for our venture there.

But things never went as well as administration hawks had forecast. KBR employees were ambushed on Iraq's highways. Restore Iraqi Oil became a very dangerous job. And as a result, KBR was spending more money than originally planned. This got people back home asking questions. One example was the cost overruns for fuel that KBR was transporting. In December 2003, an audit revealed that KBR had run up overcharges for fuel purchases to the tune of $61 million.

KBR had plenty of explaining to do. They said the overcharges came from higher prices they had been charged for gasoline by a Kuwait-based subcontractor. They complained that they'd been forced to use that particular subcontractor by political pressure from the Kuwait government and the U.S. embassy there. They said border crossing and transportation difficulties made getting cheaper gas from Turkey unfeasible. They asked for a waiver of the need to fully justify the overcharges. This was within their rights, especially as the country was still at war and needed their services badly. But again, they had one formidable force standing in their way: Bunny Greenhouse.

As the chief civilian procurement officer, Greenhouse would have to sign off on any waiver. And everyone knew she wasn't going to just let it slip by this time. Greenhouse later testified that officials in the corps decided to keep her in the dark about it. They concealed the waiver request until Greenhouse was home sick with bronchitis. There was a window of opportunity for a day or two when she would not be in the office. Officials drew up the waiver, sent it to headquarters and got it signed before Greenhouse even knew it existed. As she told *NOW on PBS* in 2005: "They wanted to get this one through without a lot of scrutiny from Bunny Greenhouse. So it was done on a day that I wasn't there. And it was done in a manner of which I was never to know about this particular document. But it just happened that this one came up as a storm in the news media. And, therefore, I had to know about it."

To get the waiver approved without Greenhouse's direct signature involved a degree of skullduggery, says Greenhouse. The corps commander, Lieutenant General Robert Flowers, had instituted a policy when he took charge that dispersed power to deputies within the corps. It was part of his management style. Flowers called it his "just do it" policy. Subordinates were issued with cards printed with those words to empower them to make reasonable decisions without running everything up the chain of command. It was designed to make things run smoother. But it relied very much on individual discretion. On that December day in 2003, with Greenhouse home sick, her deputy exercised his "just do it" authority.

At this point the press and the watchdog groups had become interested in Halliburton and the RIO contract. There was enough of a paper trail by now to enable people to start following up and asking questions. The Center for Public Integrity used the Freedom of Information Act to get a copy of the RIO contract, complete with Greenhouse's handwritten reservations. Days later, the story broke in *Time* magazine. Members of Congress started asking questions. As Greenhouse said, "My concern had found its way to the light of day." Remember, this is a woman for whom even a white lie

meant a trip to the switch tree back in her youth. Once questions were publicly asked, she was going to answer them.

Before taking on Greenhouse, the very least someone in human resources at the corps should have done is to have gone back and checked her
personnel file. A performance review noted Greenhouse was "not timid—
has the fortitude to tell it as it is," and claimed her ethics were "above re-
proach." Another review in the file highlighted her "unquestionable loyalty,
integrity and dedication to mission" and predicted an excellent future for
her at the Department of Defense.

With reporters and Congress probing the corps, Greenhouse became a
real liability for those who wanted everything swept under the rug. On October 6, 2004, she was told that proceedings were underway to demote her
from senior executive service and remove her from her position as Principal
Assistant Responsible for Contracting. At the same time she was offered an
opportunity to retire and retain all the benefits she had earned in her current position. In justifying this move, officials cited poor annual performance evaluations, two in three years (which were necessary to invoke such
a proceeding). To Greenhouse this was the culmination of a long-planned
initiative to get her out of the way. The "good ol' boys" had the patience to
wait out the two years they knew they needed. Performance evaluations at
the corps are ranked from one (highest) to five (lowest). Greenhouse had
never scored lower than two until the KBR affair began. Since that time she
had earned consecutive fives. One of the things cited in her negative review,
she says, was that they didn't like that she had taken to writing her objections on contracts by hand.

This is where Greenhouse ramped things up. Her first course of action was to go up the chain of command but still stay within the military
community. Her lawyer, Michael Kohn, noted for his work representing
whistle-blowers, wrote a letter to the secretary of the army requesting a
formal investigation by the inspector general of the Department of Defense. The investigation requested never took place, but the letter still
managed to stir things up. It got into the hands of the media and, more
importantly, Congress. Suddenly, everyone wanted to talk to Bunny

Greenhouse. And Congress was going to get first dibs, asking her to appear in June of 2005.

The corps went into damage control mode. "The acting general counsel came to me and let me know in no uncertain terms that it would not be in my best interest to have testified," says Greenhouse. But they'd already told her she was to be demoted. What were her alternatives? They were hoping she would quit. But that wasn't Bunny Greenhouse. And now Congress was expecting her to testify. Remember, the billions of dollars of contracts that she reviewed came from money appropriated by Congress. There was no way she was going to duck out from talking to the lawmakers. "In contracting, the lineage of that authority comes from Congress. So what right do I have if Congress is calling me to explain some of the improprieties or some of the concerns that I may have had?"

Greenhouse's testimony set off a firestorm about the military's ties to Halliburton and KBR. And once the word was out, Greenhouse didn't stop. She talked with reporters, began speaking in public gatherings and in late 2005 sat down with *NOW on PBS* for a comprehensive interview. The program has gained a reputation for being a place whistle-blowers like Greenhouse can go to get the word out. It has become an essential part of our government system—an antidote to the iron triangle. Whistle-blowers, Congress and the news media create an "information triangle." A whistle-blower gets the word out, then Congress and the news media start digging. That creates enough leverage to make changes.

The corps did everything they could to silence Greenhouse. The very day she went to testify on Capitol Hill, June 27, 2005, the army inspector general released the request to demote her. The official reduction in rank and reassignment came on August 27, 2005. The timing was about as bad as possible to change top personnel at the Army Corps of Engineers. That was two days before the levees collapsed in New Orleans as a result of Hurricane Katrina. The levees were the responsibility of the corps and their rehabilitation would inevitably have to pass through the office Greenhouse had run. Greenhouse would have toured the area, surveyed the damage and worked to approve big emergency repair contracts. She says her removal "caused the Army Corps' contracting function to be rendered leaderless at a time of great crisis." The inability to help her home state during that terrible disaster was a source of great pain for Greenhouse.

Many people in Greenhouse's position would have quit. Greenhouse kept fighting, in spite of additional steps she says were designed to humiliate her. Her top-secret clearance was taken away. She's continued to accrue what she calls "inappropriately downgraded performance reviews." She was moved from her spacious office into a tiny cubicle in a dead-end corner in an isolated part of the building. She had gone from being the most powerful civilian at the corps to having a glorified broom closet as an office.

Imagine what's it's like to face the angry, unfriendly stares of co-workers. She says she is treated like "a skunk at the picnic" and is shunned even by people she doesn't know. But Greenhouse reports to work every day. She does the menial tasks assigned to her. In her private time, she talks to reporters and congressional staffers about what needs to be done at the corps. She has kept at it for years.

Part of Greenhouse's strength has come from her support network—media, members of Congress and outraged citizens. But she counts on another important source for strength: religion. Greenhouse is a deeply religious person, active in church since Sunday school. And almost forty years ago, she says she received a personal calling. She can't explain it in logical terms. She came to know, she says, that God had a purpose for her. She was to be a "fisher of men." Greenhouse knew that this alluded to a story from Matthew where Jesus encountered two fishermen casting nets into the Sea of Galilee and implored them to forsake their catch and instead follow him to become fishers of men. The phrase is loosely taken to mean "followers of the Lord."

In Greenhouse's interpretation it was her sign from God that she was to have a calling in life, a special purpose that God had in mind for her. For more than three decades she did not have a clear sense of what it was to be. Then, at a terrible time in her life, as she struggled with the Army Corps of Engineers, Greenhouse realized her time to become a fisher of men had arrived. This is what she had been waiting for. A demotion in rank and pay was small potatoes compared to what she believed was her task. Even so, a transcendent call from above has not suppressed Greenhouse's sense of humor. "He told me to catch them," she says, "But not to clean them!"

In 2006, Greenhouse's efforts paid off. The army finally moved against Halliburton and cancelled their massive logistics contract with them. That was the end of the no-bid RIO contract with KBR. "The army finally got it," said Greenhouse. And Congress has now made an even bigger move. U.S. Representative Henry Waxman, the California Democrat who has long been investigating the government's use of Halliburton, recently sponsored legislation called the Accountability in Contracting Act. The bill aims to officially limit the length of no-bid contracts and compels justification for issuing such contracts in the first place. It passed in the House of Representatives by a wide margin and the Senate by unanimous consent.

Greenhouse's story shows that a single employee can have a tremendous influence on a gigantic organization. Being a "change agent" may involve pounding on the doors from outside. That's what Peggy Buryj did with the U.S. Army, in her efforts to find out what happened to her son. But change can also come from deep within. When Bunny Greenhouse was hired by the Army Corps of Engineers, she didn't leave behind her ideals. She applied them every day, sitting at her desk. Her dedication has pushed the corps toward being more ethical, more transparent and more accountable.

And the movement has gotten bigger than Bunny Greenhouse. She has become part of a network of government whistle-blowers, supported by watchdog organizations like the National Whistleblower Center. When she is not in her cubicle at the corps, working on programs to save taxpayer money, she travels the country to speak and is finishing a book about her inspirations and experiences called *Portraits of Life: Gains and Pains* that she's been writing over the course of the last few years. Those who support government reform have a saying: "Sunlight is the best medicine." Getting necessary information out into the light of day makes it much, much more difficult for sleaze to thrive.

This accidental social activist made sure someone listened when it looked like the American people were losing out. She has few regrets. She is awed at what she sees as the far greater sacrifices others have made, for example during the struggle for civil rights. People risked everything to make change possible. Some were imprisoned. Others were killed. Her sacrifice isn't the same, she says, but she sees the end goal as very similar. "Why shouldn't 'We the people' be possible?" Greenhouse asks.

PRODUCER'S SNAPSHOT: BUNNY GREENHOUSE

We reached out to Bunnatine Greenhouse in the early days after Hurricane Katrina, when word came that Halliburton had just been awarded another lucrative no-bid contract. This time it wasn't about Iraq, but about New Orleans—half underwater, half ruined. Bunny—you had to call her Bunny—was a natural choice for the interview: born and raised in Louisiana, long experience with the U.S. Army Corps of Engineers (the same folks who build Louisiana's levees), and a key player in an increasingly public dispute over past Halliburton contracts.

The stereotypical Hollywood whistle-blower stays in the shadows and speaks in cryptic sound bites. We quickly discovered that Bunny Greenhouse is no stereotype. She does not speak from the shadows. Eye contact is a big thing with her. And she is anything but cryptic. Names, places, and dollar figures pour forth with a controlled precision that speaks to a no-nonsense professionalism and a clear moral outrage at what she perceives to be a betrayal not only of her own exacting standards, but of the American taxpayer.

She is not a typical whistle-blower. She is both poised and confident, two traits that are rarely found in whistle-blowers, and for good reason. Taking on the system, placing your career in the crosshairs is not something to be done lightly or easily. Those who dare to speak truth to power set themselves on a hard course, where reputation and motivation are often the first victims of the slander and innuendo of faceless bureaucrats and politicians. Those who are not suspended or fired outright are often demoted, as Greenhouse was, to meaningless jobs in out-of-the-way corners of the federal bureaucracy. I've known some who have been issued travel orders on the eve of scheduled testimony, and others who have had their home addresses and phone numbers leaked on the Internet. They can become paranoid and suspicious of any contact, and when they do finally trust someone enough to begin to tell their tale, it often takes weeks of debriefings before they finally share enough information to make sense out of their stories.

Bunny Greenhouse is by far the most self-assured and cogent whistle-blower I have ever come across in three decades of reporting. In her presence you immediately sense the moral compass that animates Bunny and sets her apart from all the others. Most whistle-blowers we cross paths with can stand up to the constant, unrelenting pressure only when focused on tangible goals: monetary reward or a desire for revenge. In Bunny's case, there's something else going on. Bunny believes that good government requires a certain amount of transparency, and that corruption is best deterred by accountability. Her drive seems to flow from an ethical compass that places public trust over personal comfort. It is a seemingly unshakable personal resolve that guides and strengthens her convictions and sustains her in her efforts to shine a bright light into the dark corners of the government.

THE PRODUCER: TY WEST joined the staff of *NOW* as the show's senior producer in 2003, after twenty-two years in long-form production and management at the network news divisions of CBS and NBC. West's awards over the years include several Edward R. Murrow awards for spot news and three national News Emmys for investigative reporting and breaking news coverage.

10

DEMANDING THE FUTURE—NOW

BILL GRAHAM

WHAT HE'S DONE:

Graham saved an Indiana town from economic meltdown by bringing in high-speed Internet.

LOCAL HERO HIGHLIGHT:

As mayor, he refocused his rust-belt town on the future, fighting off corporate efforts to stop him.

S THERE A FUTURE FOR THE SMALL TOWN IN AMERICA? WE'VE ALL BEEN TO once-charming places where the storefronts on Main Street are covered with weathered plywood and the sidewalks and streets are empty of young people. The storyline is familiar. The town's businesses and stores can't compete against more efficient operations in outlying areas and bigger cities. They shut down, and the local economy goes downhill.

It takes a trip out to the American heartland to tell the story of one man who galvanized local business and industry to save, not abandon, an entire community. Our hero here is a mayor named Bill Graham, who spearheaded a high-tech revolution that transformed his town. The odds were against him. And just as he began to succeed, big telecommunications companies decided Graham was a competitor and set out to crush him using their political connections in the state capitol.

Scottsburg, Indiana, Mayor Graham's hometown, is just about as all-American a place as you will hope to find. You can imagine this is what inspired singer-songwriter John Mellencamp, born in a town just twenty miles up the highway, to write his song about Jack and Diane, high school sweethearts "Suckin' on chili dogs outside the Tastee Freeze." Fields of corn and tobacco surround the town. The town square is really a town square, complete with a handsome old brick courthouse in the center, ringed by small businesses, shops and cafes. In summer, local farmers lay out just-picked tomatoes, corn and watermelon for sale on the green outside the courthouse. The old Scott Theatre on the south side, with its classic green-tiled exterior and massive marquee, is now home to the weekly Ross Country Jamboree, a Grand Ole Opry–style music extravaganza.

Today's Scottsburg owes its existence entirely to the railroad. The town is named for Thomas Scott who put the train line from Indianapolis down to Louisville through this area back in the 1870s. The town's depot still stands today, recently renovated as part of Mayor Graham's efforts to rescue the town. Back then, everything in Scottsburg revolved around the train line and that depot: It was a place where the farmers of the area would come and sell their produce to be crated and run up and down the line.

For a long while Scottsburg did a good business as a local marketing hub. Then came the long decline of agriculture through the twentieth century. Other communities moved toward industry. Scottsburg stayed the way it was. It gradually became a bedroom community for more prosperous towns to the north and south. For years, many residents drove down to work in the "powder plant," an ammunition factory located thirty miles to the south, just across the Ohio River from Louisville.

In the late 1970s it appeared that boom times had arrived in Scottsburg. Construction began on a nuclear power plant at Marble Hill, just fifteen miles south of town. Many Scottsburg residents were lured away from their existing jobs by higher wages and shorter commutes. But after consuming $2.9 billion in funding, the project was abandoned due to lack of continued financing, dramatic cost overruns and outcry from environmental groups. Overnight, many residents found themselves without work. Making matters worse, this happened right at a time when the industrial sector was downsizing all across the country. There were fewer and fewer jobs to go around. And the "big box stores," retail giants like Wal-Mart, set up operations out by the interstate and sucked the life out of the mom-and-pop stores downtown.

All of these factors hit the town very hard. Never a rich place, Scottsburg now found itself ranked at the bottom of the state in terms of almost every social index. Unemployment hit more than 20 percent and the town center, which used to thrive with local businesses, was largely boarded up. Bill Graham, on the board of the town bank at the time, remembers people he knew walking through the doors to drop off keys to their properties. The bank hadn't even foreclosed on them. The business owners were just giving up. They knew there was no way they could stay afloat.

Bill Graham counted himself lucky. He had done well enough for himself in business to get by. But he couldn't escape the suffering of his community. He saw it at the bank, and he saw it at the trailer parks that he owned and managed. Many tenants were out of work. Today Graham says that he got all the training he needed for political office in those neighborhoods. "I was already mayor of that community. And you sure got to know what was important to people: roads, sewers, a park for the kids," Graham recalls.

And Graham had a deeply personal reason to find a way forward for Scottsburg. He wanted to create job opportunities for his children, who were studying in college, and for other young people. Graham had grown up in Scottsburg and wanted to spend his life there. As a young man, he wanted a good job—but in Scottsburg, like many small towns, there were no opportunities. So Graham had to move away. That's the way it is in small-town America. It's a Catch 22: You want to pursue all the opportunities the previous generation never had, but this too often has the effect of driving you away from the very community you grew up in. What if you didn't really want to leave? What if home was a special place? Graham had to face the reality that the jobs were elsewhere. He developed a good career as a construction engineer working on the U.S. interstate system in the 1960s. Graham and his wife, also from Scottsburg, lived all across the country, from Ohio to Virginia. They enjoyed their life together but missed home terribly. When the time came to have a family, they decided they would leave their comfortable life behind and find a way to move home. They wanted their children to be raised as they had, embraced in the small-town community they loved.

Graham realized he had to reinvent himself in order to raise a family back in Scottsburg. He became a businessman and entrepreneur. He invested the savings he'd put away while working on the highways and acquired a series of businesses—insurance, real estate and trailer park communities. Graham and his family prospered.

He'd done so well, in fact, that his kids were now off to college. And the cycle was about to repeat itself. His boys were going to be trained up to an extent that it would be impossible for them to return home. This struck

Graham as terribly wrong. He didn't want them to be forced to leave the community as he had. He looked at his town: depressed, the main square in a shambles, people without work. But Graham could see that underneath, Scottsburg still had a special character. It was worth saving—for himself, for his town, but also for the next generation.

In the late 1980s, Bill Graham made a decision to reinvent Scottsburg. He's been working at it ever since. Today Graham says his goal has always been to make sure everyone has an opportunity. And his own life experience has taught him something very crucial: You make sure this opportunity is there for the people at the bottom and, just as important, for those at the top. For a community to thrive, you have to have jobs for unskilled high school graduates, and you have to have jobs for an emerging group of scientists, professionals and engineers. This is the Bill Graham message. It has made the little town of Scottsburg a model for twenty-first-century civic development.

Graham likes to tell the story of how he got into politics. The year was 1988. He got together with other members of the dwindling business community to figure out how they could turn the situation around. None of them had ever been mayor—or were even interested in being mayor. Graham and a few others had served on the city council and the local planning commission. But overall, city politics had been traditionally run by Democrats. The business leaders decided they needed to take charge. And they decided Graham was their man. In many ways it must have seemed an obvious choice: Graham has a commanding presence, standing at almost six feet four inches, and he's gifted with so much energy that his friends call him "hyperactive."

Graham was unsure he wanted to run for political office. But his friends convinced him the situation was desperate, and he set out to campaign. The issue that election was simple: jobs. He came up with a slogan: "For a Better Scottsburg." Graham was elected in 1988 as the first Republican in twelve years and only the second in the town's history. He thought he was going to be a one-term mayor, but five elections later, he still occupies the corner office overlooking the town square and courthouse.

Graham got to work right away. He knew the only way he could turn Scottsburg around was to run it like a business. And something he'd always learned as a businessman was to have a plan for right away and a plan for the future.

Graham, the mayor-businessman, started looking around for opportunities. He wanted to get jobs into the community—not only stopgap jobs for the 20 percent without work, but jobs that could keep the town growing. He knew an economic renaissance was just kicking off in the region based on new investments by major Japanese automobile manufacturers. The largest Toyota plant in the world outside of Japan was being constructed at Georgetown, Kentucky. Graham wanted a piece of that business for Scottsburg. He needed three factors to attract business investments: location, available workforce, infrastructure. Being right off the interstate took care of location. The terrible unemployment numbers guaranteed an available workforce and with some basic training programs set up by Graham, they had workers ready to be hired.

Infrastructure remained the issue. The downtown of Scottsburg had become downright ugly, with 50 percent of the buildings around the square completely vacant. He realized that in order to attract businesses, Scottsburg was going to need some serious sprucing up.

Graham hatched a downtown revitalization scheme. He appealed to the town's tradition of volunteerism and community spirit. Workers and volunteers did a massive cleanup. The town installed a new series of attractive brick sidewalks all around the square. They put in new lampposts and benches. They refurbished the exterior of the landmark courthouse. Later in the scheme, they moved the old depot building, did extensive renovations and made it the new headquarters of the Chamber of Commerce and the Scott County Economic Development Corporation. Owners of downtown buildings were encouraged to invest and try to start up new businesses.

Graham's efforts began to pay off. One of the first new tenants to arrive in the town square was a gourmet restaurant and food store called Jeeves & Company. Jeeves took over three adjacent buildings that had housed a hardware store, a savings and loan and a shoe store. Graham also set up space and services on the outskirts of town for new businesses, financed with state grants and local bond issues.

Mayor Graham finally had a town he could sell. He embarked on a relentless quest to convince investors to set up operations in town. He took a mayor's job that had been a part-time affair and put in sixty to eighty hours a week. He pitched, he wheedled and he showed off the shiny new version of Scottsburg. It wasn't long before he was able to bring people around to the merits of his hometown.

Today the mayor laughs at what he considers his greatest triumph: getting a small Louisville packaging outfit called Derby Industries to expand its operations to Scottsburg. It brought only twenty jobs, but it was the start he'd been looking for. It gave the town momentum. "All of a sudden," says Graham, "We started to reverse the trend."

Derby was the start. The pivotal moment for Scottsburg came next. A Japanese company named Kokoku Steel Cord set up a facility in the new business area Graham had developed. They brought in 300 jobs. For a town of 6,000, that made a huge difference. Better yet, there were jobs at many levels: management, skilled and unskilled. Getting Kokoku hadn't been easy. The company had been looking at sixty-nine possible locations in nine different states before settling on Scottsburg. To get the plant, which made braided steel cord for steel-belted radial tires, the town had to agree to complete the downtown revitalization scheme that had been Graham's first brainchild. The mayor's hard work and businesslike approach to making plans and taking risks had paid off.

Other companies followed. Graham's reinvention of Scottsburg brought in a total of 2,000 new jobs in a ten-year period. Mayor Graham became the town hero. He has only been opposed in three of the subsequent five elections and there have been no serious challengers. At one point the town's unemployment rate went down to 1.2 percent. A town that had been shrinking actually started to grow. People started coming to Scottsburg for jobs. The city has grown 20 percent since 1990. It was astonishing to anyone who had strolled around the derelict town square only ten years earlier.

Then came another round of bad news as the twentieth century came to a close. This time it was offshoring, sending industrial jobs overseas and across the border to Mexico to cheaper labor markets. American jobs were buffeted by free trade agreements and increased automation that required less skill to operate production lines. Suddenly, retaining, not attracting, businesses became the chief goal. Graham says they were lucky to stabilize the economy at around 5 percent unemployment, around the national average. But he realized that they couldn't hold on forever.

That was the occasion for Graham's second revolution. His old model of attracting expansion factories from other places wouldn't work any more. He decided to create what he calls a TIE center—TIE stands for technology, innovation and entrepreneurship. His idea was that Scottsburg would become a place that would create and grow ideas and businesses. He thought the best way to go about this was to link up with the state's formidable universities: Purdue, Notre Dame, University of Indiana, Bloomington and the engineering powerhouse Rose-Hulman. But they stopped him cold with a single question: "How's your telecommunications infrastructure?" To Graham, infrastructure meant roads, water and electricity. As for communications, he knew the phone worked. That was about it.

Graham began learning and began asking questions around town. The results were shocking. Graham realized he was sitting on top of an impending economic disaster. Scottsburg was very much a backwater in one critical area: high-speed Internet access. To the south, Louisville had broadband Internet. To the north, Indianapolis and the surrounding towns had high-speed services. Scottsburg simply fell between the cracks. The phone and cable companies served the area, but none had invested in the infrastructure to offer broadband service. In a town of 6,000, it just didn't make financial sense. Scottsburg was a dead zone for high-speed Internet.

Many of us new digital citizens are very familiar with the frustration of waiting a long time for a web page to load, or just to get online to check your e-mail. Remember the bad old days of dial-up service? Life in the slow lane on the information highway was what Mayor Graham and his fellow citizens were used to. "I remember when going online at 7 P.M. on a weeknight meant it took an hour just to get on and then you'd probably get bounced right off," says Graham. But he just thought that was the way it was.

By 2001, Scottsburg's reliance on slow, dial-up Internet service was becoming more than just an inconvenience. It was a matter of life or death for some local businesses. A company that couldn't send files, images and other data quickly over the Internet was at a severe competitive disadvantage. It was such an impediment that a handful of the businesses Graham had fought so hard to attract were actually being forced to leave the community.

Example number one: Chrysler wanted to update its local car dealership with the same system it had implemented across the country. The company used laptops to connect mechanics to its massive real-time online maintenance database. Lack of broadband meant Chrysler couldn't roll out the system in Scottsburg. The company was threatening to force the local dealership to move to a better-connected location.

Example number two: A company called Total Concepts of Design, a metal parts fabricator, needed to be able to reliably send designs and data to their clients. They came very close to losing a big contract with the Department of Defense when they were unable to get the bid sent over the antiquated system. In a panic, they finally managed to get the application delivered by running over to the town's public library and using their connection. They too made plans to relocate to a more electronically functional place.

Graham realized he needed immediate damage control. "We were in crisis mode," he told *NOW on PBS* in 2005. "We were going to lose companies, going to lose jobs. We just had to do something. How many jobs can a small community lose?" First thing he did was reach out to the major telecom companies that served the area, SBC, Verizon, ATT, Sprint and Insight Cable. Insight Cable had just finished digging up the town to lay a major fiber optic line that brought service to big markets in other parts of the state, but not locally (five such lines ran through Scottsburg, following either the highway or rail line). Graham, the businessman, approached these companies with what he thought were solid proposals. He offered partnerships, subsidies, said he'd apply for local grants, anything to get them to agree to begin to offer high-speed Internet service. He even offered to pay the $250,000 they said would be needed to set up a local "point of presence" (techno-jargon for a high-speed hookup). But no one bit. "Economy of scale" did not permit them to invest in expanded service for the tiny market Scottsburg represented.

Graham was dismayed. The bitter truth was that his businesslike approach to serve his local business community had run aground on a corporate business decision. He was going to have to come up with another kind of solution. In fact, he would wind up creating a government service that would step in to do what business wouldn't touch. Normally this kind of approach would be anathema to the free-market Republican who counts Ronald Reagan as one of his role models. But what other choice did he have?

The City of Scottsburg solicited ideas from the technology sector to come up with plans to wire the town on their own. Six proposals came back, all with wildly differing schemes. "The only thing they had in common was that the required feasibility study was going to cost $50,000 to $60,000 and the overall installation was going to cost 5 to 6 million dollars." It was too much to invest. Graham was convinced there had to be another way, and he was right. The answer was much closer to home than he expected. "I thought we were going to have to go to California," says Graham, enunciating the name of the state as if he were saying Timbuktu, "Turns out we just had to go to Owensboro, Kentucky, two hours away."

What Graham found in Owensboro was a municipal broadband system that used radio signals to send high-speed Internet service around the city. A fiber optic line brought service to Owensburg, and the signal was routed to individual homes and businesses by radio broadcast from a series of towers. Each user had a receiver to take in the signal from the towers. Here was a technology that could solve Scottsburg's problems. And Graham wanted to do something even more cost effective. If users could be reached with this radio wave technology around town, why couldn't the same system be used to connect Scottsburg with the nearest "point of presence," twenty miles north in Seymour, Indiana? Turns out wireless would work just fine, by bouncing the signal from tower to tower to cover the twenty-mile distance. And it could be done for far, far less money than traditional methods, a fraction of what Graham had been quoted in those initial bids. The price was so good, in fact, they could afford to wire the entire county—all for $385,000.

Graham remembers first hearing about this scheme from the fellow who had been working with Owensboro, Mike Cowen. When Cowen told the mayor that he could provide a spectrum analysis to see whether the system could work in Scottsboro for only $1,500, Graham jumped. It was December 23 but that didn't matter to the mayor. He begged Cowen to stay overnight and do the work the next day, Christmas Eve. It was that vital. By mid-January the report was delivered. The plan got a green light immediately, and construction started shortly thereafter. Graham had already promised local businesses he'd solve the broadband deficiency by tax day, April 15, 2003. With Cowen's help, the mayor was able to honor his commitment.

Today, everyone in Scottsburg who wants high-speed Internet can get it from the city. Home use costs thirty dollars a month. Businesses get a 1.2Mbps connection for $200 a month. Similar T1 connections in Louisville run $350 a month, so Scottsburg was able to get businesses online at a bargain. After a three-month test drive, the system was opened up to everyone. The business plan had anticipated 100 initial customers in the first three years. They got 500. In fact, they were having trouble getting towers up fast enough to keep up with demand.

Scottsburg's Internet system is not the conventional open wi-fi service used at hotels and airports. In his research, Graham learned that system security was of paramount concern to business users. Very few were prepared to leave themselves vulnerable to easy electronic infiltration just to get a faster connection. As a result, the city created a state-of-the-art system. Scottsburg rolled out the same technology that the Pentagon began using after September 11. Each connection is provided through a frequency-hopping transmission that is almost impossible to break into from the outside.

With a high-speed system that was secure, affordable and easy to set up, Scottsburg was able to retain all the major employers in town. In addition, the service had been extended into the school system and to other town operations.

It was this unique story of how Mayor Graham was able to bring high-speed Internet to save his community that first brought Scottsburg to the attention to the producers of *NOW on PBS*. The program was examining communities' efforts to offer connectivity to their citizens. Southern Indiana, due to Graham's efforts, had become a national example. Mayor Graham had gained local hero status during his first revolution to reinvent his city. Now, the high-speed Internet venture made him famous internationally. Today it can be tough catching up with Graham, who has become a regular feature at high-tech conferences all across the country. "They've paraded me around like a circus animal," Graham told a local newspaper of his new-found fame. And towns and cities across the country don't wait to get Graham to come to them. The mayor has hosted delegations from near and far. Graham talks about the political and economic vision, and Jim Binkley, the man tasked with management of the broadband system, gives them the high-tech tour. The system has won them over 200 awards, including ones for "most innovative wireless" and "best deployment."

But it turned out not everyone was happy with Mayor Graham's experiment with municipal broadband. In fact, the very same telecommunications companies that had turned down his pleas to wire the city now cried foul. The cable and phone companies reached out to their political allies to strangle Graham's service. A new bill in the Indiana legislature, called House Bill 1148, aimed to put a stop to Scottsburg's Internet system as well as any other plans that towns in the state might be cooking up.

The "telcos" (the word Graham uses to describe them) argued that municipalities had no business muscling into their line of work and that they were ill equipped to be running high-tech ventures. Eventually Graham and others would fail, the telcos argued, and that would result in a disastrous and expensive mess. It was a galling notion to Graham. He had done everything he could to get these same companies to serve Scottsburg. "We were *begging* them to come," he stresses. Mayor Graham traveled to defend his program in hearings at the state capitol. The attacks became personal. Bill Graham, Republican and business leader, was accused of being antibusiness. In fact, one person who came in from Texas to testify on behalf of the telcos accused the Scottsburg broadband experiment of being communistic.

Graham's position in the fight was clear: "Scottsburg didn't wake up one morning and say we want to be in the broadband business. Scottsburg had business and industry that was going to leave our community because what we had was not fast enough." This wasn't about politics—it was about survival. "The last thing I wanted to do was compete with business," Graham says. In fact, he's toying with the idea of selling the broadband system to a private investor, or even getting out of the business entirely to make way for the telcos to take over. But not until he's sure there will be adequate service to satisfy the town's needs, now and in the future. "Change is happening so fast. I never want to be at the mercy of the telcos again for new technology. That scares me," says Graham.

House Bill 1148 failed to pass. So did a second attempt in 2006 to legislate Scottsburg's broadband service out of business. The program still runs today and has grown to serve 2,000 subscribers in nine counties. It has become the linchpin in the long-planned TIE center that Graham will open in late 2008. Graham believes the center, powered by the city's broadband, is the best way to keep up with the moving target that is prosperity and economic success. He is also hoping to create a Professional Teaching Training Center in Scottsburg. Folks came to him with funds for the project, he says, after they'd heard of his successes. Last summer, Scottsburg also held its first robotics camp along with Purdue University. Graham hopes to expand that in coming years and also has plans for classes on entrepreneurship and advanced training for high-tech machinery.

The story of a Republican businessman who became a social activist throws a new light on what activism is all about. A lot of people will tell you that activists are antibusiness. Call it the conspiracy theory of social activism, which goes like this: Activists say they want to help regular people, but their real aim is to attack business and corporations. Capitalism as an economic system is seen as evil, driven by nothing more than greed and self-enrichment. Put on your conspiracy spectacles, and *Your America* starts to look like an anticapitalist tract. A fast food chain refuses to give workers a tiny, almost insignificant, wage increase. An oil company profits by oppressing people a world away.

The antibusiness conspiracy theory fails as soon as you take a close look at the facts. Social activists are trying to lift up the lives of regular people. Business is a natural ally in that struggle. The American economy is driven by consumer spending and consumer decisions, and if working Americans are suffering, the economy suffers too. A healthy economy is essential for good business. A healthy economy is also the path for people to lift up their lives and for government to get the resources for a healthy society.

It comes down to whether business leaders take the long view or the short view. Bill Graham has always taken the long view of the role of business in the development of Scottsburg. He knew that bringing in more business was vital for the town, and he has worked for two decades to make it happen. His goal was more opportunities for everyone—for the workers and for the managers and entrepreneurs.

In contrast, the big telecommunications companies took the short view. Their goal was immediate profit. They didn't see a big enough customer base in Scottsburg, so they refused to provide service. When Graham figured out how to provide broadband Internet on his own, the telcos tried to use their political power to stop him and anyone else who challenged their dominance. Only now, after Graham's system in Scottsburg proved to be a big success, have the telcos begun to offer broadband service there.

Bill Graham and the reinvention of Scottsburg make a strong case that business and social activism work best when they work together. That happens when business leaders and social leaders both take the long view.

And Graham has not lost sight of the personal goals of his revolution. Remember how he wanted to transform the town into a place where his sons could stay and build lives for themselves? Graham was successful. Two of his sons live and work in Scottsburg. Now he gets to watch his grandchildren grow up, get educated and find opportunities right there in his small town. This grand experiment in tiny Scottsburg, which now serves as a model for the entire nation, all comes back to that one very personal concern. "I have two great-grandsons, a three-year-old and a one-year-old," says Graham. "What are they going to face? We have to make sure they can continue to learn."

PRODUCER'S SNAPSHOT: BILL GRAHAM

The moment he picked up the phone, I knew Mayor Bill Graham was different. Maybe it was because he picked up the phone. Most of the time when a journalist like me tries to reach a mayor, there's a thick layer of administration to punch through before you get to the person in the big chair. Not in this case. I dialed the number, it rang and then: "Hello, Bill Graham here."

I'd called Mayor Graham after reading about his unusual decision to construct a high-speed wireless Internet service for his small town of Scottsburg, Indiana. Needless to say, this is considered very un-mayorlike behavior. Local government is supposed to make sure the streets stay safe. Mayors keep the schools running and the taps flowing. But who ever heard of a government-built Internet service?

"We weren't looking to get into the broadband business," Graham told me. But, the mayor says, he had no other choice. Companies were packing up to leave, and jobs were at stake.

When Mayor Graham talks about losing jobs, these aren't numbers on a spreadsheet—they're people Graham knows by name. He runs into them at the grocery store. They've stood before him at city council meetings. When we visited him, it took us ten minutes to sit down for lunch at the local diner because Graham first had to dole out affectionate kisses and hugs to several tables of people. If all politics is local, Bill Graham is probably the greatest politician I've ever known.

In the end, this self-described technological neophyte ("cut-and-paste is a challenge for me") helped build a workable, high-speed Internet service for Scottsburg on budget and in time. The local companies that were considering leaving stuck around. New companies came to town. Far more people signed up for the service than had been initially expected. Graham lists these accomplishments with pride, but it wasn't until he handed me a photo of him and his twelve-year-old grandson, standing with arms round each other, that I really got what this was all about. Graham asked me to imagine his grandson ten years from now, a college graduate, wondering where to make his home. The idea that Scottsburg wouldn't have anything to offer a bright young man in the twenty-first century seemed to haunt Bill Graham. "We educate our young people and we turn them into young Einsteins and they have no place to come back to, and so they have to go to bigger cities to make a living. He won't be able to live here. Now am I going to reap rewards from what's being done? Sure, but nothing like I think they will if we stay ahead of the curve."

THE PRODUCER: WILLIAM BRANGHAM worked as both producer and cinematographer at *NOW* for five seasons. His work at *NOW* was twice nominated for an Emmy Award and received an award from the Columbia Journalism School for excellence in reporting on race in America. Brangham has also produced for Bill Moyers, New York Times Television, National Geographic, Frontline and ABC News.

11

POWER TO THE PEOPLE

JACKIE THRASHER

WHAT SHE'S DONE:
Thrasher is an Arizona schoolteacher who got elected to the state legislature.

LOCAL HERO HIGHLIGHT:
She's part of a new movement to get rid of the torrent of special interest money in politics.

S THERE A WAY TO GET ALL THAT MONEY OUT OF POLITICS? THE RIVER OF CASH from special interest groups causes lots and lots of damage. If you don't have a big pile of money or well-connected friends, don't bother running for office. And all those contributors aren't just writing checks for charity. They want payback—a sympathetic ear, friendly regulations and laws. The financial sleaze factor is one reason why so many people don't even bother going to the polls to vote. The whole thing seems rigged.

Travel to Arizona and you'll find there is a solution. That's where a woman named Jackie Thrasher has taught music and band in elementary school almost her entire adult life. But today, Thrasher is a politician, walking the halls of the state-house in Phoenix, Arizona. She was one of the very first Americans to take advantage of a new political system in America called clean elections. It's designed to allow normal folks to run for political office. And in the few years it has been available, it has started to change the face of politics in Arizona and Maine and other places where it operates. It's why you find somebody like Jackie Thrasher, a career schoolteacher, now serving as a member of the Arizona House of Representatives.

Jackie Thrasher has always been a participant in democracy. With a proud smile she outlines her early political history: "As soon as I could register to vote, I did . . . it was when I was in college. And I voted for Jimmy Carter." Thrasher had always wanted to help out her community. After all, you don't make a twenty-eight-year career as a schoolteacher for the money. Thrasher always had it within her to become a social activist. She just needed a way to get plugged in. The clean elections program was the answer.

"Clean elections" is the name—the branding—for a system of publicly financed elections. Candidates take a vow to use no private donations whatsoever to run their campaigns. They also swear off dipping into their personal assets for financing. In return, they receive enough money from the state to make a credible run for office. Candidates must demonstrate a base level of voter support before they qualify for public money. This is done by collecting signatures and small contributions (currently set at five dollars in Arizona and Maine). For candidates, running with clean elections money is entirely voluntary. Many races feature a mix of candidates running "clean" alongside others using traditional sources of financing. The idea is that candidates with lots of grassroots support should be competitive with traditional candidates that run with business or union support. It is a call to action for all those who wanted to make a difference but never had the means to get into politics.

The system has been put into place for many state positions in Arizona and Maine. Some cities and counties in Oregon, Vermont, New Mexico, North Carolina and New Jersey also use clean elections. The state of Connecticut is rolling out their statewide version for the 2008 election. Clean elections has been around for only four election cycles, primarily for the state Senate and state House of Representatives in Arizona and Maine. Even in these states, clean elections does not apply to federal offices such as the U.S. Senate or U.S. House of Representatives. But candidates for the governor's race in both Arizona and Maine can choose to run clean. In 2002, Janet Napolitano, Democrat of Arizona, became the first governor to use a system of public finance to get elected. She narrowly defeated a better-funded, privately financed opponent.

Consider the elections for the state House of Representatives of Arizona. Winning a seat is a daunting task. The state has one of the smallest legislatures in the country, so the districts are large and each individual race requires winning many votes. A state representative in some districts of Arizona will need ten times the number of votes to get elected compared to a candidate for the New Hampshire state-house in Concord. (The New Hampshire State House of Representatives is the third largest parliamentary body in the English-speaking world. It has 400 seats, trailing only the U.S. House and the British Parliament in total seats.) Given the type of legislature in Arizona, you might expect the House to be filled with well-funded political fat cats, supported by the business community on the right and the unions and lawyer groups on the left. You wouldn't expect to find Jackie Thrasher.

But even with the clean elections system giving her an almost-free campaign, it wasn't going to be easy for Thrasher to win. Her district was a conservative stronghold. It had delivered Republicans, and only Republicans, to the House ever since the district had been created back in the 1960s. Their U.S. congressman, Trent Franks, is considered to be one of the most conservative Republicans in Washington, D.C. Thrasher started running for office in the 2002 state election. It was the second cycle in Arizona where public money was available for campaigns. She lost, coming in third (in Arizona, each district elects two House members) and losing to two Republicans. She ran again in 2004, with the same result. Still, she managed to get more than 20,000 votes, not a bad number. And because the clean elections system makes it easy for candidates with grassroots support to run, she campaigned again for the 2006 election.

Like many people in Phoenix, Jackie Thrasher comes from somewhere else. She was born in Detroit but moved to Arizona with her parents when she was still a young girl. She calls herself "almost native," which actually means something in a state of newcomers. From an early age she showed a strong interest in music. Her parents got her started on flute lessons at age nine. Thrasher played flute and continued to study music all the way through high school and college. She graduated from Arizona State University in 1980 with a degree in instrumental music education.

Right out of college she became a teacher in the Washington school district in northern Phoenix. Twenty-eight years later she still teaches fourth, fifth and sixth graders at the Lookout Mountain School. Her music classroom is a hideaway at the back of the sun-baked campus, stuffed with cellos, a piano and lots of drums. It's clear that the students like her. Her teaching style tilts toward bubbly. During class performances she sits at the front of the class, her youthful face framed by striking red hair. She uses a conductor's wand with enthusiasm, directing the young musicians' sometimes cacophonous renditions.

Thrasher's district, where she has lived for over forty years, is typical of the city's sprawling landscape. It's vast, mostly flat and laid out in a grid pattern. Few buildings have more than one or two stories. Clustered around some of the intersections are strip malls with coffee shops, payday loan offices and tanning salons. There are also some of the features you come to expect in this part of the country: big shopping malls and golf courses. Almost nobody has a grass lawn. Street after street features stone or gravel yards, with saguaro cactus poking up out of the dusty rocks. Folks who live here are mostly white and Hispanic, with about 10 percent split between black, Asian and Native American. The district runs the entire spectrum of wealth, from poverty to a handful of the very wealthy.

Thrasher's career as a teacher led her to become an active member of the community. "As soon as you start working as a teacher, you're involved in the community. So, you have after-school events and community events that you participate in. That just seems a way of life for teachers." Once her daughter was old enough to enter school, Thrasher began to think about the entire education system in a different way. She was now both an employee and, as a parent, a client. The more she learned, the more critical she became. She was shocked to discover that the state was at the absolute bottom of the barrel when it came to funding education. Arizona had dipped to fiftieth place in the nationwide ranking of per-pupil funding in the public schools. "This is wrong," says Thrasher. "We shouldn't be fiftieth in the nation. It used to be we'd say, 'Thank God for Mississippi!' But now we can't even say that."

So Thrasher started to ask questions and follow the money. She wanted to know who was to blame. It wasn't long before she realized that the plight of the Arizona public schools was the responsibility of the state legislature. That's where change was going to have to come from. That's where the schools were being let down. "Kids don't have a voice. They don't have a voice in the legislature. Obviously, these are adults dealing with quite adult, you know, situations, as far as you know, crime in the streets, and protecting our borders and all that stuff. But what about the kids? Who's fighting for the kids?"

Jackie Thrasher was becoming empowered. She was asking questions. Thrasher the music teacher was being transformed into a grassroots activist. She came to believe she was part of the solution. Around her, others were taking up new roles. It was just after the attacks of September 11, 2001, and Americans were reevaluating their participation in the greater community to an extent that they hadn't in nearly a generation. While some, like fellow Phoenix-area resident Pat Tillman, followed the call into military service, Thrasher stuck with a cause of action much closer to home. "It was really the teacher in me, looking at those kids' faces every day that said, 'Nobody's working on behalf of these kids to improve the situation. We don't have what we need here in this building.' And I know there are schools that are not funded equitably. We've got to do better," Thrasher told *NOW on PBS* in a 2006 report.

She started paying a lot more attention to local politics. Arizona's state legislature elections are unusual in that each district elects two representatives to the state-house. She reckoned that increased the odds of her picking up a seat—even though a Democrat had never won in her district. But the elephant in the room was money. Thrasher had helped on campaigns before. She knew that races for the Arizona House of Representatives mostly don't involve big-ticket items such as television and radio ads. But she had also seen that the mailers, flyers and yard signs didn't come cheap. And campaigns required a crazy amount of the candidate's time. She couldn't afford to miss work. She relied on her paycheck just like anyone else. Running for office looked to be out of reach.

Clean elections had already been in place for the election held in 2000, when fourteen state legislators used the program to secure office. But it was still new and hadn't been fully tested for a big statewide race yet. Jackie Thrasher remembered the headlines from 1998 when Arizona voters narrowly approved the system through a ballot initiative. The idea for clean elections hadn't been born in Arizona. Progressive groups such as George Soros's Open Society Institute had poured money into the campaign for clean elections from afar. But Arizona's recent history—the state had gained a notorious reputation for political corruption—provided an extraordinary boost to passing the clean elections initiative.

The list of political misdeeds in Arizona is robust. Some say it goes all the way back to the days of pioneers and cowboys. But the modern-day poster child of corruption was Republican Evan Mecham. A former car salesman, Mecham became governor in the late 1980s. He drew national ire for canceling the Martin Luther King Jr. holiday in Arizona. That action kicked off protests and boycott movements. The NFL, which had been planning to hold the Super Bowl in Phoenix in 1993, moved it to California instead. And that wasn't Mecham's only problem. After only a few months in office, he'd managed to alienate friends and allies in and out of government. Republicans from Barry Goldwater to John McCain pleaded with him to resign. But he refused to go quietly. In fact, Mecham has the rare distinction of having been simultaneously the target of a recall effort, criminal prosecution and official impeachment proceedings. In the end, his downfall was a sizable loan he'd failed to declare during his run for office. It led to his removal and successful impeachment.

With barely a moment to catch its breath after the Mecham saga, the state's political system was splattered with another bucket of sleaze. In 1990, the local county attorney's office in Phoenix got a tip through an undercover gambling operation that members of state government had expressed willingness to accept bribes. They set up an elaborate hidden-camera sting operation, even going so far as to hire an ex-mobster from Las Vegas. The sting became known as Azscam. With cameras rolling, the ex-mobster offered politicians money in exchange for supporting his efforts to legalize gambling in the state.

Several state legislators took the money while hidden cameras recorded the exchange. Some reached right across the mobster's desk to grab the loot. Others sat and counted the booty in full view of the camera. Azcam produced some memorable quotes. State Representative Bobby Raymond, as he took the bribe, said, "I don't give a f—k about issues." And State Senate majority whip Carolyn Walker explained to the mobster, "The least I want to do is die rich."

The story broke in the *Arizona Republic*, but once the videotape of the sting was made available, the sheer arrogance of corruption was there for all to see. Tom Jarriel, an ABC News reporter who covered the story for the program *20/20,* had a classic tagline: "This state's motto is 'God Enriches,' but for some of Arizona's legislators, that wasn't enough."

As the years went by, sleaze erupted again and again in the state's politics. By 1998, Arizonans were jaded, exhausted by the headlines and fed up with dirty politics. That's what brought clean elections activists to the state, with the belief that the idea would be an easy sell in Arizona. It wasn't a perfect fit. Arizona prides itself on being very independent in thinking and is often libertarian in politics. Even if the clean election movement was going to eliminate dirty money, it was still a government program. Opponents seized on the idea that clean elections sent the bill to taxpayers for speech they didn't endorse.

Then the intellectual heirs to native son Barry Goldwater weighed in. The Goldwater Institute became a key opponent to clean elections. It served as the public face of a business-oriented coalition that included the state Chamber of Commerce, the Firefighters Association, and the Arizona Farm Bureau. The folks at the Goldwater Institute built their argument around the U.S. Constitution. The allegation was that clean elections steps on the right to free speech, one of our nation's most cherished values. But wait a minute. Isn't free speech supported, even broadened, by opening elections to people without a lot of money? Not so, says the Goldwater Institute. They point to the 1976 Supreme Court decision in *Buckley* v. *Valeo,* in which the court famously equated political contributions with constitutionally protected free speech. In other words, if a rich man spends a million dollars, that's a form of speech. Ben Barr of the Goldwater Institute told *NOW on PBS:* "We allow everyone in society, rich or poor, to be able to engage in free speech. You know, politics costs money. Speech costs money."

The clean elections people came up with an end run around the free speech argument. Their solution: make clean elections optional. You didn't have to run clean if you didn't want to. If you didn't opt to run clean, you could express all the free speech money could buy. And they also came up with a clever approach to the financial cost of clean elections. They knew voters would never go for clean elections if it required a tax increase. So they designed a funding mechanism around court judgments. If you got a speeding ticket, you'd have to pay an extra 10 percent to the clean elections fund. Plus, they put in voluntary payments: those five-dollar contributions to candidates and an optional check-off on state income taxes.

The referendum vote in 1998 was extremely close. Arizona voters decided to give clean elections a try, approving it by 51 percent to 49 percent. Across the country, Maine had already voted to approve clean elections in 1996. Both states implemented the program at the same time, for the 2000 election cycle.

Jackie Thrasher knew all about the tough debate in Arizona over clean elections. She was proud that her state did something to go beyond its reputation for scandal. But it wasn't until she became inspired to run for state office that she really started to pay attention. She decided to run for state office to do something about education. She started to investigate her options and found that clean elections was exactly what she needed. "Once I learned a little more about it, then I realized that was the only way I was ever going to have the opportunity to do it," recalls Thrasher. "I didn't have a bankroll of money. I didn't even know how I was going to come up with it. But once I decided to do it, I knew about clean elections. I knew there would be a way."

The first thing Thrasher did was sign up for a clean elections boot camp. There are a lot of rules that come along with that free money. Already there have been tough consequences for those who have violated them. A Republican representative named David Burnell Smith won a seat in the Arizona House in 2004. Then it emerged that he had spent $6,000 more than he'd been given by the clean elections fund. That meant that outside money had to have seeped in, the cardinal sin of clean elections. The legislation contained sweeping powers, not only to demand money back but to force violators from office. Burnell Smith fought in the courts but he eventually ran out of appeals. History was made in the process. Burnell Smith is now the only politician in the nation to have been removed from office by anything other than impeachment, criminal prosecution or recall vote.

Thrasher signed up for clean elections and started pounding the pavement. She needed 210 five-dollar contributions to qualify for funding.

Thrasher soon discovered that it wasn't that easy to get hundreds of people to sign a statement of support and pay five bucks. "The first few times poor little Jackie got her feelings hurt when the door got slammed," Thrasher says. "I was like, 'Oh, my God. How could this be?' But, you toughen up after the first two or three. And then, you get over it."

Thrasher was a Democrat running in a conservative district. She was called an "abortionist." She was berated for having "no moral fiber." She'd often get into discussions about what to do about illegal immigration, a topic on many voters' minds in this border state. Sometimes she was confronted with apathy rather than anger: "'I don't do politics,' I heard," recalls Thrasher. But there were rewards, too. "I've had so many people when I knock on their door and say 'Jackie Thrasher, I'm running for the legislature, I'm a teacher and I hope you'll support my campaign,' and they're like 'You're a candidate coming to my house? I never had a candidate knock on my door before!'"

In fact, one of the goals of the clean elections movement is to empower voters as well as candidates. In gathering signatures, candidates talk face-to-face with hundreds of voters. The voters get a better sense of who is running and how they'll handle the issues. And they realize their vote matters. It's politics at the grassroots level. That's what drew Janet Napolitano to the system. She has won the Arizona gubernatorial race twice, each time running an effective, "clean" campaign. She couldn't realistically go door-to-door to get five dollars each from the 4,200 contributors she needed. So Napolitano set up community house parties across the state. She phoned in during the house parties and talked to the groups by speaker-phone. It was a perfect way for her to connect with prospective voters, living room by living room, patio by patio, all around the state. "These are what politics in a way, I think, started out as. You invited your neighbors over, your colleagues from work, the other parents at your child's school," Napolitano told *NOW on PBS* in the middle of the 2006 campaign.

At the house parties, neighbors and friends got together to socialize, talk politics and contribute their fives. It worked for Jackie Thrasher too—a resident of her district held a house party to raise support for the Democratic ticket. Thrasher picked up about twenty contributions from people she hadn't seen before.

Voter by voter, Thrasher got her 210 contributions. By August of 2006, she was officially certified as a clean elections candidate for that November's election. She got a lump sum check for $11,945. But the system is set up to escalate a candidate's funding depending on who is in the race. If a "clean" candidate faces a contested primary, there's a larger check. And there's another check for the general election. There's even a mechanism that boosts support if the opponent, using traditional financing, is spending lots of money. The "clean" candidate can apply for matching funds, up to a maximum amount, to stay competitive. Jackie Thrasher did not have an opponent in the primary, but in the general election she faced the well-funded Speaker of the House, who financed his campaign the old-fashioned way. This meant that Thrasher eventually got the maximum, a total of $68,304, to campaign.

The national discontent with Republicans in 2006 delivered a perfect storm to Arizona District 10. The eternally Republican district was unhappy with Iraq and unhappy with the party's domestic policies. The clean elections system allowed a Democrat to stage a well-funded campaign. And a determined woman, driven to bring change to the community, had the resolve to get the word out and never stop trying. Thrasher was elected to the Arizona House of Representatives on November 7, 2006, by a margin of 231 votes. Only a last-minute rally by the state GOP to save the seat of the Speaker of the House prevented Thrasher from coming in first in the two-seat district. In the end both the speaker and Thrasher got elected and the district's other Republican, a popular two-term incumbent, was knocked out.

That same election saw Napolitano win reelection as governor, again running "clean." So does the clean elections system favor Democrats? After all, the movement was launched by progressive groups who wanted to increase the participation of more diverse and more liberal candidates. But a close look at the way that clean elections has played out in Arizona shows that politics is full of unexpected results.

It turns out that the extreme right wing in Arizona was just waiting for a chance to express itself. The state's Republican establishment had largely shut them out. That was due to a moderating effect on the political process exerted by business interests, most often represented by local chambers of commerce and other civic organizations. Pro-business candidates were favored in the primary, and extreme elements were weeded out. Local Republican Party branches supported this arrangement: They wanted candidates moderate enough to win in a general election. Clean elections cut the legs out from under these traditional gatekeepers. Suddenly, in Arizona, hardliners who had been muzzled by consensus could collect 210 contributions and get public funding to mount a bid for office. And it turned out that once they were allowed to run, some of the right-wingers had the votes to win.

That's what happened in 2004. There was a bloodbath in the Republican primary. New right-wing candidates running "clean" wiped out moderate incumbents. Several went on to win seats in the Arizona House. And suddenly the face of government changed. Some of the newly elected had a single driving interest, such as opposition to abortion. And none of them saw any need for getting along with others on the state-house floor. A place that for generations had functioned on a respect-each-other's-differences mentality became poisoned and polarized. In fact, clean elections has made it more difficult to govern in Arizona, say insiders. There's more infighting, more squabbling over legislation. But to a certain extent, this is true democracy at its most raw. And it isn't always pretty. For years, the Republican establishment ran things. Now there are new players on both the left and the right.

Still, Thrasher sees the overall effect of the system as enhancing the debate and allowing more open participation. She believes it's helped the Democrats. "It has put candidates out there where you may not have seen Democrats run in a typically Republican district. You are seeing more of that now, where you have Democrats in almost every race." In 2006, 76 percent of Democrats used public financing for state-house races, as opposed to only 47 percent of Republicans. And the election did bring a reshuffling. At least two of the right-wing hardliners who had won in 2004 are no longer in office.

Remember Bobby Raymond, caught on camera as he took a bribe, saying, "I don't give a f—k about issues"? There are far fewer legislators in the Arizona House these days who ignore the issues and just follow their party leader's instructions on how to vote. Legislators across the political spectrum are grappling with the urgent problems facing the state. Sixteen freshmen representatives entered the state-house along with Jackie Thrasher in 2007. She says they have brought a breath of fresh air and have made a name for themselves by voting their consciences, no matter what party they belong to. They have big disagreements about what the problems are and how to solve them, but they do want to make the state a better place. Clean elections—at least in Arizona—has transformed the political landscape.

Politics over the last decade in Arizona provides a fascinating window into scaling up community activism. The clean elections movement benefited from the public disgust at fraud and corruption. Arizona, like many other western states, makes it relatively easy to put an initiative on the ballot, and that was another plus. Imagine a different scenario in which incumbents in the state legislature have the power to approve or kill clean elections. Why would they ever say "yes" when their campaigns are fueled by truckloads of special interest contributions?

The famously liberal state of Massachusetts became a test case to see how receptive a sitting legislature would be to the introduction of clean elections. Voters there approved a clean elections system in a 1998 referendum. You'd think the Massachusetts state legislature, dominated by Democrats, would be happy to endorse clean elections. What happened? Elected officials in Boston didn't like what they saw and refused to fund the program. Critics charged that the Beacon Hill establishment didn't want to face the competition that they feared publicly financed elections would bring. The people had voted the system into place, but with no money to run it, it simply died.

Indeed, efforts to expand clean elections across the country have been hit or miss. Maine's system was also enacted by popular referendum back in 1996 and has thrived. Connecticut, which rolls out clean elections in 2008, took a different path. That state's system was created not by referendum, but as a law crafted by a Democratic legislature and signed by a Republican governor. A legacy of recent scandals played a big part in the success in Connecticut. But the movement suffered a huge defeat in California in 2006, when a clean elections system was on the ballot as Proposition 89. Millions of dollars on both sides poured into the battle. Three-quarters of California voters said "no."

In Arizona, the opponents of clean elections haven't gone away. They've vowed to keep fighting until they've succeeded in killing public financing for elections. In 2004, probusiness groups put a half million dollars into an effort to overturn clean elections. They pushed to get a proposition on the ballot called the "No Taxpayer Money for Politicians Act." Feelings ran strong on both sides of the debate. In July 2004, the opponents suffered a setback when a state legislative council took issue with the exact wording of the initiative and, fearing it might confuse voters, sent it to the courts. In the end, the proposition was not on the ballot. The Arizona Supreme Court threw it out, ruling that the proposition violated the "single-subject" rule for initiatives.

The clean elections folks in Arizona knew they needed to grow the movement to keep it alive. They worked to get support from lots and lots of stakeholders. All those door-to-door visits by candidates were a big plus for voters. And there was early success in getting candidates to adopt public financing. In the 2006 elections, the governor and over half the candidates for the state House of Representatives ran clean. That's a big marker for long-term success. It's also gratifying that Arizona's clean elections system has brought many new people into politics. Jackie Thrasher and others who have won running clean are regular folks who are fighting to improve their communities, their state and their nation.

How has Jackie Thrasher done in her new career as a state legislator? She says it's a merry-go-round that won't stop. "Sometimes it was thrilling and other times I thought I was going to be sick!" she told supporters and friends in an e-mail. She says she loves the job, and actually likes being a legislator. She has a Blackberry now. She's figured out how to work effectively on the floor. She's gotten to know the lobbyists that hover around the state-house. They are still a force to be reckoned with, even though clean elections clipped their wings. Thrasher got extra attention as a freshman legislator because of her upset win and how close she had come to unseating the speaker. From day one she was an instant celebrity. She puts it differently—"I'm a zoo attraction!"

What has surprised her is how much the phone in her office rings. "I didn't realize how many people would call for help," says Thrasher. These aren't fellow politicians asking her to support a bill or lobbyists with a cause to pitch. The callers are real folks with real problems. They ask her help on everything from dog bites to collecting overdue child support. Thrasher says it has been very rewarding to help out, or at least point them in the right direction.

For a while, Thrasher trimmed her teaching schedule at Lookout Mountain to one day a week. When the legislature was in session, that one day of teaching was crucial, no matter how tired she was. She says it was her reality check, getting her back to the real world and real world issues. She has now resumed a full schedule both in class and in government. Too bad, she says with a laugh, that she can't enforce discipline on the floor of the state-house the way she does in the classroom.

Thrasher is empowered and making a difference. In early 2007 she cosponsored a bill called the Teen Driver Safety Act, which requires young drivers to get more practice behind the wheel before being granted full driving privileges. She also has had success with increased childcare subsidies for low-income workers and higher pay for teachers. Getting more money and resources for education remains her number one priority. Her plan is to work with other legislators and build a coalition that will invest in the young people of Arizona.

She also found herself in the middle of a tough political battle on a hot-button issue. A conservative Republican sponsored a bill to stop teachers in public schools from expressing anything that smacked of political opinion. Thrasher saw this is as a dangerous muzzling of speech and a

severe impediment on the ability to teach without fear. As a teacher herself, she knew the chilling effect it would have in the classroom. She told
a local newspaper that, taken to an extreme, this law might make her second guess teaching Tchaikovsky for fear that a student would accuse her
of endorsing homosexuality. She spoke to the press, wrote an op-ed in a
local paper and let everyone know she would fight the bill. In the end, the
bill never got to the floor—the legislation was hung up in committee and
is considered dead.

The campaign to get reelected in 2008 has already heated up. Arizona
state representatives have two-year terms so there is not much time between
campaigning. Her previous opponents, the Speaker of the House and the
incumbent she knocked out, have filed their campaign papers. It's shaping
up to be another big fight, this time alongside a presidential campaign that
is sure to bring out a lot more voters on both sides. Thrasher and at least
one of her opponents will run clean—so they'll be able to battle over the issues without pleading for funds from special interest groups.

Thrasher has become a vocal advocate for what she believes is the future of our political system. "I think that changing the way democracy
works is a big part of the clean elections debate," she says. "And I think it
comes back to who is it that's running. Who is it that's able to participate?
And if it's only going to be a certain type of person, a certain brand of person, then I think democracy suffers." In her time as a state legislator, she
counts as a major accomplishment something that goes beyond her votes
and the bills she's passed. By merely being there, she points the way forward
for others. "I wanted regular people to see that you *can* do this. That an average woman can do something," says Thrasher.

Thrasher is one of those "real people" who have become energized
about grassroots politics and are changing America. She wants to see clean
elections adopted across the country. "There are people out there that really
do honestly just want to serve. And this will give them a chance. And yes, it
will change the face of politics, not only in Arizona. But I think if we can
get it going nationally on a federal level that would really help. We'd see
some different folks running."

PRODUCER'S SNAPSHOT: JACKIE THRASHER

Honest, real, and down to earth—these may not be the first words that come to mind when describing most politicians, but then again, Jackie Thrasher is not most politicians.

The first time I met Jackie she was walking down a hallway at her school surrounded by a gaggle of nine- and ten-year-olds. She floated along, asking and answering questions, clearly engaged with all the students. Thrasher seemed to have perfected the balance of enthusiasm and discipline that marks good teachers. Important note: This was before our crew arrived. She was not putting on a show for the camera—this was Jackie Thrasher being herself.

As I worked with her, I found that Thrasher is passionate about making change. She wants to transform education and transform democracy. She speaks with genuine urgency about what needs to be done. Other politicians might deliver a bunch of poll-driven sound bites. Not Jackie Thrasher. In fact, Thrasher is not polished. She was nervous about doing an interview for television. As the interview progressed, she opened up. What happens to the children in school, she asked, when Arizona comes in dead last in educational funding? And what happens to voters in Arizona, when the legislature is full of corrupt politicians? As a producer, I'm as hard-boiled as the next guy, but I was touched. This woman was speaking from her heart. She was allowing herself to be vulnerable. Among politicians, it is a note often reached for but rarely hit or held. For Jackie, this was not a performance. She said what she felt, talked about what she thought was broken, and laid out her ideas about how to fix it. And you believed her.

We conducted the interview a few weeks before the general election. To be honest, I didn't think she was going to beat her opponent. She was running against a two-time incumbent with lots of support. She absolutely should be in government, I felt, but how could she get there? When she spoke the truth, it moved me, as it might move lots of people. But it doesn't generally trump the power of established incumbents.

Jackie Thrasher went on to squeak out a victory. After she won, I sent her a congratulatory e-mail. I told her that it didn't seem right to call her a politician when that term has been so cheapened and debased by others. Jackie, I wrote, you are my favorite "elected official." It is so refreshing and even inspiring to know that Jackie Thrasher is working right there in the midst of the professional politicians. Arizona's politics are headed for some big changes.

THE PRODUCER: CHRIS THOMPSON had his first assignment with *NOW* in 2006 as an associate producer on the program's special report about publicly financed elections. Back then he was a freelancer and had worked for many news organizations. Thompson joined the staff of *NOW on PBS* in 2007.

GREENING THE GULF

DIANE WILSON

WHAT SHE'S DONE:
Wilson forced a major corporation to stop
dumping toxic waste into Texas bay waters.

LOCAL HERO HIGHLIGHT:
As captain of a shrimp boat, she saw the
pollution firsthand, and created a guerrilla
campaign to protect her waters and her
livelihood.

D IANE WILSON DIDN'T SET OUT TO BE AN ENVIRONMENTAL ACTIVIST. SHE was captain of a shrimp boat in the gulf waters off the Texas coast. Pollution and toxic discharges outraged her, then empowered her. She found out the hard way that the environment was not on the minds of local officials, or even most of the local population. So she had to become an organizer as well as an activist, step by painful step. And she realized she couldn't succeed with only local support. She had to enlarge her movement, scale it up so that she could count on help from activists as far away as Washington, D.C., and Asia.

The first thing to know about Wilson's activism is that she is the opposite of a technocrat. She puts the "active" in activism. She has gone to jail, and even came close to death on a hunger strike. Wilson says she has taken this approach—what she calls "misbehavin'" and "monkey-wrenchin'"—because of the kind of fight she has faced. She took on a massive, well-connected and well-funded corporation: the plastics manufacturer that was discharging harmful chemicals into the waters where Wilson lived and worked. It would be remarkable for a senator or a U.S. representative to try to pull this off. But when she started the fight, Wilson had never even met a member of Congress. She was a shrimp fisherwoman with no more than a high school education. She had only the power that she herself could summon.

Diane Wilson credits her boldness to her early years growing up in a family that was immersed in the Pentecostal church. She describes it as "hard-core Pentecostalism," with snake handling, prophesying and speaking in tongues. She says her upbringing gave her an inner power that has enabled her to move beyond conventional concerns like "what will others think?"

That's not to say that Diane's church approves of her activism. The church has a strict set of rules for living and any departure from the rules is forbidden. Wilson says that when she began her first campaign, her mother told her that she'd joined a path that was leading her "straight to hell." That was a big change from her childhood years where she carefully followed church teachings. Wilson says, she was "peculiarly quiet" as a young girl: She wouldn't speak to anyone and even used to hide from people. She took intensive speech therapy classes that helped her eliminate a stutter. She found solace in reading, even though reading anything but the Bible was considered by her church an act of idleness and therefore a sin.

Wilson was born and raised, and still lives, in Seadrift, Texas. Located on the Gulf Coast about two-thirds of the way from Galveston to Corpus Christi, Seadrift bills itself as "the only city on San Antonio Bay." To call Seadrift a city is a stretch. There is no grocery store in town. No hospital, no mall, no multiplex cinema. No public library. Cell phone service seems to depend on which way the wind is blowing. The local government calls Seadrift the "last of the lost frontier towns." Wilson has watched her town shrink. There are a handful of cafes, general stores and three bars (what would a fishing town be without bars?). There used to be a bunch of seafood shacks; now only one is left, the Chunky Monkey. A few years before Wilson was ready for the ninth grade, the high school closed. She rode a bus eighteen miles north to Port Lavaca every day to study.

The town's population of about 1,500 is mostly white. There are still some descendents of the German settlers who established Seadrift as a city in 1911. But recent times have seen the port town grow more diverse. There's a remarkable sign in the window of the town's general store giving details about fishing boat safety inspections by the U.S. Coast Guard. The placard is written in a combination of three languages you only find on the Gulf Coast of America: English, Spanish and Vietnamese.

The different groups haven't always gotten along. On the night of August 3, 1979, long-brewing tensions between white and Vietnamese fishermen boiled over. Two Vietnamese men shot a local white crabber. The incident led to riots and reprisals against the Vietnamese community, including the burning of fishing boats and the firebombing of a residence. Seadrift had become ground zero for the resentment felt all across gulf coast fishing communities from Pensacola, Florida to Corpus Christi, Texas. Local fishermen felt that Vietnamese immigrants, refugees who fled Asia after the collapse of South Vietnam, had taken away their livelihoods. A 1985 Hollywood film called *Alamo Bay* starring Ed Harris memorialized the events of that August night. Today most Seadrift residents have moved on. The town's ethnic groups have figured out a way to live peacefully together.

Vietnamese, Hispanic or white, the character of Seadrift is firmly entrenched in fishing. The town's main roads all head right down to the port. Some twenty shrimp boats creak and bob at the docks, adorned with names like *Janet Lee* and *Mary Sue II*. The *Leila C* has a "For Sale" sign taped to the side of the pilot's cabin. Some vessels look like they haven't seen open water for months or years. There's a pontoon party boat in sad shape, with the words "Back Bay Tours" optimistically printed on the side. The center of action is clearly the Harbor Inn, a small seafood café located right across from the docks where locals congregate to chat over fried shrimp and oysters and lots of iced tea.

Diane Wilson's activism has made her a celebrity in Seadrift. Everyone knows her red pickup truck, whether it's parked in front of the tiny post office or down at the Harbor Inn. And everyone knows what she's accomplished. One afternoon she'd just left the Harbor Inn, when a man she'd been talking to turned to the waitress and said, "You know, she's always been nice." The waitress replied, "Yep, and she's saving our waters."

The waters have been central to Wilson's life and to generations of her family. Her grandfather, a Cherokee Indian, moved to the area from Arkansas and began to fish. He went for redfish, the area's prize catch until it was overfished and banned for commercial fishing in the mid-1980s. Her dad was the first to get into shrimping. Diane started going out on the water with him when she was eight. It was a bit unusual then, as now, to find a female out working the bay. Wilson says her ability to quickly repair a net won her a place at her father's side. She got her first boat, for crabbing, when she was twenty-four. She upgraded to shrimp with her second boat when she was twenty-seven. Even in her subsequent life as a civic activist, Wilson never abandoned her seagoing sensibilities. It went along with the independent spirit and boldness that she would later make her trademark. Her appearance is just as bold: a wild tangle of hair, rough-and-ready work clothes, and an intensity of gaze that is part Pentecostal, part sheer determination.

Back on shore, Wilson married and began to raise a family of five children. She was happy to have a family, but her real love remained the sea. "I love the silence," says Wilson. "I love the quietness of it." She worked alone on her boat, often the first to leave every morning and the last to return to port with her catch. Then the fishing and the shrimping got bad. Pollution, as Wilson was later to learn, played a part in the deteriorating stock of shrimp. At one time there were a hundred boats working out of Seadrift harbor. At peak times in the season, the boats even had to line up out in the water and wait their turn to dock to unload their catch. Back then Seadrift's entire harbor front was lined with brightly colored shacks selling fresh seafood that was loaded directly off the boats behind them and thrown onto beds of fresh ice. Now, very few boats were going out at all.

The decline had been gradual but noticeable. It started with fishermen dropping their standards. Wilson remembers her father's reaction: "Dad never cursed but when he saw those boats going for smaller shrimp, he yelled 'son of a bitch.'" Lower standards cascaded into a struggle to keep up. The community had long honored certain traditions. There were unspoken rules. Now, fishermen were going out at odd hours or out of season, trying to beat each other to the remaining stocks. And there was pressure to go for ever-smaller shrimp. Some even resorted to selling their prized shrimp licenses, which can fetch up to $8,000 from eager sports fisherman looking to get into the game.

As the shrimp stocks kept shrinking and the price of gas kept going up, Wilson realized she couldn't keep going. After a particularly bad algae bloom in the late 1980s, Wilson tied up her forty-two-foot shrimper, the *SeaBee,* and took a job working in her brother's fish house. Wilson was able to pay her bills and stay in touch with what remained of the shrimping community.

It was a chat with a shrimper named Bill Bailey that forever changed Diane Wilson's life. The year was 1989. Bailey was sick and hadn't been out on the bay that day. He stopped by the fish house to chew the fat and commiserate about the shrimp catch. But he had something with him: a folded-up newspaper clipping that he was eager to share. It was an article from the local paper about a new report by the Environmental Protection Agency (EPA) on the release of chemicals by U.S. companies nationwide. The article stated that Calhoun County, which includes Seadrift, had one of the worst rates of release of toxic emissions in the country.

It's a surprising fact that until the late 1980s, the U.S. government did not require industry to disclose the amount of toxic chemicals being released into the nation's water, air and land. In 1986 that all changed. The Emergency Planning and Community Right to Know Act mandated compulsory annual reporting to the federal government. The law came about because of the tragic release of toxins from a Union Carbide facility in Bhopal, India, in 1984 that killed over 3,000 people and injured many more (the complete death toll from related illnesses may be as high as 15,000). Not long afterward, there was an incident in West Virginia with similar circumstances although no loss of life. Congress rushed to legislate a program of monitoring companies using toxic chemicals, and laying out contingency plans for emergencies.

That inaugural report, called the Toxic Release Inventory, showed tiny Calhoun County, with a population of only 19,000, as the most polluted place in the entire nation. It was number one in the nation for release of toxins on land, Wilson says, number three for exporting toxins, number six for polluting groundwater and number twenty-one for airborne releases. Texas led the nation in releases, followed closely by Louisiana. Between the two of them, the gulf coast neighbors represented a quarter of all toxic releases in the United States.

No one in Seadrift could claim that they'd never had suspicions. Highway 185, which runs down to the San Antonio Bay from the nearest sizable city, Victoria, features massive chemical plants lining both sides of its two lanes, the twisted steel pipes of their towers rising out of the alfalfa fields. All the big names are present and accounted for: DuPont, Union Carbide, BP/Amoco. Alcoa is nearby. Some plants are so large that they have their own set of railroad tracks inside their perimeter fences.

Folks in Seadrift all knew someone who worked in one of the plants. Apart from fishing, the chemical plants were the only show in town. Diane Wilson herself had once worked at the Union Carbide plant. She had driven a cousin there to look for work and recruiters convinced both of them to sign on. She remembers the water in the bathtub turning yellow when she washed her hair after a shift. Wilson left after a few weeks. Now, years later, she realized that the yellow coloring that streamed from her hair had been a clue about the massive pollution all around her.

The Toxic Release Inventory contained shocking information for Seadrift and many other communities. But there was a big problem. The community reporting law had no mechanism for enforcement, or even guidelines aimed at reducing discharges. The only requirement was to report the toxic release. The EPA administrator, William Reilly, issued a press release along with that first report saying:

> We are in an era of citizen involvement in environmental decision making. As information about toxic chemical emissions is made available to all interested citizens, they will be able to examine the extent of the problem in their own communities. They will be armed with information they can use to ask the right questions and demand appropriate action from government and industry to control toxic chemical releases that present a risk to their health or environment.

Two people, two different paths. William Reilly, after leaving the EPA, became a director at DuPont. Diane Wilson, standing beside a pile of ice in that fish house in Seadrift, Texas, read the news about pollution in Calhoun County and began her path to activism.

Wilson had no illusions of grandeur. She only knew that something had to be done. It all started coming together in her mind: the toxic releases, the decline of the shrimp stocks. She realized that she and her community needed more information. They needed to get together and find out what they could do. As Wilson explained in an interview with *NOW on PBS* in 2005, she started small. "I did something I never did in my life," recalled Wilson. "I called a meeting. The backlash from just calling that meeting was so tremendous. It totally bewildered me."

Just a couple of days after she'd gone down to city hall to register her meeting and schedule a time, the president of the local bank showed up in the fish house where Wilson was shoveling ice. He started asking questions. He was looking for assurances that she wasn't going to attack industry. Wilson began calling local politicians to see if they would send representatives. Some agreed but later canceled. Next she rang up the county's emergency coordinator. She got an earful about falling for the lies contained in the Toxic Release Inventory report and was told that the numbers were made up to justify the environmentalists' paychecks. And then city hall got involved. She received a visit from the town's secretary, a friend, who begged her to either move the meeting out of town or postpone it indefinitely. She was told the county was up for an economic development grant and that the planned meeting had set off alarm bells in Washington, D.C. Wilson was bewildered at the level of resistance she was suddenly facing from calling a simple meeting. "None of it made any sense," she says. "I was walking into a huge mess and I knew nothing about it."

Wilson would soon learn that at that very moment one of the biggest manufacturers of plastic resin in the world, the Formosa Plastics Corporation, was negotiating a billion-dollar investment in a new factory facility in nearby Point Comfort. The plant would sit on the next bay over, twenty-five miles east of Seadrift. Formosa, which as its name suggests is a Taiwanese company, is a leading manufacturer of polyvinyl chloride, the main component in the white plastic piping widely used in home construction. The company had been formed in the 1950s with a loan from a United States economic aid program. The company's founder, Wang Yung-Ching, built a

very successful company and turned the Formosa brand into a massive con-
glomerate dealing in everything from cars to circuitry. He is ranked as one
of the world's richest men.

Formosa already had a small plant in Point Comfort. What was now
being discussed was a major investment, touted as the biggest in the history
of Texas. The factory alone would cost $1.5 billion to build. Construction
would bring 4,000 jobs to the area for years and 1,200 permanent jobs once
operational. Development was already well underway and county officials
had gone all the way to Taiwan for talks. Now, out of the blue, there was a
lady in Seadrift who looked to be kicking up a fuss. The concern was obvious. Everyone's greatest fear was that Wilson would generate negative publicity and scare off Formosa. Local officials were sure that Louisiana had
put in a rival bid for the Formosa plant. The two states compete for the
chemical industry. During the long struggle that followed, Wilson would
often be accused of being a "Louisiana spy."

Wilson learned about the proposed Formosa expansion from an anonymous letter containing an article about the deal. She wasn't against the
plant. She just wanted to stop pollution. The news sent her on a fact-finding mission. She learned that the environmental history of Formosa was not
pretty. She was told that Formosa had been caught releasing vinyl chloride,
a substance that has been linked to cancers, birth defects and spontaneous
abortions. One report in a Dallas newspaper alleged Formosa was a persist-
ent violator of the Clean Water Act. And all that pollution just came out of
their small existing plant. Wilson wanted more information for her community. Instead of canceling the meeting, she made Formosa and its plans
for expansion the main subject.

That got the attention of members of the local business community and
county officials. They attacked her and then begged her to stop. They even
offered to set up meetings with experts they would bring in. The local
banker who had come to the fish house that first day even suggested that if
she changed her tactics and embraced the needs of industry, they'd be able
to set her up with a well-funded environmental group and give her a comfortable existence.

Opposition to Wilson's initiative went beyond the town's business leaders. Many local residents worked in one of the chemical plants or had friends or family members with jobs there. They saw in Formosa's proposed expansion a boost to the entire local economy, with more jobs and more income for all.

Diane Wilson had counted on the fishing community to be one hundred percent behind her. The whole idea was to get cleaner water and a bigger catch. But hard times had turned the fishermen into a demoralized bunch that didn't have the will to fight city hall. She discovered that fishermen were more comfortable heading out to sea than sitting in committee meetings. Given their dislike of communal decision-making and action, her efforts to organize them into a protest movement were doomed.

Wilson found that even her family was against her. Her mother disapproved of her activism. Her husband was angry that she was spending so much time away from him and the kids and spending what little money they had.

But Diane Wilson could count on one enormous asset: herself. She had become empowered. She had come to believe that she could make a difference in her community. She knew the next step for a civic activist was to grow a base of supporters and allies. So she looked beyond Seadrift for support, and discovered some powerful resources. One was Jim Blackburn, a Houston environmental lawyer. From the very start, Blackburn lent his expertise to Wilson, all pro bono. Another was Rick Abraham, an environmental activist. There was also Donna Sue, Wilson's co-worker at the fish house. Donna Sue acted as a sounding board as Wilson searched for a way forward. She also egged Wilson on when her determination flagged.

Wilson's efforts got her a meeting with Formosa's plant manager. "The first time I even talked to them, I said 'Do y'all have any environmental problems? Do you, like, have any releases?' And I still remember what the plant manager said. He said, 'Oh, we had this little pop valve release.' And he said, 'It's kinda like a garden hose springing a leak.'" Wilson was skeptical but did manage to get Formosa to agree to conduct a community-wide liver screening. In exchange, she agreed to drop a request she'd filed to hold a public hearing on the project's permits.

The trouble was now that she'd started looking into Formosa, more and more information kept coming in. A reporter from Houston who had been investigating Formosa drove out to Seadrift to ask Wilson questions. He ended up teaching her a lot she didn't know about the company. She went to the Texas Water Development Board in Corpus Christi to look at some records and a clerk leaked evidence to her of more Formosa releases that hadn't been reported. A steady stream of Formosa whistle-blowers got in touch with her, people who worked in construction, security, management. Some had been made sick by working at Formosa's existing plant, others decried unsafe work practices there. It wasn't all done over coffee at the Harbor Inn. One man refused to give his name and insisted they meet in a Wal-Mart parking lot miles away. As she began to collect evidence, her emerging focus was to find a way to compel Formosa to conduct a comprehensive environmental impact study before they got their expansion facility running.

At the same time, Formosa moved into high gear. The company threatened to sue Wilson and anyone who supported her. They sent stenographers and video crews to her meetings and protests, telling her they were on the lookout for lies. They organized a citizens' letter-writing campaign to tell local officials that they supported the investment. Formosa reneged on the liver screening they'd promised her. Even a two-hour meeting with Formosa's chairman got only the offer of a junket to the company's plants in Delaware and Taiwan. Wilson refused.

Diane Wilson was gathering important information, but she was still having trouble expanding her base of support. In fact, the more she tried to find new ways to thwart Formosa, the more she added to the ranks of her opponents. At a protest outside a local chamber of commerce banquet for Formosa's visiting chairman, Wilson, Donna Sue and the ten other people they'd managed to bring out were outnumbered and outshouted by a rally of 300 Formosa workers. Regular folks in the community opposed Wilson because they wanted all those jobs. One of Wilson's brothers started working for the company and stopped talking to her. Her other brother, Froggie, who was also her boss, fired her from the fish house because he was afraid retribution would be carried out against his business.

In the course of her fight to stop Formosa and compel them to do the environmental impact study, Wilson went through every agency she could find: the EPA, the Texas Parks and Wildlife Department, the Bureau of Land Management, the Texas Air Control Board, the Texas Water Commission. She contacted the offices of every representative and senator for the area. She sued Formosa and the EPA in court. She went to the state attorney general. She met with the governor's staff. All to no avail. Some weren't interested. Some said they had no power to do anything. And many actually supported Formosa. One congressman told her that taking up her cause would be political suicide. It was a tough time for Wilson. Everyone seemed to be in Formosa's pocket. "I find out real quick that the regulatory process does not work when your politicians are just like that with the corporations," recalled Wilson in her *NOW* interview. "We had a mayor who had a contract with them, the senator had a contract with them. These are the people that endorse their permits." Wilson says the experience was so bad, she took her list of contact information for local politicians and "ripped it to shreds." From that point on, Wilson refused to work with political figures.

Wilson was getting desperate. She had six shrimp boxes filled with documents. She had put together compelling evidence of environmental, workplace and contract violations committed by Formosa. She'd assembled a paper trail linking the company to former Senator Phil Gramm. Formosa had made campaign contributions to Gramm while he was senator. Now, according to Wilson, a former Gramm campaign advisor was in charge of the EPA in the district where Formosa wanted to build its new plant. She'd managed to get media coverage but that hadn't changed what was happening in front of her eyes. Formosa's project was moving forward undaunted. Even a string of mishaps and bad publicity didn't throw it off track. There was a serious leak of hydrochloric acid from Formosa's existing plant, causing the evacuation of the area around the plant. Then Formosa was fined over $8 million for violating the Resource Conservation and Records Act, the second biggest such fine in history. But even these blunders didn't turn the regulators against the massive new project. In fact, Formosa managed to negotiate for the fine to be cut in half.

The biggest push by Wilson and her supporters was to force Formosa to do the environmental impact study. They sued the company. They badgered the EPA to require the study and eventually sued them, too. They pleaded with Formosa to do it voluntarily. Months and months of effort brought only bitter defeat. "EPA May Grant Exemption to Formosa Plastic," read the headline in a Dallas paper. The agency had issued what's known as a FONSI, a "finding of no significant impact" for the Formosa expansion plant. The fight had been lost. And that's when Wilson got unreasonable. As she told *NOW on PBS*, she made up her mind right away: "I said 'they're not getting it.' I love that bay. And I was like, 'nope, they're not getting it.' And so, I did a hunger strike. It came off the top of my head, 'I'm going to do a hunger strike.'" Wilson recalls the look on the face of her ally, Rick Abraham, the environmental activist: "He just laughed. And he said, 'Diane, they don't do hunger strikes in Texas. That's California style, you know? And especially a woman. They're going to laugh you out.' And I kept saying 'Nope, I'm doing it.'"

Wilson had exhausted many of the traditional methods of bringing change to a community. She'd held hearings and protests. She'd gone to her local elected officials for help. Activism of the civil disobedience type came as a last resort. The big corporation she was up against was always going to be able to outspend her, but that didn't mean it was going to be able to outlast her. Diane found that through being unreasonable, and sticking with it, she had a way to leverage the fight. "I'm into boldness," says Wilson. "I found out boldness works." For Wilson, exercising power meant being unreasonable.

Of course, being unreasonable has deep roots in the consciousness of America. Henry David Thoreau tapped into it with his 1849 essay *Civil Disobedience*, a work, Diane Wilson says, that has guided her in her struggles. And it goes back even further: to the Boston Tea Party in 1773 when the Sons of Liberty dumped British tea in Boston Harbor to protest the crown's new tea tax. Those colonial activists had disguised themselves as Native Americans. But Wilson doesn't believe in pretending to be someone she's not. She doesn't make herself out be a high-powered political operator. Instead, she boldly embraces her every-woman background and makes it one of her most powerful tools.

Wilson planned her hunger strike to have maximum visibility. She managed to borrow a shrimp boat that was docked close to Formosa's operations. Right on the boat's deck, in full view of Formosa workers, Wilson sat and fasted. For days, she was ignored. A handful of Formosa workers stopped by to make fun of her. A week into her hunger strike, she started to get noticed. The result: the shrimp boat owner evicted her, concerned for his liability. Wilson moved her protest on land, right at the gates of Formosa. Her brother, who worked at the plant, urged her to quit and told her that Formosa was watching her every move.

Eventually, she decided to take her hunger strike on the road. She traveled around the state, from Houston to Austin to Dallas. She asked for meetings. She told anyone who would listen about the danger presented by the planned Formosa plant. Still, her focus was on getting that environmental impact study. When a meeting with a top EPA official went well, Wilson decided that was enough progress to stop her strike, but when she learned Formosa had not stopped construction on the expansion, she stopped eating again. Then Wilson got a frightening call from home. A helicopter had flown over the house. The family dog had been shot twice and killed. The helicopter returned that night and buzzed the house. The authorities were never able to find out who it was. Wilson was terrified and made plans to return home. Her husband told her it would be safer for the family if she stayed away. She did.

Wilson was by this time long into her hunger strike. She was weak, dizzy and growing delirious. She began having hallucinations. She'd almost run out of hope. Then, completely out of the blue, Formosa's chairman, Mr. Wang, showed up in Wilson's lawyer's office in Houston. He wanted to make a deal to get Wilson to stop.

Wilson and her supporters were offered a raft of concessions, including workers' benefits, environmental audits, waste reductions, citizen's inspections and tougher air emissions standards. Wilson stopped her strike immediately, celebrating with pizza. She was ready to declare victory. But then Formosa backtracked on part of the deal. Wilson was angry and frustrated. After a long hunger strike, she thought she'd gotten a breakthrough, but now the company's promises were unraveling. She couldn't trust Formosa. She decided it was time to pull out of the negotiations with the company. This led to a serious breakdown between Wilson and her lawyer, Jim Blackburn. He'd been at her side since day one. Now he told her he couldn't help her any longer. He began to negotiate with Formosa without Wilson. She'd hit an all-time low. "I reached bottom," says Wilson. "I couldn't do it any more, but I couldn't stop. I didn't know what to do."

Wilson has written an eloquent book about her evolution as an activist, called *An Unreasonable Woman*. The book is full of hope and energy, but it also chronicles Wilson's darkest moment. She cranked up the diesel engine of her shrimp boat and headed out on the bay. She brought along two packages of sleeping pills and a few bottles of strawberry wine.

> I was a woman leaving and on marked time, and whether I had thirty years or thirty days or thirty seconds, the place was going to be the same when I arrived. I moved in the night by instinct, not turning on the depth meter or the running lights or the radio, and the only light was the faint green smear going south with a bit of east in it. Then I had nowhere to go. I had arrived. So I pulled down the throttle and shut off the motor, and while the bay lay still and the lapping water was a cat's mouth on the wooden hull, I stood in the cabin and opened the wine bottle and the package of sleeping pills.*

Wilson began drinking and taking pills. She lay herself down on the stern of the boat, hoping that when she fell asleep and began to die, she would roll off into the bay. That's where she wanted to be. But sleep never came. All through that long night, she lay awake, prone on the exposed deck. For a while it became hard to breathe, but her tough constitution carried her

---

* Diane Wilson, *An Unreasonable Woman: A True Story of Shrimpers, Politicos, Polluters and the Fight for Seadrift, TX* (White River Junction, VT: Chelsea Green, 2005), 327.

through. There is a note of resignation as she describes how she took the boat back to port, went home and got in bed.

The next morning there was news of a historic agreement reached in Austin by Jim Blackburn and Formosa. Very little of what Wilson wanted had been achieved, but to the outside world, the long struggle against Formosa had made a big step forward. Wilson hadn't even been there for it. She was utterly defeated. She had tried everything she could and had only managed to wreck her own life. Even her unreasonableness had failed her.

But then came a call inviting her to the other side of the world. After nearly two years doing battle with Formosa, Diane Wilson had made a name for herself in Taiwan, the plastic company's home base. Her efforts were admired by activists overseas, who had also been in pitched battle with the company. They wanted to fly her over for a series of meetings and talks. So Wilson got her passport and boarded a flight for Taipei, her first time out of the United States. Again, Wilson's life was transformed. Her frustrations at getting results with Formosa had made her into an unreasonable woman. The trip overseas radicalized her. She gained a visceral understanding of what it meant to be an activist in an illiberal society. Until 1987, Taiwan had been under martial law, constantly preparing for war with mainland China. Social protest was outlawed. Here, activism could cost lives. Wilson met Lin Yi-hsiung, a dissident who had been imprisoned for organizing prodemocracy demonstrations. While he was in prison, his twin daughters and mother were murdered. The murders have never been solved. Many suspect it was political retribution for Lin's activism.

Wilson gained new energy from her trip. The determination of the Taiwanese activists was contagious. "My life was corrupted by a radical germ," she writes in her book. When she stepped off the plane back in the United States, she was ready to take up the fight again. The agreement with Formosa reached by Blackburn hadn't really achieved what Wilson felt was needed. There was still no guarantee that the new Formosa plant would reduce toxic emissions enough. And there was good news waiting for her. During the hunger strike tour, she'd met with that EPA official who said the agency would compel Formosa to do the environmental study. Now the

EPA was about to officially announce that they were ready to move forward, not only for the Texas operation, but also for one in Louisiana.

Shortly after returning home, a new concept began to form in Wilson's now radicalized mind. An engineer had called her to suggest that Formosa adopt a "zero-discharge" system, one where waste is recycled and not sent into the bay at all. The engineer sent Wilson literature to convince her that it could be done. If effective, this would solve everyone's problems. So Wilson made "zero discharge" her new mantra. For this campaign, she realized that she was going to need new allies. Her fishing buddies had never helped her. She'd alienated her lawyer, Jim Blackburn. So she did something no one expected. She turned to the Vietnamese community for help.

In the years that followed the violence of the 1970s, the Vietnamese community and the white community had maintained an uneasy peace. They lived side by side but never had much to do with each other. When Wilson approached Vietnamese community leaders with a request to support her push for zero discharge everyone in town was surprised. But it turned out to be the right move. Soon she had hundreds of people coming to her meetings. There were eager volunteers for the protest lines outside Formosa's plant. For the first time, Wilson was able to generate political pressure by growing her movement in numbers. That got results. Empowered, Wilson appealed to an EPA board in Washington and got them to agree to a last-minute hearing on Formosa's wastewater permit.

Then Formosa engaged in a final deception. Wilson learned of it by accident. She called the EPA in Dallas for an update. The lawyer on the phone mistook her for a Formosa staffer. The EPA woman began to discuss Formosa's ongoing and active discharges. Wilson was shocked. There weren't supposed to be any current discharges. Formosa was legally barred from discharging at all until a judge ruled on the permit appeal. What's worse, the EPA knew about it and didn't appear to be planning to do anything. The woman at the agency told Wilson it was up to their discretion to act or not. Wilson was furious. She'd been lied to by Formosa for the last time.

In her interview with *NOW on PBS*, Wilson recalls her anger: "It did not matter that they were violating the law. The EPA knew it. The state

knew it. Formosa was discharging. Me, the little community activist following the letter of the law—I was the only one that didn't know it. I was so
outraged because that says something about the whole government. And I
did the most outrageous thing I could think of. And I knew it had to deal
with me: it had to be my risk, my boat. And so I took the thing I valued
most and took it out there. I'm just going to sink it right on top of that discharge. It was going to be a monument to their crime."

The plan was hair-raising, even deadly. And she had to figure out how
to carry it off. She knew that she would have to first remove the diesel engine of the *SeaBee*. She couldn't very well sink her boat in protest over environmental practices if she was going to foul the waters of her beloved
bay with diesel fuel. From Seadrift, it was more than forty nautical miles
around the headland to the Formosa plant. In the end it was her brother
who came through. He still worked at Formosa but that didn't stop him
from throwing her a line from his own boat and towing her out and
around the headland.

It was going to be the finale of Diane Wilson's long fight. As soon as
they'd made it out into the gulf, a violent storm hit. At times, Wilson could-
n't even see her brother's boat ahead from the waves and the rain. Then
three U.S. Coast Guard vessels appeared. They'd been tipped off about Wilson's plan. The coast guard chased the shrimp boats and shouted through
megaphones for them to give up. The shrimp boats were in no shape to out-
run coast guard cutters, and they were quickly caught and towed to shore.
The *SeaBee* was impounded. Her brother was allowed to leave with his boat.
Wilson was threatened with imprisonment and hefty fines, even accused of
committing "terror on the high seas," but was not actually arrested. That
very day a makeshift armada of about 15 other shrimp boats showed up to
start a blockade of the bay in solidarity. A fleet of Vietnamese shrimp boats
were en route from nearby Palacios. But the fisherman's boats proved no
match for the coast guard and were dispersed in short order.

It was another defeat for Wilson. Then came another shock. Formosa
came around to Wilson's position. Why? The attempted sinking was one unreasonable act too many for the company. Maybe the last-minute show of

support from the ersatz armada showed a degree of community mobilization that scared Formosa. Maybe they were simply afraid of what Wilson would come up with next. "The end result was that Formosa Plastics was sitting there watching the whole thing. And they were like, 'What is it going to take to shut her up?' And I was like, 'Do zero discharge. Recycle your waste stream.' So that's how I got zero discharge from Formosa Plastics."

Wilson had taken on a gigantic multinational company. She faced the hostility of local officials and the indifference of the regulators. She discovered Formosa had been spreading money around as campaign contributions. She struggled to build a base of support. But she prevailed. The years of struggle and hard work had finally paid off.

In fact, Diane Wilson did more than win a major victory over a corporate polluter in her community. She also helped point the environmental movement in a new direction.

Wilson's activism came at a time when a crisis was brewing in the environmental movement. Here's what happened. For decades, environmental groups put lots of energy into studies and less energy into mass organizing. They relied on a 'technocratic' approach. And, for a long time, the data-crunching approach worked. Environmental groups and scientists came up with new information about the hazards of a particular chemical, and then presented that information to Congress and regulatory agencies like the EPA. That led to hearings and impact studies and then new regulation. The result: new, safer limits for everything from lead to asbestos to the gasoline additive MTBE.

At the same time, the big environmental organizations like the Sierra Club became professionalized. There was a big shift from being a network of part-time community activists to having a paid staff, lots of fundraisers and even lobbyists in Washington, D.C. Members were recruited by the millions in order to pay for all this.

The technocratic approach required bipartisan consensus. And, in fact, the 1970s and 1980s had witnessed broad cooperation on the environment between the Republicans and Democrats. After all, Richard Nixon signed into law the Clean Air Act and the Clean Water Act.

All that worked fine until something extraordinary happened. The environment became a partisan battle. Political hacks began rewriting public policy papers that had been drafted by teams of scientists. A wave of appointees in the Department of the Interior and in the EPA came from industry and made it clear that industry was going to be their priority.

The result was that environmental efforts in the United States went backward. Coal-fired electric plants pump out more mercury and greenhouse gases than a decade earlier. An unprecedented number of oil and gas leases have been signed for surveying or extraction on national lands. Coal companies have been given the green light to use a technique called mountaintop removal that has a spectacularly destructive impact on streams and hillsides.

In the face of these reverses, environmental groups have raised a hue and cry. But that has had little impact. And it gets worse. Environmentalists have been unable to persuade the United States to take a leadership position in combating global warming.

Environmental groups stuttered and sputtered. They brought suit in state and federal courts. But things continued to go backward. Here is where the weakness of the technocratic approach became blindingly clear. The environmental groups did not have a mass base that gave them power. Their mailing lists were full of people who donated twenty-five dollars or fifty dollars a year as a charitable deduction. Those millions of people approved of doing something about the environment, but they were not empowered or active themselves. The Sierra Club and the other big groups were unable to wield real political power. They couldn't force a recalcitrant administration to take action on the environment. They had millions and millions of people on their side, but these people were not civic activists. Technocrats, with studies and position papers, got nowhere.

Some environmentalists have taken note of the failures of the last decade and have struck out in an innovative direction. They are working to create a new generation of community activists. They are organizing people around a set of civic rights for all communities: clean air, clean water and food that doesn't poison you. Each and every person on earth has these rights. The air that your child breathes is as important as protecting wilderness areas—maybe (heresy of heresies) more important. Every community has the mission of fighting for their rights in their local area.

And that's exactly the direction of Diane Wilson's activism. She is an authentic representative of her community, fighting for clean water and fish and shrimp that aren't full of toxic pollutants. In fact, Wilson's fight harks back to the beginnings of environmental action in the United States—when local activists fought to clean up their communities.

And Wilson has continued the fight. She really did get radicalized, whether it was inspired by her visit to Taiwan or because she'd finally achieved such an immense victory against Formosa. Today, Wilson has made activism a full-time career. One cause cascades into the next seamlessly. Just as justice is achieved in one instance, another injustice reveals itself and demands her attention. Wilson is a cofounder of an in-your-face outfit called Code Pink, which has seen her take part in demonstrations and actions around the world, targeting the current administration. She has stood outside the president's Crawford, Texas, ranch alongside Cindy Sheehan and protested the war in Iraq. She describes the organization as a "rowdy bunch."

In the end, Wilson proved that her community could indeed have their cake and eat it too. Today the Formosa expansion factory stands in nearby Point Comfort and indeed employs 1,600 workers, even more than first promised. But at the same time, because of her efforts and refusal to quit, Formosa now recycles fully 33 percent of its waste. It's not zero-discharge, but a massive improvement, one that the company even crows about on its website: "Over 25 percent of [the expansion] investment was spent on environmental protection features, including a state-of-the-art wastewater treatment facility." And it turns out Wilson's idea was catchy. Now Alcoa uses the same wastewater system that Formosa agreed to put in at their nearby facility. And while the sea has yet to lure Wilson away from the life of an activist, she has the satisfaction of knowing the waters are in much better shape now than when she set out on her quest.

PRODUCER'S SNAPSHOT: DIANE WILSON

Diane Wilson was on the run. She told me this over the phone in our first conversation. I've never had an interviewee tell me that they were on the lam, but it was the first of many firsts with Diane.

Diane had been arrested in Texas in August 2002 when she scaled a Dow Chemical plant and unleashed a banner that read "Dow Responsible for Bhopal." She was arrested and charged with criminal trespass, convicted and sentenced to four months. She was ordered to report to prison but at the time she was on a nationwide book tour. The book's title, *An Unreasonable Woman*, seemed to describe everything I needed to know about Diane. Jail would have to wait.

Based on what I'd learned about Diane, I expected a tough fisherwoman with a weathered face and rough demeanor. But her voice over the phone was soft, friendly, almost shy. And in person, Diane is charming, her smile and laugh contagious. There's no pretense about her. Diane immediately makes you feel at ease, as if you've been lifelong friends.

Nevertheless, I knew that Diane had faced death threats, held hunger strikes, fought with family and friends, got fired from her job, all because she couldn't stand by and watch giant corporations do terrible things. I couldn't help but wonder where this woman got her courage, sense of power and her unrelenting will to confront injustice.

Just as she says, she's unreasonable, but it's more than that. I've met hundreds of activists in my years working in television, but I recognized that Diane comes from a different place. She didn't receive a degree in environmental studies or draw a salary from an advocacy group. It's not a career for her. Something really bad was happening right where she lived, and Diane Wilson decided she couldn't turn her head and walk away. Hoping that someone else would come along and fix it wasn't going to fly. Diane often talks about following her instincts and her instincts always tell her to stand strong.

Diane is an extraordinary woman, but she's also ordinary. She's a mother of five and grandmother to ten (although not like any grandmother that I've ever met). This wife, mother and grandmother empowers and in-spires others to realize that truly anyone can take up the struggle and fight.

But I don't know if Diane sees it that way. She would probably say that she's a shrimper first, like her father before her and her grandfather before him. That may be true, but there is no denying the impact that she's had on the environmental and social justice movement. Her brand of activism res-onates with a lot of people who are out there fighting to make a difference.

After our interview, Diane flew back to Texas to protest at a fundraiser held for former congressman Tom DeLay. I called Diane to go over a few things. Her daughter answered the phone and told me that when her mother came back to Texas, the criminal trespass charge caught up with her. She was in prison doing her time for the Dow Chemical protest. Diane Wilson would miss the airing of her interview. How fitting, because in her work she has never sought the limelight.

Later I wasn't surprised to hear that Diane spent her time in prison advo-cating for the rights of the other women imprisoned with her. So for Diane, the fight continues. We can only hope that she remains unreasonable.

When our interview with Diane came to an end, I asked her to auto-graph a copy of her book for me. She wrote "From one unreasonable woman to another." I can only hope.

THE PRODUCER: GINA KIM came to *NOW* after six years of producing interviews for television shows, including Phil Donahue on MSNBC. She has also worked for filmmaker Michael Moore and spent several years working on environmental issues for NYPIRG, the public interest lobbying group.

13

A RIVER RUNS THROUGH IT

LYNN AND DEVONNA OWENS

WHAT THEY'VE DONE:

Lynn and Devonna Owens helped save the wide open spaces of Montana's Madison Valley.

LOCAL HERO HIGHLIGHT:

These ranchers teamed up with former enemies—environmentalists—to create a world-class community alliance.

THIS STORY UNFOLDS IN THE EVOCATIVE COUNTRYSIDE OF SOUTHWEST MONtana, where broad, mile-high valleys are framed by the jagged ridges of the Rockies. It's one of the few places left in America where there are still true-life cowboys, moving cattle up to seasonal pastures and protecting herds from predators. They really do saddle up as the last stars fade with the dawn. And deer and antelope really do play.

But how do you keep it that way? That's the big challenge, and that's where plenty of discouraging words are heard. Why? The place is so beautiful that city folk are flooding in, buying up property, laying down roads and making a mess. It makes you wonder—does every inch of America have to be paved over? Will this entire country become one giant suburb? That's what the ranchers of Madison Valley are up against as they fight to preserve the wide-open spaces and a way of life. And they've come up with some pretty startling rodeo tricks to lasso and hog-tie those developers.

Visit the ranch of Devonna and Lynn Owens and you'll get a taste of the changes in Madison Valley. The Owenses have been running cattle on their land for four decades. Drive up the dirt road that leads to their ranch and you are as likely to pass a Hummer with California license plates as a beat up Chevy Silverado. Walk up to the top of "the bench," a plateau that sits above the Owenses' house, and you can see what's changed and what has not. In one direction, a herd of pronghorn antelope grazes. Ennis Lake is visible far beyond, framed by the Madison Range of the Rocky Mountains. But turn in the other direction and you are confronted with a line of fifty homes, all recently built, all set on their own twenty-acre parcels. This is the community named Shining Mountains West. The developer bought the land from a ranch family that wanted to get out of the business. Lynn says it hits him in the gut every time he sees that subdivision. He and his fellow ranchers are fighting to keep developers from doing the same thing to the entire valley.

Lynn and Devonna Owens both come from ranching families, and both grew up in the Madison Valley. Neither planned to stay and ranch. Devonna went to nursing school up in Bozeman and Lynn got an electrical engineering degree. After they married, they moved around a lot. Lynn worked in the power industry, traveling all over the west, from Billings down to Phoenix and even up to Alaska. But in the 1960s they heard the call of the valley. At first Lynn's father refused to consider passing on the family ranch. He reckoned they'd never be able to readjust to a life of ranching cattle. Lynn and Devonna worked on the ranch for a year. They proved their commitment, arranged a loan from the bank and bought the property from Lynn's father. The way Lynn sees it, it's because he and his wife left and came back that they truly appreciate how special life is in the Madison Valley.

The Owenses run a cow-calf-yearling operation. They keep a steady stock of reliable heifers and every June the animals give birth to a batch of calves. Both parent and offspring spend the summer out on the range, roaming, grazing and putting on weight. They keep the calves for another year and sell them as yearlings. Devonna says she has an emotional attachment to each and every cow they have, even if their ultimate fate will be the dinner table. Lynn says he spends more time around cows than people: "As far out as the eye can see, I can tell you which exact cow it is just by the shape and the color and way it moves. But with people, especially if they changed their whiskers, I wouldn't know who they are."

A little over ten years ago, the Owenses realized a transformation had begun. The subdivision nearby became suddenly popular after the mini-series *Return to Lonesome Dove* was filmed there. People snapped up the lots and construction really ramped up. Suddenly there was an endless procession of construction vehicles along the dirt road that passed right outside their ranch house. Cars with out-of-state plates were turning around in their driveway. The dust kicked up on the dirt road coated windowsills, furniture, the floor. Finally, Lynn and Devonna moved the house a quarter of a mile inside the ranch, away from the traffic. Even today, Lynn says, several cement trucks drive up the road each morning.

You really see how far development has taken hold when you drive through the region's main city, Bozeman. It's earned the nickname Boze-Angeles with all the new coffee shops, trendy bars and boutiques. And sprawl: The town's population has grown by more than 20 percent since the year 2000.

Does that mean that tract homes will carpet the valleys of southwest Montana? Real estate developers are licking their chops. These valleys are more than just unspoiled and magnificent (as if that weren't enough). They have location, location, location: not far south is Yellowstone National Park. So, southwest Montana is stacked high with multimillionaires and billionaires. Ted Turner has his 113,000-acre Flying D Ranch nearby. Tom Brokaw, Mel Gibson and Whoopi Goldberg have all owned ranches in the area in recent years. This remote location even features the most expensive home in the world, a 53,000-square-foot, ten-bedroom property going up in an exclusive enclave called the Yellowstone Club. According to *Forbes* magazine it was recently priced at $155 million. By comparison, Donald Trump's place in Palm Beach and Bill Gates' mansion in Medina, Washington, each weigh in at $125 million.

Turns out that those guys aren't the main problem. It's the merely wealthy, who don't have the cash for a truly big spread. They want to snap up their very own twenty-acre patch of heaven. As one local rancher, John Crumley, says, "I didn't realize that everybody else in the United States wanted to be a cowboy." Developers are in the midst of a makeover of Paradise Valley, and nearby Bitterroot Valley. They are still beautiful, but transformed. You are far more likely to see a fancy lodge in the middle of a pasture than a herd of yearling cattle.

For the Owenses and other ranchers, new construction brought a host of new problems. New neighbors meant new pets. Soon dogs were getting after the cattle. They could bloody a calf or chase a cow and cause a broken leg. And the owners of the new houses wanted improved services, including roads better suited for school buses, fire trucks and ambulances. Land values went up, and that inevitably meant property taxes jumped.

Higher taxes were a blow for the Owenses. Ranching has never brought big profits. Over forty years, the price of beef has risen fourfold. Sounds nice, huh? But everything a rancher needs has increased by a factor of ten. Raising cattle out in a place with such a short growing season is even tougher. It's much more about the land than it is about the cows. As rancher John Crumley sums it up: "We make our living converting sunshine into grass which cattle convert into food for humans."

On paper, Lynn and Devonna Owens were now millionaires. In fact, from a purely financial point of view, it was crazy to keep ranching. They could sell the land and cash out. But that would mean changing everything about their lives and pointing the valley even further toward development. They didn't want that. Rather than sit at home and stew, Lynn Owens, his wife and six other ranch families decided to take action. They wanted to have a say in the future of Madison Valley.

The decision to form the Madison Valley Ranchlands Group was monumental. Ranchers are like all those fishermen Diane Wilson had so much trouble bringing together. They are rugged individualists, ornery folks who don't take to meetings and group activities. Except that now they were banding together for action.

The rancher group knew their first task was to rope in more people. They needed allies to grow their movement and their political power. Lane Adamson speaks for the entire Ranchlands Group when he says it turned out to be easier than expected. "We discovered a real earth-shaking truth that we didn't realize. There are other people that love this place as much as we do. And, they're as willing to invest time, energy and resources into addressing those issues. They're great partners."

Their first target: wealthy new residents. The ranchers knew the newcomers had been attracted by the beauty of the valley and its wide-open spaces. The ranchers called these folks "money people." The Owenses, Crumley and other ranchers reached out and talked to them, family-to-family, neighbor-to-neighbor. The money people learned a lot about what the ranchers were facing. The ranchers showed them how their cattle spreads were helping to keep Madison Valley from being carved out into subdivisions. The Ranchlands Group began winning lots of supporters among the money people.

Next target: environmentalists and wildlife advocates. This was a thorny subject for ranchers. There had been an outcry when the U.S. Fish and Wildlife Service made the decision to reintroduce the gray wolf into Yellowstone Park in 1995. The wolf had been wiped out of the entire region seventy-five years before by early settlers and government trappers. Ranchers and cattlemen hated wolves because they attacked cows, killed calves and scared herds. But the Wildlife Service and environmentalists wanted to restore this endangered species, with the idea that the wolves would restore an ecological balance to the Yellowstone region as a predator of elk and deer.

A total of sixty-six wolves were brought in. The Yellowstone Wolf Project knew that the wolves, if they thrived, would head beyond the boundaries of the park. Sure enough, a decade later, there were over a 1,000 wolves and they were roaming up into the valleys of Montana, Idaho and Wyoming.

Some ranchers were outraged. Over in Paradise Valley, *NOW on PBS* spoke with fourth-generation rancher Martin Davis. "Wolves and livestock don't mix," he said. "That's the reason they were eradicated back when. I look at them as a predator instead of something cute and fuzzy." Wolves attacked one of Davis's heifers and killed a calf. Even though wolves account for only a fraction of the cattle that don't make it each year, wolves mean ranchers must spend extra time and money checking on their herds.

So why would ranchers cozy up to wolf-loving environmentalists? Because cattle and wolves both need lots and lots of open space. Cattle need space for grazing—different pastures for different seasons, and land to grow hay for winter feed. Wolves need space because, as predators, wolf packs can't be close together. Each pack needs a big area to roam around, hunt and raise its pups.

But can wolves and cattle coexist? The ranchers know that the wolves are not going away so they are willing to try to live with them. But they needed help from environmentalists. They also discovered that environmentalists could help boost their political power.

Actually, it was one of the money people who became a pioneer in managing cattle and wolves on the same property. Roger Lang, a Silicon Valley entrepreneur, bought a big ranch at the southern end of Madison Valley. The 18,000-acre Sun Ranch had been owned by actor Steven Seagal. When Lang first went out to the Madison Valley to take over the ranch, he was skeptical about cattle, but enamored of wildlife, including wolves. Cattle often get a bad reputation for being environmentally unfriendly. There are the stories about parts of the rainforest in the Amazon being cut down to create grazing grounds for cattle.

But once out in the valley, Lang learned that cattle, when managed properly in their grazing habits, can provide a biological benefit to the environment. These ranches are not feed lots: In the Madison Valley cattle herds are carefully moved around the rangeland so they don't overgraze. Lang wanted to run the Sun Ranch as an experiment to see if cattle, wolves, grizzly bears and a large herd of migrating elk could all share the land.

All the same, when a new wolf pack moved into the valley and onto the Sun Ranch, conflict erupted. Lang became a test case for new schemes to try to manage the wolves and train them to avoid cattle. They were fired at with shotgun blanks and rubber bullets. Strings of plastic flags were set up in strategic areas with the hope that the flapping sound they created would startle the wolves. A predator-deterrent specialist slept out with the cows at night, based on the theory that wolves avoid humans. The Ranchlands Group along with the environmental group Keystone Conservation created an effort called the Range Riders: groups of people hired to stay with the cattle twenty-four hours a day during grazing season to keep the wolves at bay in areas throughout southwest Montana.

The wolf management measures helped, but nevertheless there have been problems. When wolves attacked cattle on the Sun Ranch, Lang's crew shot two wolves and the feds shot three more. The environmentalists are still working closely with the cattlemen, but the shooting of five wolves was a big bump in the road.

Up where Lynn and Devonna Owens run their cattle, wolves aren't much of a problem yet. But they are facing a different wildlife problem. The elk have been causing them trouble. Every fall the voracious herds eat grass and alfalfa that the Owenses desperately need for their cattle. And yet here again there is a calculus that makes development one of the main culprits. You see, the rancher up the hill from the Owenses sold his land a few years ago. The new owner, not in the cattle business, decided to stop allowing hunting on his property. In years past, hunters were able to get up after the elk during official hunting seasons and manage the herds. But now, their number has been permitted to grow unchecked. By the time the grazing in the hills is depleted and the elk are forced down onto the Owenses' land, they have moved into a more developed, populated area where hunting is not as practical or safe. So they just roam freely, eating the alfalfa and busting up the fences.

So this became another issue confronting the Ranchlands Group: how to manage wildlife in the face of a changing valley. Deer and elk needed these open spaces to roam and graze, and the recently reintroduced populations of wolves and grizzly bears depended on well-fed deer and elk. The diverse groups of ranchers, money people and environmentalists needed to work together for it all to function. It wasn't all milk and honey. The ranchers' cows still dropped manure on the land of the vacation homeowners. Cattlemen still headed out with a rifle if a wolf attacked a cow. But the groups were able to unite around the common goal of maintaining the open spaces of Madison Valley.

Their success shows the importance of framing the goals and objectives of a group and finding commonalities. Ranchers figured out how to unite with Silicon Valley millionaires who had bought ranches as well as with environmentalists at the nearby university. Some of these folks would normally be enemies. They worked on what they all had in common and strategically avoided what divided them.

But this is also a story about people banding together to provide oversight and control because the state had failed them. Montana has some of the most permissive laws in the country regarding land use and develop-

ment. Only five of the state's fifty-six counties have countywide zoning regulations. Until very recently, the population was so low that extensive rules
and regulations simply weren't needed. In some counties like Madison,
there are no building codes, almost no permitting processes and no zoning
except in a few of the towns. With the encroaching development, the old
system wasn't working anymore for these ranchers. As ranch after ranch was
sold to a builder or developer, they found a too-literal application of the
"freedom of the west" was actually killing the spiritual freedom the region
was built on.

There is a profound irony here. These real-life cowboys would have
never imagined themselves as advocates for zoning regulations. But in
2006, their Growth Solutions program persuaded Madison County to
adopt restrictions on building within 500 feet of the Madison River and
within a hundred feet of its tributaries. Now that's real land regulation. The
Ranchland Group's mission statement reflects this conflict. They support
"protecting private property rights" but also say "rapid, unplanned development" is turning "the values we cherish" into "little more than memories to
tell our grandchildren." Lane Adamson explains his own evolution of thinking on the issue: "I was a typical rancher. I was antiregulation. But, as we've
gone through this process, I've come to understand that the reason communities have done zoning, or regulations, in the past is to protect private
property rights. And, that was something I hadn't understood. You know,
we just thought they did zoning because somebody needed the job. And so,
they sent 'em out to harass people."

To understand just how hard it must be for these ranchers to come together and push for regulation, it's important to understand cowboys and
their culture. When we say cowboys, we really mean hard-core cowboys.
These are hat-wearing, tobacco-chewing, truck-driving, God-fearing cattlemen. They are up at dawn and out working until dusk, day after day, all
year. Take Lynn Owens. On a recent summer morning he came in from fixing a water pump that had gone down in the alfalfa field. He wore dunga-
rees and hip-high rubber work boots, a cowboy shirt and, of course, a
cowboy hat. The wear on the clothes, the dirt on his hands, the sun-etched

creases on his face made clear this was no extra from a Hollywood western. And Owens and his colleagues don't share Hollywood sensibilities, either. These individuals are not given to concepts like social activism and community organizing. It is a surreal experience to stand with a tough rancher beside his ATV on the edge of his massive ranch and hear him talk about "collaborative stewardship." But this isn't a time to get worried about rhetoric and politics. This is about survival.

That's not to say that this remarkable social experiment has been easy. John Crumley, a former rodeo rider, lifelong rancher and today the president of the Madison Valley Ranchlands Group, says that he refused to attend the group's first four meetings held back in 1996. "I wasn't going to belong to any communist organization," recalls Crumley, only half joking. Ranchers are reluctant to reach out to others for help. Crumley says, "There's something with the way we were raised. You feel good when you accomplish something and you get it done by yourself."

But ranchers have never been shy about getting together for a good time. Many come to Madison Valley's premiere social event, the annual Weed Dinner. It is held each summer around the first weekend in August.

In cattle country there are few things as loathed as noxious weeds that crowd out the grass and alfalfa the ranchers grow to feed their animals. The canny ranchers know weeds are one of those unifying issues for the entire community. Vacationers find them unsightly. Fishermen hate the way they spoil the trout-spawning shallows. Environmentalists see them as alien species usurping the native flora and fauna and destroying the natural habitat. So they all get together—ranchers, money people and ecologists—to raise funds through an auction to fight a common enemy: noxious weeds. As John Crumley says, "It's something that everybody in the valley can get behind. It doesn't matter whether you're a Democrat or a Republican. Whether you're a full-time rancher or a part-time landowner. You had to do something about the weeds and so everybody got behind that."

Controlling pests like spotted knapweed, yellow toadflax or salt-cedar is also a community issue that requires a community response. Weeds on one property will, in time, lead to weeds on neighboring ranches. Seeds are carried by the hooves of migrating elk or simply the Chinook winds. This was why actor Steven Seagal had earned himself a lousy reputation in the valley when he owned the Sun Ranch. Perhaps familiar with the ill effects of pesticides he'd witnessed in California, Seagal did not pursue aggressive weed management on his massive property. Locals say the beautiful, productive grasslands were quickly transformed into a giant weed patch.

So after Roger Lang bought the ranch, the Madison Valley Ranchlands Group paid a visit to talk about weeds. Lang was on board right from the get-go and not only started to restore the grasslands on the ranch, but was the one to first suggest having a fundraiser auction. That year they held the first Weed Dinner on the Sun Ranch. Today, Lang is on the board of the Ranchlands Group. He's still a regular feature at the Weed Dinner. This year he showed up with his father, his son and his ranch manager.

On display at the Weed Dinner is the full spectrum of diversity of all the people committed to community action. In the auction, lot number thirty-two is for "oil change, gloves, jumper cables, tow-straps, fleece jacket," while lot forty-two is an elegant silk pashmina. Cowboys mingle with vacationers and wildlife advocates under the wide-open skies. Waiting in line for the buffet, one of the environmentalists remonstrated with Lang for the recent shooting of a wolf on his land. Overall, though, the vibe was harmonious. Everyone was in full western attire, including the wealthy part-time residents. In fact, the only way to tell the ranchers from the new-comers was observing who among them took notice of the small plume of smoke rising from the adjacent ridge, caused by a lightning strike. None of the ranchers would be able to enjoy their prime rib without the assurance that the start-up blaze had been extinguished.

What began as an effort to contain development has now evolved into grassroots activism that responds to community needs. As property changes hands, new solutions are needed. Water is one example. The subdivision near Lynn and Devonna Owens' ranch is located upstream on the creek that runs through their property. Instead of the creek water being used for irrigation on a single ranch, it was now feeding the lawns and horse pastures of all the individual twenty-acre lots. So water control became another issue for the Ranchlands Group. They held a well-attended forum to start addressing the issue last July.

The original group of Ranchlands Group members never dreamed they'd be handling such a diverse range of individual issues. All they'd wanted to do was make sure traditional ranching remained viable in the valley. Now they are managing growth, water use, weeds, wildlife and more. It got to be so much work that in 2001 they hired Lane Adamson to be their full-time project director. Lane gave up the ranching life to staff their headquarters in the town of Ennis, Montana.

The Ranchlands Group has even reached out to the subdivisions to make new friends and allies. One subdivision called Sun West Ranch agreed to allow some of a local rancher's cattle to graze on the 1,600 acres of common land the development maintains. This goes a long way to solve a serious problem ranchers face as ranching gets ever more costly. Ranching is all about the ability to grow grass. How many cattle you can raise and later sell is restricted only by the amount of grass you can grow. Although the cost of living and operating a ranch may increase, the amount of grass available on your land cannot. So by finding additional pasture to lease on good enough terms, ranchers can leverage their operations. They can rest their own pasture, making it more efficient, and can even raise more cattle than their land would normally allow.

Folks that sink a million or so dollars into a house aren't going to want to watch for cow manure as they stroll their property. But Lane Adamson and other members of the Ranchlands Group were able to convince the new homeowners of Sun West Ranch to cooperate and help out the ranchers. It also brings some of the new residents together with the ranchers. More people and more cooperation lead to more joint action. The management company that oversees the subdivision even sees marketing potential in this. Their website says: "Sun West Ranch was the first ranch in the Upper Madison Valley to join the Madison Valley Ranchlands Group effort to protect the ranching way of life and the biologically healthy open spaces on which ranching depends." The Ranchlands Group hopes to expand this type of positive coexistence.

The coalition built by the folks who live in Madison Valley has worked wonders. It's the flip side of Diane Wilson's story. Wilson is all about the power of the single person whose ferocious dedication brings results. The story of Montana's Madison Valley is about building partnerships that have real political power.

But can their political power match the raw power of money? The Ranchlands Group has been grappling with that big question for the last decade. Is there a way to give economic incentives for ranchers not to sell off their land to developers? The Ranchlands Group investigated the idea of putting ranch land into conservation easement. The way this worked was that the family ranches would sign away any right they (or any successor) had to develop or subdivide the land. The land would then be protected, safe from development forever, and the ranchers would get the value of those development rights as a tax break. The problem with this scheme was that people running a family ranch don't have much they can do with a tax break. They're lucky if they break even and by the time they've done their official paperwork, almost none of them end up in the black. And by giving away the development rights, they were drastically reducing the overall value of their land. As Lynn Owens explains it, "They didn't fit us. People don't want to sell their God-given rights on anything."

For a while they focused on trying to find donors—wealthy environmentalists who were willing to buy the easements. In other words, pay the ranchers to put the land into easement. But in ten years of searching, they were never able to find the generous and deep-pocketed folks they needed. So they went back to the drawing board. They've now begun to develop a new approach that might just work. John Crumley credits Roger Lang with developing the idea. Lang had already put a lot of the Sun Ranch into conservation easement—he was one of the money people and could afford to give up some of the land's value. But even he couldn't resist the pressure of the market. He began to look into the possibility of shaving off just a few select home sites to sell for big money, which he would use to fund the Sun Ranch Institute, a research and educational nonprofit he started in 2007.

Lang's scheme to market a very small number of plots, each with very little acreage, has attracted the attention of the rest of the Ranchlands Group. The idea is that you sell a small home site but grant the buyers land use rights for your entire property. You guarantee they'll never have many neighbors and give them a massive wonderland in which to play. The small plot thus commands a much higher price than the acreage would normally allow. And then you get to keep the great majority of the land to yourself and keep the ranch alive. The Ranchlands Group calls the idea "exclusive conservation homesites," or ECHO. (You know ranchers have become true activists when they start dreaming up names for projects that are easy to turn into acronyms.)

Already Crumley is in on the game. He and two partners have three sites that they're looking to sell in a prime location over on the west side of the valley just outside historic Virginia City. The three prospective buyers would have small plots but access to 6,000 acres to use as they please. The tradeoff is that Crumley and his partners' cattle will spend a few weeks grazing down the grass.

The Owenses are looking to do the same thing. Lynn has his eye on a small patch of land on his ranch that backs up on his massive alfalfa field and the creek that runs across the property. The Owens ranch is too small to carve out more than a couple of home sites, but the way the real estate market is going, that might be all the Owens family needs. One would be more than enough to pay for their grandchildren's college educations. They also aim to help cover their retirement so they can pass the ranch along free and clear to the next generation.

That's good news, because Lynn and Devonna's son Brett has just returned from Iraq where he was finishing up a career with the Air Force. He's hoping to take over the ranch, with his military pension as backup. His parents are delighted. A love of their life under wide-open skies is what keeps them here and what keeps them fighting to make that life possible for their children and grandchildren. Lynn Owens looks out over his alfalfa field and tells a visitor that the Madison Valley is so pretty that working here isn't really work. Over to the east, on the outskirts of his ranch, John Crumley echoes the sentiment. "My daughter keeps asking me why I don't just sell the place, retire and go travel, see the world," he says. "What she doesn't understand is that I enjoy life every day. I wouldn't want to be anywhere else."

PRODUCER'S SNAPSHOT: DEVONNA AND LYNN OWENS

Covering land use issues around Yellowstone National Park is never relaxing. Wandering wolves, bison with brucellosis, property rights disputes and the pressure of development produce contentious debates.

But in the Madison Valley the discussion seems unusually civil. Ten years ago the traditional cattle ranchers there, in an attempt to address the inevitable pressure on their way of life, formed their own conservation organization, the Madison Valley Ranchlands Group, now based in Ennis, Montana. The group sets the tone for dialogue on wildlife and development issues in the Madison Valley and is a model for other small communities.

I went to meet one of the group's founders, Lynn Owens, to find out why they started the Ranchlands Group. Just after dawn on a cool spring morning I found Lynn, seventy-seven, splashing around in wading boots while diverting water to a new channel in an irrigation ditch. He was like a kid at summer camp. When he was done, we picked up his wife Devonna and were off to feed their cattle herd, marked with the family "KO" brand that goes back three generations.

Up on a hill overlooking their 1,500-acre spread, Lynn tinkered with a towering new computerized pivot sprinkler system while Devonna checked on some new trees planted as a windbreak. She whistled at the meadowlarks and smiled when they answered back.

A large herd of antelope grazed in the upper pasture as Lynn pointed out the encroaching development. New subdivisions to the north and east meant thousands of acres of rangeland once leased for grazing were no longer available to the local cattle ranchers.

The Owens's house is modest, but their living room window looks out on a thirty-mile view of the Madison Valley ringed with snow-capped mountains.

After the morning chores, Devonna sat at the computer to see if there was e-mail from their son serving in Iraq. Lynn and I talked about the politics and issues that gave rise to the Ranchlands Group while a kitten played with Lynn's foot. A cattle dog lounged on the porch, watching a distant herd of deer.

I still drop in on Lynn and Devonna as often as I can to get a briefing on local issues. I have to get up early to catch them. They invite me along as they move about the ranch, and it's often hard to keep up. There are times when I need help understanding the politics of ranching, but when Lynn talks about the need to preserve a "way of life," I now know exactly what he means.

THE PRODUCER: BILL CAMPBELL, a freelance news producer and photographer who lives and works in Livingston, Montana, has done many pieces for *NOW on PBS*. Campbell spent two decades as a reporter and photographer covering Africa. In 1989, he decided to leave behind the excitement of the war zone and return home to focus on issues of the environment and nature.

14

AN AMERICAN STORY

I F YOU'VE GOTTEN THIS FAR IN *YOUR AMERICA*, YOU'VE SEEN PLENTY OF EXAMPLES of people who are making a big difference in their local communities. But it's fair to ask the next question. Does it really count at the national level? You might admire what they're doing but conclude that the country's problems are so big and the system is so broken that their efforts are insignificant.

America is a great county, but there's a lot that has gone wrong. Wages are stagnant. The health care system is in tatters. The country's infrastructure is falling apart. Millions of homeowners face foreclosure. Very, very bad things are happening in the environment. Big corporations demand ever greater profits while regular folks struggle to get by. After years of engaging in a "war on terror," we are less and less safe.

What are politicians doing about all this? For the most part, they're yelling at each other about who is to blame. Today, the money that roars through the nation's capital and state legislatures can deafen politicians to the needs and interests of working Americans. The story of Jack Abramoff is a cautionary tale. Abramoff, the poster boy of the slick and connected lobbyist, wrought a fine business out of bartering alleged access for enormous sums. He bilked Native American tribes out of nearly $80 million and solicited $9 million from the government of Gabon for a meeting with President Bush (a meeting did, indeed, take place, though it has never been conclusively tied to Abramoff or any payment). Abramoff laundered money through a fake think tank to protect his profits, and bragged and threatened and cajoled potential clients based on his "friendship" with the leader of the Republicans in the House of Representatives, Congressman Tom DeLay.

Abramoff came to represent the epitome of the monetization and privatization of politics. His case is not simply one of a willing buyer but also of willing *sellers:* people in Congress and the executive branch who put up their services for a fee. Take Randy "Duke" Cunningham, elected to Congress in 1990 as a Republican from California. He used his position to amass a personal fortune from weapons contractors and lobbyists. In 2006, he was sentenced to eight years in prison after pleading guilty to accepting millions in bribes.

The good news is that Duke Cunningham is the exception, not the rule. There are lots of honest politicians out there. But consider a recent statistic: The number of registered lobbyists in Washington has doubled since 2000, to over 35,000. That works out to sixty-five lobbyists for every member of Congress. How do these "K Street bandits" (many of their offices are on K Street in Washington, D.C.) earn their keep? They ask Congress for lucrative favors. An individual member of Congress can insert an earmark into a big spending bill. The earmark rewards a town, a company, even a single person. The appropriations bills are favorite targets for earmarks because they are so huge that multimillion dollar earmarks seem like a rounding error. Case in point: There were 12,881 earmarks inserted into the 2008 appropriations bills. In all, the earmarks added up to over $18 billion— money collected in taxes from you and me, taken out of the pool available to help solve America's pressing problems.

The power of the lobbyists extends far beyond securing billions of dollars in earmarks. Lobbyists are taking active roles in governance. They are helping to craft legislation and regulation. And they are even turning up inside government—appointed to oversee the very industries that were paying them as lobbyists. For instance, J. Steven Griles was one of the country's most powerful lobbyists for coal, oil and natural gas companies. Then President Bush appointed him in 2001 to be deputy secretary of the Interior. Griles went from energy lobbyist to chief operating officer of the government agency that oversees all the natural resources in America. During the three years he spent there, the Department of the Interior moved aggressively to open up federal lands for drilling and energy extraction. In 2004, Griles went back to being a high-profile lobbyist, his Rolodex now stuffed with the names of his former colleagues in government. He was sentenced to prison in 2007 in a plea deal, after he admitted that he'd lied to a Senate committee about his ties to Jack Abramoff. Some might see cosmic payback at work. But J. Steven Griles sitting in a prison cell doesn't undo the thousands of new oil wells and massive strip mines on public lands. It doesn't reverse the relaxed standards for pollution. Griles and the army of lobbyists and the river of money tied to special interests are a national disgrace. Is our democracy so corrupt that the public interest is for sale to the highest bidder?

Enter civic activism. Activists are working to remake the American political system so it is responsive to the people. And they're drawing on a rich tradition that stretches right back to the American Revolution. Again and again, grassroots activism has been a source for change and renewal. What did the American colonists do when Britain passed the Stamp Act of 1765 to raise money for the British troops on American soil? They protested loudly and effectively—everything from refusing to pay the tax to threatening tax collectors with tarring and feathering.

Fast forward a century and look at the whirlwind of activities pushing for the right to vote for women. Susan B. Anthony and other national leaders spoke in towns and communities across the country. Local organizations succeeded in getting women's suffrage approved in a dozen states by the early 1900s. And Jane Addams put civic engagement to work from the ground up. She founded Hull House in Chicago in 1889 as a community center for the poor and as the locus of a social reform movement. Addams showed by doing: She fought successfully to get a seat on the Chicago Board of Education. She even served a term as a garbage inspector. Addams became a key voice backing the Nineteenth Amendment (finally ratified in 1920) that gave women the right to vote. She showed that civic activists at the local level can and do have a huge effect on moving the nation forward.

In modern America, civic activism has a key role to play. Community leaders lift up solutions and possibilities. They provoke politicians into doing the right thing. Take Bill Graham—the mayor of that small, rural town in Indiana. He just wanted fast, low-cost access to the Internet, in order to keep local businesses competitive. He wasn't looking to face off against his own state legislature, heavily lobbied by huge telecommunications companies. But that's what he had to do. Graham's quest not only changed the lives of his constituents but also turned his town into a model for economic development in Middle America. What motivated Graham wasn't a reach for higher office or press attention. He just wanted to make life better. He ended up spearheading a movement.

Back to the question posed at the beginning of this chapter: How exactly is grassroots activism going to make a difference across the country? Each of the people you've read about in *Your America* took a different path to get things done. But there are common elements, and they add up to a blueprint for change.

Change begins inside each of us with empowerment. The essential first step is to grab hold of a new relationship between citizen and democracy. Think of citizens as cocreators of democracy. It means that the actions that all of us, taken together, bring about the democracy we live in. It means that what you think and what you say and what you do are all democratic activities. Thus, if you believe that you are empowered to create a different America and act on that belief, you are creating democracy.*

The democracy that you and I create lives alongside the conventional view that we all learned in school, about the three branches of government

---

* Harry Boyte, a civic activist who teaches at the University of Minnesota, coined that resonant phrase, "the citizen as co-creator of democracy." His book is an important resource: Harry C. Boyte, *Everyday Politics: Reconnecting Citizens and Public Life* (Philadelphia: University of Pennsylvania Press, 2004).

and the importance of voting. We've all come to realize that conventional democracy doesn't always work so well in practice. Representational democracy depends on other people we elect to represent our interests. But they don't always represent what we want. The torrent of money and special interests sometimes points them in a different direction.

In the cocreator view of democracy, it's very important to vote, but that's only the beginning. So for the citizen-creator, how do you get things done? Well, you start out by empowering yourself to make change happen. You show people by your actions where the country should be heading. In fact, the essential democratic activity is doing. Now, there's nothing wrong with asking a politician to make a change or protesting something that government has screwed up. But those steps put you, the citizen, in the role of petitioner. You're asking somebody for a favor. You are saying you don't have power, and you're asking someone who does have power. But you do have power. That's what being a cocreator of democracy means: Each one of us has the power to achieve things. And the first step is to get out there and do something.

The next step is to get others to climb on your train. The goal is to attract lots of people and win them over by your actions and your example. You make a difference with what you do, and lots and lots of people make a much bigger difference. An empowered group of citizens is the essential force for change. In fact, many of the activists in *Your America* make a special point of reaching out to diverse and even antagonistic segments of the community.

The idea is that a group of citizens acting together becomes a powerful political force. The group has the force of example: We are empowered to start making changes right now. When the call is, "Join with us!," mayors listen. City councils listen. Congress listens.

This is the essence of a healthy democracy. Elected officials take heed when people get organized and point the way toward change. The activists create results, and along the way they help create a democracy that is more supple and responsive to the real needs of the citizens.

In fact, the more you can grow your movement, the more impact you'll have. In the world of politics, numbers count. And we're not talking about sending around a petition by email. Civic activism is all about doing. You scale up by inviting more and more people to take action. Local action in dozens, even hundreds, of communities creates a gigantic force for change. The challenge is to grow the movement so that new members also become empowered as cocreators of democracy. This is a "talk-the-talk, walk-the-walk" approach.

As grassroots activism scales up, it intersects with old-fashioned electoral politics. The enlarged movement becomes a more and more important constituency. Political power translates into new laws, new regulations and better ways of doing things. But this time the approach is from the bottom up, creating political incentives for representatives to act for the benefit of the community. That brings about a reinvention of politics, thanks to democracy's local heroes.

AFTERWORD

by John Siceloff

THIS BOOK GOT WRITTEN BECAUSE REGULAR PEOPLE GAVE THE MEDIA ELITE A kick in the rear end. Confession: I'm a card-carrying member of the media elite, and I was the one who got booted in the behind. I worked at the news divisions of CBS, NBC and ABC. Then came 9-11. PBS turned to veteran journalist Bill Moyers to create a weekly public affairs series that could respond to the dearth of in-depth scrutiny behind those tragic events. I came over to PBS to work as the show's executive producer. When it launched in 2002, *NOW with Bill Moyers* occupied a unique place in the American television landscape. It was a call to action with a mission to engage citizens in a way that wasn't being attempted on television—to cause debate, to inform, to motivate, to cultivate their spirit of citizenship and to foster their participation in our democracy. Bill Moyers and his long-time collaborators Judith Davidson Moyers and Judy Doctoroff O'Neill helped people see the world and care about the world in a new way.

David Brancaccio became host in 2005, and the show title changed to *NOW on PBS.* Lots of the two million people who tune in to watch our reporting on the urgent issues that face America write to us. They tell us what they love, and what they can't stand. Then came the email that delivered that kick in the behind, from a viewer who wrote that she and her family watch *NOW* every week without fail. She said they don't call the show *NOW*—their name for it is "Kill me *NOW.*" Give us hope, she wrote—tell us about ways forward for our generation and our children's generation.

That was the first of many e-mails from folks who told us that they love our tough investigative reporting, but want something more. They've come to understand that America is confronting profoundly difficult problems and they want to know what regular people can do to start solving them. We've responded by lifting up and celebrating stories of people and communities. David Brancaccio and I call this "solutions-oriented journalism," and the goal is to provide tools for the engaged citizen.

As we told more of these stories, I realized that they point to a larger narrative about reinventing democracy from the ground up. That led to *Your America*. I joined forces with producer Jason Maloney to write the book, and we began by choosing a dozen people whose stories had appeared on *NOW*. We approached the project as a completely new reporting effort, not a rehash of the reports that had appeared on television. Jason traveled around the country to interview each of our subjects and investigate what they had accomplished. We wanted to know what got them started and what kept them going when things got tough.

The "Snapshots" at the end of each chapter in *Your America* were written by the production teams at *NOW* who did the television stories. Their challenge was to tell these complicated stories in a few minutes of air time. The snapshots give their impressions of a group of truly amazing people.

RESOURCES

READY TO LEARN MORE? READY TO START MAKING A DIFFERENCE? WE'VE SET up a special website, so jump onto the Internet and head for: www.pbs.org/now/youramerica. You'll find lots of Internet resources and books to read, as well as opportunities for action. You can learn more about the people profiled in the book and watch the stories that appeared on *NOW on PBS*. If you're hopelessly hooked, you can even buy the *Your America* DVD.

ACKNOWLEDGMENTS

Thanks to my mother and father, Elizabeth and Courtney Siceloff, whose lives illuminate a path that begins with love. Thanks to Birgit Jorgensen, who believed in the journey. Thanks to Sam Stoloff at Frances Goldin Literary Agency, who charted the reefs and shoals of publishing for a couple of TV guys. Thanks to Jake Klisivitch, at Palgrave Macmillan, who understood where we wanted to go. Thanks to the staff of *NOW on PBS*, who plunge ahead in our narrow skiff in the wine-dark sea. And thanks to all the local heroes, who urge us onward.—*J. S.*

My profound thanks go to each and every one of the individuals mentioned within these pages, particularly to our chapter subjects who invariably took significant amounts of time to talk with us in great detail about their accomplishments. Additionally, thanks to the folks who worked with us to better understand the issues and campaigns that surround our characters—in particular, Julia Perkins and the staff of the Coalition of Immokalee Workers who sat with us in their headquarters and served as our guides through the town of Immokalee; Ben Moynihan, coordinator of National Initiatives for the Algebra Project who agreed to work with us over a holiday weekend to make sure we understood the organization; Barb Lubin, Robbie Sherwood and Howie Fischer, our sherpas for navigating the exceptionally complex world of Arizona politics.

Beyond helping get the facts straight, there are a handful of people who made this project possible from the perspective of encouragement, guidance and logistical support. Thanks to Kira Kay for her endless help proofreading, advising, listening to ideas, fact checking and, when necessary, reassuring. To Maryanne Vollers, whose encouragement made a daunting task seem, for the first time, approachable. To Joyce Griffin and Gordon Brawn who opened their doors and turned their home into a writers' sanctuary. To my father, and to Joan Griffin, my mother, for a lifetime of encyclopedias.—*J. M.*

INDEX